Music Education for Social Change

Music Education for Social Change: Constructing an Activist Music Education develops an activist music education rooted in principles of social justice and anti-oppression. Based on the interviews of 20 activist-musicians across the United States and Canada, the book explores the common themes, perceptions, and philosophies among them, positioning these activist-musicians as catalysts for change in music education while raising the question: amidst racism and violence targeted at people who embody difference, how can music education contribute to changing the social climate?

Music has long played a role in activism and resistance. By drawing upon this rich tradition, educators can position activist music education as part of a long-term response to events, as a crucial initiative to respond to ongoing oppression, and as an opportunity for youth to develop collective, expressive, and critical thinking skills. This emergent activist music education—like activism pushing toward social change—focuses on bringing people together, expressing experiences, and identifying (and challenging) oppressions. Grounded in practice with examples integrated throughout the text, *Music Education for Social Change* is an imperative and urgent consideration of what may be possible through music and music education.

Juliet Hess is Assistant Professor of Music Education at Michigan State University, where she teaches secondary general methods in music education, principles in music education, and philosophy and sociology of music education.

Music Education for Social Change
Constructing an Activist Music Education

Juliet Hess
Michigan State University

NEW YORK AND LONDON

First published 2019
by Routledge
52 Vanderbilt Avenue, New York, NY 10017

and by Routledge
2 Park Square, Milton Park, Abingdon, Oxon OX14 4RN

Routledge is an imprint of the Taylor & Francis Group, an informa business

© 2019 Taylor & Francis

The right of Juliet Hess to be identified as author of this work has been asserted by her in accordance with sections 77 and 78 of the Copyright, Designs and Patents Act 1988.

All rights reserved. No part of this book may be reprinted or reproduced or utilized in any form or by any electronic, mechanical, or other means, now known or hereafter invented, including photocopying and recording, or in any information storage or retrieval system, without permission in writing from the publishers.

Trademark notice: Product or corporate names may be trademarks or registered trademarks, and are used only for identification and explanation without intent to infringe.

Library of Congress Cataloging-in-Publication Data
Names: Hess, Juliet, author.
Title: Music education for social change : constructing an activist music education / Juliet Hess.
Description: New York ; London : Routledge, 2019. |
Includes bibliographical references and index.
Identifiers: LCCN 2019003877 (print) | LCCN 2019006436 (ebook) | ISBN 9780429452000 (ebook) | ISBN 9781138322523 (hardback) | ISBN 9781138322530 (pbk.)
Subjects: LCSH: Music--Instruction and study--Social aspects. | Music--Social aspects. | Social action.
Classification: LCC MT1 (ebook) | LCC MT1 .H49 2019 (print) | DDC 780.71--dc23
LC record available at https://lccn.loc.gov/2019003877

ISBN: 978-1-138-32252-3 (hbk)
ISBN: 978-1-138-32253-0 (pbk)
ISBN: 978-0-429-45200-0 (ebk)

Typeset in Bembo
by Taylor & Francis Books

In honor of the 20 activist-musicians who contributed to this volume.

Thank you for your work. The world is better for it.

Contents

Acknowledgments viii
About the Author ix

Introduction—Catalysts for Change: Activist-Musicians in Music Education 1

1 A Critical Pedagogy for Music Education 15
2 The Potential of Music 40
3 Music Education as Connection 62
4 Honoring and Sharing Lived Experiences in Music Education 85
5 Music Education as Political 107
6 The Dangers of Activist Music Education 127

Conclusion: A Tri-Faceted Pedagogy for Future Activism 150

Afterword—Taking Courage: Implementing Activist Music Education 162

Appendix: The Activist-Musicians 169
References 177
Credits 198
Index 199

Acknowledgments

This book truly has a community behind it. I would first like to offer immeasurable thanks and gratitude to the activist-musicians who shared their ideas and philosophies with me. The world is better because of your work, and without you, this volume would not exist.

Numerous people contributed to this work by reading sections and providing feedback. Barbara Applebaum, Julie Beauregard, JoAnne Halpern, Karen Howard, Athena Madan, Judy Palac, Kintla Striker, and Kelly Thomas offered valuable insights that helped refine this work. I want to thank Deb Bradley in particular for reading multiple versions of this book in its entirety and providing invaluable feedback and critique to push this project forward.

Since I began this project, being in conversation with many people has greatly informed my thinking. In particular, I would like to thank Carina Borgström Källén, Elizabeth Bucura, Elisa Dekaney, Teri Dobbs, Lori-Anne Dolloff, Mary Rose Go, Lyn Goeringer, Brandy Jensen, Monica Lindgren, Sarah Long, Jamie Magnusson, Nasim Niknafs, Carol Ochadleus, Jen Shangraw, Sandra Snow, and Cara Stroud. Michael Largey provided helpful insights throughout the entire project, and I am extremely grateful for his mentorship.

This project was partially funded by the Humanities and Arts Research Program (HARP) through Michigan State University in 2017/18 and by a visiting scholar position at the Academy of Music and Drama at the University of Gothenburg in fall 2017. Many thanks to both institutions for committing to this work. I would like to specifically thank the music education community at Michigan State University—both colleagues and graduate students—and the College of Music administration for supporting this project and facilitating a research leave in fall 2017.

Thank you to the entire Routledge team and Constance Ditzel in particular for believing in this project from the beginning and supporting it through fruition. I would like to offer thanks as well to the four anonymous reviewers who provided immensely helpful feedback on the text.

On a personal note, love and thanks always to my family for the continual support. I am immensely grateful for the community who helped to produce this work.

About the Author

Juliet Hess is an assistant professor of music education at Michigan State University, where she teaches secondary general methods in music education, principles in music education, and philosophy and sociology of music education. Juliet received her Ph.D. in Sociology of Education from the Ontario Institute for Studies in Education at the University of Toronto. She previously taught elementary and middle school vocal, instrumental, and "world" music at a public school in the Greater Toronto Area (GTA). Her research interests include anti-oppression education, activism in music and music education, music education for social justice, and the question of ethics in world music study.

Introduction—Catalysts for Change
Activist-Musicians in Music Education

Vignette 1

The day following the January 20, 2017 inauguration of Donald J. Trump as President of the United States, hundreds of thousands of people descended on Washington, D.C. and cities across the country to attend the Women's March (Hartocollis & Alcindor, 2017). Conservative estimates of attendance marked the Women's March as the largest protest in U.S. history (Waddell, 2017). In the midst of the Washington, D.C. march, a small group of singers, led by artist MILCK (Connie Lim), sang a song called "Quiet," written by Lim and Adrianne Gonzalez.[1] Women wearing pink "pussy hats" (Garfield, 2017)[2] and carrying signs saying "Dissent is Patriotic" came together in what some would call an anthem of the march (Tan, 2017), to adamantly refuse to "keep quiet." MILCK's powerful lyrics rang out loudly:

> But no one knows me no one ever will
> If I don't say something, if I just lie still
> Would I be that monster, scare them all away
> If I let them hear what I have to say
>
> I can't keep quiet, no oh oh oh oh oh oh
> I can't keep quiet, no oh oh oh oh oh
> A one woman riot, oh oh oh oh oh oh
>
> I can't keep quiet
> For anyone
> Anymore

This song brought people together in resistance against the blatant sexism, misogyny, and heterosexism[3] pervasively emanating throughout the campaign leading up to Trump's election. In an interview about the song, Connie Lim (MILCK) noted that

> As a songwriter, I like writing something that's completely true to me and sing it so truthfully that it's true for other people even though it's a

different truth. I think if great work is honest, it will resonate with people. So my job is to be very vulnerable and very open about how I want to express myself.

(Tan, 2017)

This musical moment went viral on YouTube with 13.6 million views (Tan, 2017). In this instance, a song rooted in Lim's defiance against her experience being stereotyped as an Asian American woman (Tan, 2017) resonated with millions.

Vignette 2

On May 17, 1964, Nina Simone addressed a mostly-White audience at Carnegie Hall: "This is a showtune, but the show hasn't been written for it yet" (Brooks, 2011). She launched into "Mississippi Goddam," a fierce indictment of the state of race relations in the United States:

> But that's just the trouble
> "do it slow"
> Desegregation
> "do it slow"
> Mass participation
> "do it slow"
> Reunification
> "do it slow"
> Do things gradually
> "do it slow"
> But bring more tragedy
> "do it slow"
> Why don't you see it
> Why don't you feel it
> I don't know
> I don't know
>
> You don't have to live next to me
> Just give me my equality
> Everybody knows about Mississippi
> Everybody knows about Alabama
> Everybody knows about Mississippi Goddam[4]

Simone wrote "Mississippi Goddam" immediately following the murder of four African American children—Addie Mae Collins, Cynthia Wesley, Carole Robertson, and Carol Denise McNair—attending Sunday School in the 1963 church bombing in Birmingham, Alabama, and the murder of civil rights activist Medgar Evers in Mississippi on June 12, 1963. The bombing "was the catalyst that ultimately encouraged the performer to risk the lucrative security of her career in order to pursue activism—the medium at the forefront of this activism was her music" (Talbot, 2015, p. 5). The first "political anthem" for Simone (Brooks, 2011), "Mississippi Goddam" forced White audiences to grapple with Simone's anger and the state of racism and race relations in the country and further indicted the Civil Rights Movement for "doing it slow" in the face of White supremacist terror like the Birmingham bombing and the murder of Medgar Evers. The upbeat accompaniment runs contrary to the accusatory lyrics, perhaps making them felt even more deeply. "Simone and her band effectively check the tempo of the nation, calling attention to the historically glacial pace of this country's racial reform even as the galloping, staccato rhythm section marches forward and forecasts the nation's impending damnation" (Brooks, 2011, p. 187). The song was banned in Mississippi and other southern states (Brooks, 2011), demonstrating the power of Simone's political anthem to resonate with and mobilize listeners.

Vignette 3

In 1976, the South African apartheid government implemented the use of Afrikaans—the language of Dutch settlers in South Africa—as the medium of instruction in schools, forbidding the use of Xhosa, Sotho, and Zulu. In June of that year, high school students in Soweto protested this policy en masse in the Soweto Uprising. Beginning on June 16, thousands of students took to the street, focusing their protest on language specifically, rather than the entire apartheid system (Brown, 2016). Over the next several days, the police became violent, firing into the crowds, killing children. Up until that point, murder "had come in secret: in prison cells, and in packages through the mail. It did not happen in public, on the streets" (Brown, 2016, p. 167). Students responded, throwing stones. Outside of Orlando West High School, students protested the use of Afrikaans as ten police cars arrived with approximately 30 officers. In defiance, as police launched tear gas into the crowd, the youth sang "Nkosi Sikelel' iAfrica"—the song that would become the official South African national anthem—in the Sotho language. Students threw stones in response to the tear gas, and several police officers fired their weapons, killing two students (Brown, 2016, p. 166).

In 1977, South African singer and activist Miriam Makeba released a song written by Stanley Todd and Hugh Masekela called "Soweto Blues,"[5] memorializing the Soweto Uprising. Both artists resided in New York after the apartheid government exiled them from South Africa. Makeba sang,

> The children got a letter from the master
> It said: no more Xhosa, Sotho, no more Zulu.
> Refusing to comply they sent an answer
> That's when the policemen came to the rescue

Children were flying bullets dying
The mothers screaming and crying
The fathers were working in the cities
The evening news brought out all the publicity:
"Just a little atrocity, deep in the city."[6]

The lyrics of "Soweto Blues" heart-wrenchingly described the uprising and further helped to heighten international awareness of the apartheid regime in South Africa.

Introduction

These three musical moments emerged in response to oppressive regimes and marginalization. Lim and Gonzalez, Simone, and Makeba, Todd, and Masekela spoke powerfully about identity and conditions that affected them personally, refusing, as Lim sings, "to keep quiet." These activist interventions through music and across multiple time periods illustrate moments when artists spoke difficult truths in relation to identity and oppression. Music, in these instances, resonated with many, bringing different groups together to unite in struggle. The small group of students who sang "Nkosi Sikelel' iAfrica" in Sotho during the Soweto Uprising further provides a significant example of youth asserting themselves as political agents through music. Activism and music are enmeshed and inextricably connected. Music education and activism integrate similarly. Music learning intrinsically involves exploring social, political, historical, and cultural contexts, while musical activism can provide a significant mechanism for music learning. How might youth interact with music in music education in ways that validate their experiences and help them to develop their own unique voices? How might such interaction with music education contribute to social change?

Presently, "alt-right" and racist ideologies proliferate throughout the world (Giroux, 2017b; MacKinnon, 2017; Marsh, 2017; Nowak & Branford, 2017; Taylor, 2016; Thompson, 2017). Hate continually manifests in both new and familiar ways. While oppressive instances and events may be situated and specific, the presence of oppression is consistent across time, simply shifting in form and content. Rising up against both oppressive ideologies and material violence seems urgent and imperative. These musical moments initiated by Lim and Gonzalez, Simone, and Makeba, Todd, and Masekela demonstrate that music has a role in resistance. Historically, music has always contributed to anti-oppression movements (see for example Gilbert, 2007; Hirsch, 2002; Kanaaneh, Thornsén, Bursheh, & McDonald, 2013; Moore, 2006; Turino, 2008; Tusty & Tusty, 2007). Recognizing the importance of thoughtful resistance to the ubiquity of oppression, music educators might consider ways to envision a climate of increased social justice and equity. As a music educator with experience both as a public-school music teacher and a postsecondary music teacher educator, I have reflected deeply on ways that music education may play a role in enacting anti-oppression practices and fostering equity and justice.

In the fall of 2014, immediately following the events in Ferguson, Missouri, I initiated a project to conceptualize activist music education. The death of Michael Brown at the hands of the police in Missouri left me angry and wanting to mobilize. The demonstrators who "interrupted" the St. Louis Symphony in October 2014 by singing Florence Reece's song "Which Side Are You On" ("Requiem for Michael Brown")[7]—a musical response to violence that had ravaged Ferguson—prompted me to seriously consider what may be possible through music and music education. The number of people of color—predominantly Black men—killed by the police during the year before Michael Brown's murder in August 2014—was staggering, and included Jordan Baker, McKenzie Cochran, Yvette Smith, Victor White, III, Eric Garner, Tyree Woodson, and John Crawford, III. Following the subsequent murder of Tamir Rice, at age 12, in November 2014, rising up against such violence through music education seemed imperative. Police violence killed 1114 people in the United States in 2014.[8]

Inspired by the organizing around me and the clear emphasis on bringing people together to oppose injustice, I wondered what such activism might look like in music education. While this situation was specific, given the continual manifestation of oppression in different forms, finding ways that music education can contribute to resistance may allow music educators to formulate a distinctly anti-oppressive pedagogy. Such pedagogy aims to address the sexism, racism, Islamophobia, anti-Semitism, heterosexism, cisgenderism, classism, ableism, anti-immigrant sentiments, and other oppressions so prevalent in society. To imagine what role music education might play in challenging an epidemic of ongoing oppression that keeps claiming lives, I decided to speak with people involved in both activism and music. Over the course of four months, I spoke with individuals who defined themselves in some way with both activist and musician identities. These conversations with activist-musicians provided a means to conceptualize activist music education for school music. At the time, I imagined that activist music education in schools would likely look quite different from activism in the streets. The emergent activist music education, like activism pushing toward social change, focuses on bringing people together, expressing experiences, and identifying and challenging oppressions. Music education can help address immeasurable injustices. Local, national, or global tragedies prompt me to turn first to education to consider how it may be possible to teach in such a way that different outcomes may emerge from similar future circumstances. Music education has a role to play in anti-oppression; this project considers how enacting a music education informed by the perspectives of activist-musicians might look. This project became a way to envision what music educators might do in the face of ongoing, unspeakable violence and oppression.

Amidst rampant oppression aimed at many identities, police brutality, climate change, and violence targeted at people who embody difference, music educators have the agency to identify ways that music education can contribute to changing the social climate. In this context of hate and violence, activist music education may help youth foster connections within and beyond their communities, learn to assert their voices strongly in the world, and develop a practice of critique. Music education can sharpen youth's demand for justice by modeling and engaging together in the critique, analysis, and disruption of oppression. To resist oppressive ideologies circulating nationally and globally requires more than just an active stance that encourages youth to think deeply about what they encounter in the world and to trust their own experiences and voices; such resistance also requires broader mechanisms for expression, communication, and knowing. Music education innately provides such opportunities.

This book explores the common themes, perceptions, philosophies, and ideas of 20 activist-musicians involved in social change across the United States and Canada, positioning them as catalysts for change in music education. Participants articulated both the various roles that music can play and potential implications for an activist school music education that strives for social change. It is essential to explore these implications in any climate of inequity. The perspectives of these activist-musicians offer a crucial way to reimagine the social climate through formulating what I call *activist music education* for K-12 education. Such an education aims to equip youth across three main areas: (a) fostering connection with Others;[9] (b) honoring and sharing lived experience; and (c) developing the ability to think critically about the world. The tenets for such a music education emerge directly from activist-musicians' musical practices. Looking to the perspectives and experiences of activist-musicians provides important insights for how music educators can honor the intrinsic integration of activism and music education toward a different possible imaginary than those reinforced by the oppressive ideologies presently circulating in society.

Defining Activism

Many people currently hesitate to label themselves as activists. Indeed, some see the term as "contentless," distinct from similar terms, such as *abolitionist, unionist,* or *suffragette,* located in specific social movements (Smucker, 2017). In constructing activist music education, I employ the term *activist* precisely because of its openness. The association of activism with social change and change-making situates my work firmly on the left side of the political spectrum. To use such a term in education, however, must allow flexibility for diverse contexts. The challenges youth face vary widely, and activism as a concept allows them to address their specific conditions. The term *activism* is versatile; it allows youth to apply the skills they learn under the purview of activism to create change in their own worlds. I draw upon Kuntz's (2015) definition of activism for the purposes of this book:

In a general sense, to engage in activism is to in some way work for social change. As such, activism requires an imaginative or creative element—the ability to understand ourselves as other than we are. More specifically, activism involves the determined intervention into the normative processes and practices that govern the world in which we live. As a practice of intervention, activism necessarily remains grounded in the realm of the material; activist practices are material practices. Through activism one might seek to generate new meanings, new ways of considering and engaging within the world.

(p. 28)

As I explore the potential of activist music education, drawing upon the experiences and perspectives of activist-musicians, I put forward a music education that works toward social change and involves creative imagining and envisioning. The material element of activism furthermore demands tangible changes. Given the norms and regulations that govern school as institutions, any conceptualization of activism as a practice in schools will look substantially different from activism and mobilizing that occurs in communities. The music education offered by these 20 activist-musicians aligns with many of the tenets of Freirian critical pedagogy. I explore Freire's ideas and approaches in Chapter 1, alongside some of the critiques leveled against critical pedagogy, and examine the ways critical pedagogy is employed in music education. This book, in some ways, suggests a different type of practical enactment of critical pedagogy for music education. While activist music education aligns in many ways with music education for social justice as scholars have taken it up so far (see for example Benedict, Schmidt, Spruce, & Woodford, 2015; Gould, Countryman, Morton, & Stewart Rose, 2009), I employ the term *activism*, following Kuntz (2015), to underscore the importance of both action and imagination—aspects not necessarily intrinsic to definitions of social justice education.

The Activist-Musicians

The perspectives of activist-musicians provide a vital means to formulate activist music education. The hyphenated activist-musician identity offers a unique praxis-oriented[10] position. For many of these activist-musicians, their activist-self centers equity and critique while their musician-self allows them to actively insert these ideologies and critiques into the world. Activist-musicians are uniquely positioned to "name the world" (Freire, 2000/1970) through music and to work to transform it. Holding both identities simultaneously, these activist-musicians put forward music with educative potential and speak profoundly to education as praxis in the Freirian sense, as defined in Chapter 1.

I recruited the activist-musicians through connections within my own activist networks by requesting participants who identified as engaging in activist work through music. Because of the geographical nature of my own connections, participants were predominantly from the Toronto area in Ontario, Canada (6), and, in the United States, the New York City area (5), multiple cities in California (6), the Boston area in Massachusetts (2), and Vermont (1). Activist-musicians were diverse musically and demographically. They held an array of socioeconomic positions and ranged in age from late 20s to 70s. Most participants were under 40. I interviewed three participants in their 20s, ten participants in their 30s, two participants in their 40s, four participants in their 50s, and one participant in her 70s.[11] The participants identified as White (8), Asian American or Asian Canadian (10), Black (1), and mixed race (1). Nine participants identified as men, nine as women, and two as gender non-conforming. While I did not inquire about sexual orientation, eight participants identified as LGBTQQIA[12] without prompting. Activist-musicians spanned the musical genres of hip-hop (6), punk (2), indie pop (1), indie/hip-hop/soul (2), metalcore (1), jazz (2), contemporary classical music (3), world music that included Korean drumming, Japanese Obon, and traditional Chinese instruments fused with Western styles (3), musicals (2), and indie rock (1). Several artists participated in or fused multiple styles. One deejay participant moved between hip-hop, rock, funk, soul, house, and reggae. Lyrics, when applicable, presented a diverse range of topics that included personal experiences, identity politics, discussions of social issues, and beyond. While I did not look for involvement in education as a prerequisite for participation, many of these activist-musicians taught in some capacity. Two participants were classroom teachers at the time of the interview, and two others had past classroom teaching experience. Two participants also taught at the postsecondary level. Twelve participants taught in other capacities—as teaching artists in schools, as educators in community music contexts, and as workshop facilitators across multiple topics. As a result, the majority of participants discussed education with some pedagogical experiences. Of the 20 activist-musicians interviewed, two participants did not identify as musicians. One participant was a writer who was in the process of writing the book for a musical she was producing. The other participant ran an organization that linked musicians to activist initiatives for purposes that included, but were not limited to, educational contexts. Because of their intensive involvement with music and activism, they offered valuable perspectives for this project. I employ the term *activist-musicians* for the purpose of group description. It does not necessarily capture the way all participants described themselves—a point important to keep in mind while reading this book. I use it for ease of discussion. The Appendix provides a short biographical statement for each activist-musician, and I provide additional details whenever pertinent within the chapters themselves.

The diverse perspectives of these activist-musicians are instructive for music education. The 20 individuals hold a range of different identities in terms of gender, race, class, sexual orientation, immigration, age, geography, religion, spirituality, and disability. Between them, they span many genres of music and lyrical styles and have vast musical experiences, as well as activist and educational experiences. Drawing on their experiences of music, activism, and education, their perspectives inform the construction of activist music education for K-12 education. This volume focuses on activist-musicians' ideas about education, rooted in their own experiences of activism and musicking rather than technical elements of their musical skill development. Many of their own technical learning processes align with the now-significant body of music education literature on informal learning processes and strategies initiated by Lucy Green (2001, 2008). Rather than reiterating variations on the strategies Green (2001) details, I focus instead on what the activist-musicians' musical skills have allowed them to create and facilitate in the world, as well as the implications of their perspectives for music education.

The music and artistic work of these activist-musicians offer a model for creative engagement in local and extended communities. Their varied musical styles provide critiques of a range of issues, explore identity, examine themes about humanity, point to environmental concerns, and urge both critical thinking and engagement in the world. Their creative praxes reveal profound potential for music and for music education. They model community engagement and take an active stance in their communities. Eschewing passivity, they demonstrate a way for youth to engage conditions that both concern and affect them. These activist-musicians further exemplify the ways in which the "personal is political" (Hanisch, 2006/1969), engaging their own experiences to draw connections to larger social movements. They often use their music to ask important questions and grapple with critical issues. Activist-musicians share what it can mean to explore serious issues through music and to use personal narratives as a "way in" to address vital social and environmental concerns. These individuals also model ways both to challenge injustice creatively and accessibly and to trust one's own voice and assert it publicly.

Historically, activist-musicians have enacted key roles in social movements, as the vignettes that open this introduction demonstrate. Music, for example, played an integral part in the U.S. Civil Rights Movement (Turino, 2008), in the anti-apartheid movement in South Africa (Gilbert, 2007; Hirsch, 2002), in Palestinian resistance (Kanaaneh, Thornsén, Bursheh, & McDonald, 2013), in socialist Cuba (Moore, 2006), and in the Estonian protest against Soviet occupation (Tusty & Tusty, 2007). Individual artists have also addressed specific issues powerfully across multiple time periods. In the U.S. context, musicians such as Billie Holiday, Barbara Dane, Joan Baez, Pete Seeger, Woody Guthrie, Tupac Shakur, Edwin Starr, Tracy Chapman, Lady Gaga, and A Tribe Called Quest, among others too numerous to name here, demonstrate the rich tradition and legacy of activist and protest songs. These artists spoke about events such as the Civil Rights movement, the Vietnam war, and the presidency of Donald Trump, for example, and raise awareness about issues that include, but are not limited to police violence, racism, sexism, homophobia, class issues, and immigrant struggles. Honoring the possibilities of music alongside the rich history of music's integral role in resistance underscores the importance of listening to activist-musicians as music educators consider how to music anti-oppression.

As oppression and hate continue to evolve in both new and familiar incarnations, activist-musicians' perspectives offer ways to engage and challenge injustice, individualization, and passivity in the face of justice concerns. The ideas they suggest vary in explicitness and focus more on community building, connecting to Others, honoring lived experiences, and thinking critically than on making any kind of unequivocal political statement. Their ideas for music education offer a community-based approach that emphasizes relationships and valuing the perspectives of Others. Rather than a "top-down" refusal of oppressive conditions, activist-musicians offer a "bottom-up" relational approach to community engagement[13]—a student-driven approach rooted in love, hope, care, and optimism, rather than the opposition that the word *activism* may suggest. Their music provokes thought and encourages listeners to consider perspectives of which they may not otherwise be aware.

The Potential of Music Education

As a music educator in troubled times, I often look first to music to consider ways to move forward. Indeed, music education offers unique ways to address injustice and oppression. Drawing on Small's (1998) multi-faceted definition of *musicking* as a verb[14] that encompasses taking part "in any capacity in a musical performance, whether by performing, by listening, by rehearsing or practicing, by providing material for performance (what is called composition), or by dancing" (p. 9), musicking creates opportunities to speak to dominant discourses, to express ideas, responses, and emotions, and to participate in a community. I extend Small's (1998) definition to include what Tobias (2012) terms "hyphenated musicianship"—musicianship that allows youth to take on multiple roles simultaneously, including those of songwriter, performer, sound engineer, recordist, mix engineer, and producer, in a way that honors the multiplicity of skills youth participants demonstrated in the songwriting and technology project that Tobias examined. The multi-faceted nature of musicking offers an important medium for youth to further develop their sense of justice through, for example, a creative practice of songwriting engaged to identify and critique oppressions occurring in lived experiences.

Activist-musicians elucidated the potential of music to foster connections with Others, tell stories and share experiences, and engage politically in the world. The emergent activist music education draws upon these same ideals—connection to Others, to histories, and to contexts; the honoring and sharing of lived experiences through music; and thinking critically about the world. This type of education encourages youth to trust their own voices and assert those voices in their communities. In a climate of widespread injustice, learning to think critically through music education allows youth to recognize and challenge oppressions. Music educators might argue that the possibilities such a music education provides may nurture critically engaged citizens (Elliott, Silverman, & Bowman, 2016; Hess, Watson, & Deroo, 2019).

At a time in their lives when they are quite vulnerable, youth grapple with issues of classism, racism, sexism, heterosexism, cisgenderism, ableism, ageism, and all of their intersections. In putting forward activist music education, it is important to recognize that youth of privilege may not encounter injustices daily; thus, within any given school population, there may be students keenly aware of injustices perpetuated against marginalized populations and those who are less aware of the injustices faced by their peers. In addition, in an era of increased racial and class segregation in the United States, youth may have fewer opportunities to encounter peers with significantly different backgrounds (Kozol, 1991; Lareau, 2011; Lareau & Goyette, 2014). Poverty, school violence, trauma, and police brutality affect some youth daily, and youth from marginalized communities in particular face systemic injustices routinely. Music educators, however, have the power to affirm youth's activist sensibilities—to encourage youth to challenge injustice and help those students less aware of oppression to recognize and resist it.

Music offers tremendous potential as a force for expression and activism. Buck-Morss (2003) asserts that art could play a significant role in society as a "grassroots, globally extended, multiply articulated, radically cosmopolitan and critical counter-culture" (p. 72). Combining the potential of art with the ideas that fuel critical pedagogy (detailed in Chapter 1) positions activist music education to address injustice and hegemony through critical education. Escobar (1994) argues for the imperative of art to do political work in times of injustice:

> Only after the creation of a society without social classes, without the exploitation of man by man [sic], could art become a truly free, disinterested activity. In the meantime, art must be employed in the service of class struggle and human liberation.
>
> (p. 37)

He continues, "By nature, art is desire materialized or realized in visible or concrete form and, as such, the most powerful and sublime means to express problematic aspects of active or passive human existence" (p. 51).

Music, then, provides an important platform to speak back to dominant discourses in society. Educators and society often view youth of color, particularly urban youth of color, through a deficit framework (Castagno, 2014; Delpit, 2006/1995, 2012; Howard, 2013; Vass, 2013). Youth in school music programs may engage music to tell their own stories and speak back to the deficit discourses that affect their lives.[15]

Critical Pedagogy and Activist Music Education

Many of the perspectives of these 20 activist-musicians resonate with the tenets of critical pedagogy in the tradition of Paulo Freire. Freire adamantly maintained that educators must not simply replicate critical pedagogy—they must reinvent it for their contexts (Dale & Hyslop-Margison, 2010; Freire & Macedo, 1998). I did not approach this research with critical pedagogy in mind; rather, its significance emerged through the alignment of its tenets with the ideas that the activist-musicians expressed in the interviews. Because of the resonance of activist-musicians' perspectives with critical pedagogy, in this book, I draw upon our conversations to consider what it might mean to actualize critical pedagogy as a practical activist music education—not as a method or a template, but rather as a set of principles for music educators to reinvent for their own classrooms. A critical pedagogy for music education may help youth to identify the conditions that shape their lives and work to transform them (Freire, 2000/1970). Activist-musicians' perspectives help us consider what such political engagement may look like through artistic practice, and how educators may create the conditions for this type of engagement in school music education.

Book Outline

This introduction draws upon the perspectives and experiences of 20 activist-musicians to delineate the importance of fostering activist music education given the different oppressions that youth may face. Considering the manner in which activist-musicians' ideas aligned with Freire's critical pedagogical approach, Chapter 1 introduces key tenets of critical pedagogy, alongside their critiques and their use in music education, and subsequently re-actualizes these tenets in alignment with activist-musicians' perspectives. Chapter 2 examines what activist-musicians perceived as the role of (their) music in the world. They assert that music fosters connections, facilitates storytelling, and provides potential for political engagement. They argue, however, that music can also be dangerous and may, at times, become fascistic. The subsequent chapters draw upon the concepts that the activist-musicians put forward in Chapter 2 and examine the ways in which music education can also encourage connections, honor lived experiences and facilitate sharing them, and engage politically, as well as become dangerous.

Chapter 3 introduces the potential to enact music education as connective. Activist-musicians suggested ways that music education can build community locally, connect musics to their rich histories and contexts, look for links across disciplines, and help youth connect to what I call *unfamiliar Others* through musical practices. Practical implications for teachers in this chapter include developing skills as a facilitator and community builder, contextual knowledge of various musical practices, and familiarity with a range of musical traditions.

Chapter 4 focuses first on the ways that educators can honor youth's lived experiences through providing a "place-based education," and subsequently encouraging the sharing of their realities through a practice of songwriting—a creative and performing practice of music education advocated by these activist-musicians. The final section of Chapter 4 explores possible difficulties that may emerge for youth when they share their experiences.

Chapter 5 actualizes Giroux and Giroux's (2004) "culture of questioning" as political music education and offers practical implications for teachers and for pedagogy. Chapter 6 explores the possible pedagogical dangers that emerge from enacting the type of activist music education suggested in Chapters 3, 4, and 5. Topics examined include issues of hierarchization, cultural appropriation, stereotyping, exoticization, empathy, audience desires, trauma, "empowering," and microfascism.[16] Drawing upon the perspectives of activist-musicians, I offer suggestions for navigating these important concerns.

The Conclusion draws upon all previous chapters to offer a tri-faceted pedagogy for activist music education—a pedagogy that includes fostering connection, honoring and sharing lived experiences, and engaging in critical thinking. I return to Kuntz's (2015) definition, offered in this introduction, in conjunction with critical pedagogy and consider a way forward for activist music education. The Afterword subsequently addresses some of the challenges and risks teachers may face when choosing to implement activist music pedagogy.

Notes

1 See videos of "Quiet" on the #icantkeepquiet website: http://icantkeepquiet.org/song
2 Significantly, pussy hats have been critiqued for being trans-exclusive and White-centered (see for example Kozol, 2017; Woo, 2018).
3 The Women's March predominantly focused on sexist oppression. While multiple speakers featured at the march, including Angela Davis and Janet Mock, articulated an intersectional feminism that opposed racism, some have criticized the march for promoting White women's interests over those of women of color (see for example Grigsby Bates, 2017).
4 See Brooks (2011, p. 186) for this Carnegie Hall version of the lyrics.
5 "Soweto Blues" was released on Hugh Masekela's album *You Told Your Mama Not to Worry* (Masekela, 1977).
6 See www.metrolyrics.com/soweto-blues-lyrics-miriam-makeba.html for the complete lyrics.
7 See www.youtube.com/watch?v=T_7ErkQFduQ to view this demonstration.
8 This pattern of police violence continued, and the website *Killed by Police* (http://killedbypolice.net) documented 1222 deaths in 2015, 1171 deaths in 2016, 1194 deaths in 2017, and 1166 deaths in 2018.
9 I capitalize the term *Other* to indicate that particular groups have been marked "Other" as distinct from the self in a way that typically involves a process of dehumanization. The focus on connection in this book works to bridge this distance between self and Other.

14 *Introduction—Catalysts for Change*

10 My use of the word *praxis* follows Freire's (2000/1970) work, as I define later in Chapter 1. It builds in some ways on praxial music education (Elliott, 1995, 2005; Elliott & Silverman, 2015; McCarthy & Goble, 2005; Regelski, 1996, 2005a, 2005b).
11 Interviews took place in fall 2014. Ages and demographic information were accurate at that time. The ages and perspectives shared throughout the text are consistent with participants' comments in 2014.
12 *LGBTQQIA* is an acronym for lesbian, gay, bisexual, transgender, queer, questioning, intersex, and asexual individuals.
13 Sotomayor and Kim (2009) distinguish institution-driven and community-driven engagement projects and point to a youth internship program in which youth shape the program initiatives as an example of a community-driven approach.
14 Forms of *music* as a verb, including "to music," "musicking," and "musicked," appear throughout this book.
15 See Hess (2018a) for an example of youth countering deficit discourses in a community songwriting program.
16 I use the term *microfascism* following Deleuze and Guattari (2005/1987), who differentiate fascist and totalitarian regimes from microfascist impulses—smaller-scale authoritarian moves that thread through capitalist society.

1 A Critical Pedagogy for Music Education

Many of the ideas activist-musicians expressed about both music and music education align with critical pedagogy. While I did not approach this research with critical pedagogy in mind, the striking resonance of activist-musicians' ideas with the tenets of critical pedagogy led me to draw upon these tenets to underpin their perspectives. Indeed, activist-musicians' ideas provide a way to re-envision critical pedagogy in a manner that positions music and music education to purposefully address oppressive systems in the 21st century.

Like many active learner-centered approaches, critical pedagogy encourages youth to construct their knowledge through rigorous assessment of the material they encounter. Active-learning theorists including Dewey (1966), Vygotsky (1978), Piaget (1972), and Bruner (2006) consider the social context for learning while eschewing passive approaches to education. In constructivist learning, educators and education theorists center processes of knowledge construction rather than acquisition and honor the experiences learners bring to the classroom. Critical pedagogy similarly embraces active learning and calls upon learners to dialogue with each other and with the teacher to co-construct knowledge while fully accounting for learners' social contexts. The emphasis on critical pedagogy in this volume emerged from activist-musicians' espousal of ideas consistent with Freire's (2000/1970) work, making the use of critical pedagogy emergent rather than imposed. Gordon (2009) calls for a pragmatic discourse of constructivism that moves beyond abstract ideas about knowledge to focus on educational praxis for teachers. By focusing on critical pedagogy, activist-musicians' perspectives facilitate the elaboration of a deeply practical critical pedagogy for music education. Critical pedagogy is one approach among many to active learning and knowledge construction in education. As such, I invite educators to consider where critical pedagogy converges with and diverges from other constructivist approaches to learning.

In this chapter, I first examine the tenets of critical pedagogy, as envisioned by Brazilian pedagogue Paulo Freire, that resonate with ideas shared by activist-musicians. I explicate Freire's (2000/1970) construct of praxis and its interrelated processes of reflection and action toward transformation, drawing on multiple critical pedagogues to extend Freire's ideas. The subsequent section examines the proliferation of Freire's work in North America, followed by an exploration of the ways in which music education scholars take up Freirian concepts. The fourth section of this chapter offers several critiques of critical pedagogy, including its potential to exacerbate power hierarchies between teachers and students, as well as to further reinscribe colonialism, patriarchy, and Whiteness. The penultimate component of this chapter re-actualizes Freire's tenets in light of both the criticisms leveled against his work and the perspectives of the activist-musicians. Activist-musicians' ideas provide an important mechanism for reinventing critical pedagogy for music education. The final section identifies how these tenets underpin the chapters that follow.

Freire and Critical Pedagogy

Applied originally in Brazilian literacy contexts, Freire's early work challenged students to "name the word and the world."[1] He argued that when students learn to read, they become literate more quickly if the words they learn directly address issues, ideas, and objects in their lived experience. In encouraging students to name the world, Freire urged them to identify the conditions that shaped their lives. He challenged students to be critical of the political powers that influenced their lives locally and shaped their labor conditions in Brazil.

Born in 1921, Freire came of age during the Great Depression, which greatly influenced both his perspective on education and his concern for the socioeconomic challenges different groups encountered in Brazil (Gadotti & Torres, 2009). His early work in literacy in the 1950s and 1960s connected education to citizenship and development (Gadotti & Torres, 2009). The "coming-to-consciousness" or *conscientization* Freire aimed to provoke in the people with whom he worked resonated with ideas emerging from the Frankfurt School (Freire, 1998b; Giroux, 2009), as well as from Gramsci and Marx (Darder, Baltodano, & Torres, 2009; Freire, 1998b). In my interviews with activist-musicians, many pedagogical tenets they discussed aligned with critical pedagogy, leading me to engage critical pedagogy or Freirian praxis as a framework to construct activist music education. Freire's (2000/1970) construct of praxis and its interrelated processes of reflection, action, and transformation provide a helpful framework to actualize activist-musicians' ideas for pedagogy.

Freirian Praxis

Praxis, as defined by Freire (2000/1970), is the integration of thoughtful reflection and action. Freire argues that the word is the essence of dialogue and must contain reflection and action. Noting that reflection without action is verbalism, while action without reflection is activism, he instead advocates for both reflection and action as *praxis* (pp. 87–88).[2] Freire (2000/

1970) reminds us: "Arriving at this [critical] awareness cannot be purely intellectual; it must involve action as well as reflection, for only then will it be praxis" (p. 77). Praxis remains fundamental to transformation. It has no particular destination; rather, praxis aims to ever-improve the human condition through measures of social justice, equality, and humanization (Dale & Hyslop-Margison, 2010, p. 98).

Freirian praxis, interwoven with reflection, action, and transformation, involves several interconnected components. The very basis for enacting praxis requires honoring the lived experiences of all individuals within a classroom community, as well as working to develop mutual relationships between students and teachers. Once all participants in the education community establish this environment of mutual respect, the focus becomes reflection. Integrated approaches to reflection include the Freirian practices of conscientization and problem-posing education. Having reflected, processes of naming the world, dialogue, and dreaming connect that reflection to action leading to transformation. Ultimately, Freirian praxis may lead to what Freire calls liberation, empowerment, and "coming to voice." Praxis' demand for both ongoing reflection and action creates the foundation for activist endeavors. The activism for which I advocate in this book refuses Freire's assertion that activism lacks reflection. Rather, activist-musicians put forward a deeply reflective activism, with the embedded critique Freire so richly values. Moreover, examining Freirian ideas as originally conceptualized provides a foundation for reimagining these concepts based on critiques as well as activist-musicians' perspectives.

Creating the Conditions for Critical Pedagogy: Honoring Lived Experiences and Fostering Mutuality between Students and Teachers

Praxis requires a pedagogy of respect among members of the classroom community, creating an environment that both honors the lived experiences of all classroom constituents and fosters mutuality between students and teachers. This practice of honoring students' realities and striving for mutuality creates the conditions necessary for critical pedagogy to occur.

Freirian pedagogy places lived experiences at the center of education. Rooted in Freire's early literacy work, Freire and Macedo (1987) argue that any literacy practice should draw directly upon people's own experiences. Lankshear and McLaren (1993) identify six learning principles from Freire's work and include among them the necessity for learners to connect to their lived experiences when teachers engage critical pedagogy (pp. 43–44). Dale and Hyslop-Margison (2010) argue that

> Every person's epistemic perspective is affected by her/his lived experiences. We live, we love, we laugh, we work, and we cry. Human actions

and interactions within their respective historical and social contexts shape their consciousness and moral judgments.

(p. 22)

When facilitators honor students' diverse epistemic perspectives and lived experiences, they work alongside participants in education to grow together. Critical pedagogues intentionally draw upon students-teachers' lived experiences in shaping a curriculum rooted in the needs of educational participants.

> When . . . learning is grounded in the personal experience and interests of students, it also goes a long way to responding to the pedagogical imperative of building upon the existing experience of the learner in the way that Myles Horton speaks of when he writes, "you have to start where people [students] are, because their growth is going to be from there, not from some abstraction or where you are or someone else is."
> (Mulcahy, 2011, p. 83, citing Horton, 1998, p. 131)

Critical pedagogy privileges participants' lived experiences over imposed ideas and centers individuals' distinct locations.

Critical pedagogy also emphasizes mutuality between teachers and students. Freire (2000/1970) reframes the hierarchical "teacher-student" relationship, redefining the role of the teacher as "teacher-student" and the role of the students as "students-teachers" (p. 83), highlighting the reciprocal relations between educational participants and underscoring that teachers have much to learn from students. For Freire, both teachers and students play a key role in education. Freire (2000/1970) explicates the horizontality:

> Through dialogue, the teacher-of-the-students and the students-of-the-teacher cease to exist, and a new term emerges: teacher-student with students-teachers. The teacher is no longer merely the-one-who-teaches, but one who is himself [sic] taught in dialogue with the students, who in turn while being taught also teach.
> (p. 80)

The emphasis on mutuality and horizontal relationships communicates to students the value of the knowledge they bring to the classroom. Practices of both honoring the lived experiences of classroom community members and striving toward mutuality create the foundation upon which critical pedagogy becomes possible.

Processes of Reflection: Conscientization and Problem-Posing Education

As a fundamental element of praxis, processes of reflection ideally lead to action and ongoing transformation. Freirian concepts of *conscientization* and *problem-posing education* provide possible mechanisms through which students may come to reflect on their experiences and develop their abilities to critique the world around them. Moving to any kind of meaningful action requires a practice of deep reflection.

Conscientization, or "coming to consciousness," describes a process through which people become aware and reflect upon the conditions that shape their lives. Bergman Ramos, the translator for Freire's (2000/1970) *Pedagogy of the Oppressed*, notes that the "term *conscientização* refers to learning to perceive social, political and economic contradictions, and to take action against the oppressive elements of reality" (p. 35). Freire extends the term *conscientização*, or *conscientization*, to differentiate this fluid and inquisitive learning process from learning concerned with acquiring facts and information (Ryan, 2011, p. 86). The contextual process of conscientization, then, occurs in stark opposition to the type of learning that takes place in what Freire (2000/1970) terms *banking education*—a process of education that positions students as objects waiting to be filled with knowledge, rather than active participants in their own learning.

Banking education directly contrasts with Freire's (2000/1970) *problem-posing education*:

> In contrast with the antidialogical and non-communicative "deposits" of the banking method of education, the program content of the problem-posing method—dialogical par excellence—is constituted and organized by the students' view of the world, where their own generative themes are found.
>
> (p. 109)

These generative themes emerge directly from students' experiences. The teacher then presents these themes back to students as "problems" in order to collectively address them. In the banking model of education, the teacher offers a narrative through which students receive a set of facts or "deposits"; a problem-posing education operates dialogically, respectfully acknowledging all participants in education and encouraging them to consider the conditions that shape their realities. The banking model puts forward the teacher as subject and positions students as objects waiting to be filled with knowledge. Problem-posing education, conversely, recognizes all participants in education as subjects. In representing students' realities as "problems," problem-posing education challenges students to reflect upon such representations critically, with an eye toward transforming these conditions. Freire (2000/1970) argues that educators committed to liberation "must abandon the educational goal of deposit-making and replace it with the posing of the problems of human beings in their relations with the world" (p. 79). Intrinsically dialogical, problem-posing education values relationships between teachers and students; it works to unsettle the power dynamics in such relationships, as teachers work alongside students to address the challenges or problems students face. Both conscientization and problem-posing education serve as means to reflect critically on the world before moving to action to transform the issues identified as problems.

Reflection toward Action and Transformation: Naming the World, Dialogue, and the Imperative of Dreaming

Moving from reflection to action toward transformation involves the interrelated processes of what Freire (2000/1970) calls *naming the world* and *dialogue*. Both concepts involve action and integrate reflection. Dreaming, moreover, becomes imperative for any movement toward transformation. As a society, having a vision for the future will help inform our present actions.

In Freirian critical pedagogy, problem-posing education invites participants to pursue conscientization and name the world—that is, they identify the conditions that influence their lives. Together, teacher-student and students-teachers collaborate to name oppressive conditions and work to transform them. Naming the world within critical pedagogy necessarily involves transformation. If problem-posing education calls upon students to address the challenges they face, naming the world involves identifying the problems, conditions, and ideologies that shape students' experiences and collaboratively considering them.

Naming the world with clarity also necessitates coming to terms with any internalized oppression (Fanon, 1963; O'Brien, 2011).[3] This process thus also involves attending to the self, focusing on both internalized oppression and imposed oppression. For Freire, identifying oppressive conditions facilitates educational participants' agency to transform their lives and continually strive for improved conditions.

Upon naming and subsequently acting to transform conditions, this process repeats through Freirian dialogue (Freire, 2000/1970). Dialogue within critical pedagogy includes reflection, naming the world, action, reflection, and renaming, explicitly recognizing transformation as an ongoing, meaningful process (Darder, 2017). In enacting change, participants in education can address oppressions or problems previously beyond reach, always striving for improved conditions. As a means of continual human transformation, dialogue, then, is dynamic and "assumes a constant state of becoming" (Dale & Hyslop-Margison, 2010, p. 98). "[T]he agents in the dialogue not only retain their identity, but actively defend it, and thus grow together. Precisely on this account, dialogue does not *level* them, does not 'even them out,' reduce them to each other" (Freire, 1998b, p. 107). Dialogue within critical pedagogy further underscores the emphasis Freire placed on mutuality and horizontal relationships.

Freire (1998b) also explicitly emphasizes the importance of dreaming. He argues: "Dreaming is not only a necessary political act, it is an integral part of the historico-social manner of being a person. It is part of human nature, which, within history, is in permanent process of becoming" (p. 81). Dreaming, he asserts, fosters change. When we imagine a possible future that moves beyond the "mechanical repetition of the present" (p. 82), something more becomes possible in our refusal of automatic reinscription. Freire (1998b) centers the agency inherent in dreaming—the ability to make change and create a different possible future. He grounds this notion firmly in reality; rather than pointing naively to some kind of causal relationship between dreaming and change, he notes that without dreaming, change remains impossible. He contends that

> The understanding of history as an *opportunity* and not *determinism*, the conception of history operative in this book, would be unintelligible without the *dream*, just as the *deterministic* conception feels uncomfortable, in its incompatibility with this understanding and therefore denies it.
>
> (p. 82, italics in original)

Imagining and dreaming thus comprise fundamental aspects of critical pedagogy. We must have vision for the future in order to create the transformation that critical pedagogy demands.

Liberation, Empowerment, and Coming to Voice: What Critical Pedagogy Makes Possible

The processes of reflection, action, and transformation that make up praxis may make possible Freirian ideals of *liberation, empowerment*, and *coming to voice*—key goals of emancipatory education. *Coming to voice* involves students asserting their perspectives about the conditions that shape their lives—a process entangled with empowerment and liberation. Students, according to Freire, become empowered and liberated when they engage in conscientization and problem-posing education in collaboration with the teacher. He describes liberation not as an act of bestowal or independent achievement, but a mutual process. Such educational collaboration encourages student empowerment, liberation, and the assertion of one's perspective.

When students assert their own perspectives, they begin the process of what Freire calls liberation through problem-posing education in collaboration with the teacher or teacher-student, seizing control of their realities and working to transform them. This shared responsibility between teacher-student and students-teachers positions them as co-investigators in the pedagogical process (Kirylo, 2011, p. 156). Liberation then occurs through cognitive acts. Freire (2000/1970) asserts that students come to voice and empower themselves: they become active contributors in their own education, engaging in conscientization, participating in problem-posing education, and articulating their realities. Such empowerment may encourage students to continue the work of reflection and action toward the ongoing process of transformation.

These elements of the reflection, action, and transformation process intrinsic to critical pedagogy praxis—the importance of lived experiences, mutuality between students and teachers, conscientization, problem-posing education, naming the world, dialogue, the imperative of dreaming, coming to voice, liberation, and empowerment—align with many of the ideas activist-musicians put forward in this study. Their perspectives drive the process of reimagining critical pedagogy for the 21st century; thus, this volume both draws upon and diverges from previous work on critical pedagogy in music education and literacy education.

The Proliferation of Critical Pedagogy: Freire in North America

Freire's ideas have significantly influenced international scholars. Accused of being a communist and a subversive, Freire was exiled from Brazil in 1964 and did not return until 1980. He moved to Bolivia and subsequently Chile, where he wrote *Education, the Practice of Freedom* and *The Pedagogy of the Oppressed*, his most influential work (Gadotti & Torres, 2009). Originally published in 1970 in Spanish and English rather than the original Portuguese, *The Pedagogy of the Oppressed* resonated with readers in Latin America and far beyond. Harvard University invited Freire for a visiting scholar residency in 1969, and articles he published in the *Harvard Educational Review* in 1970 (Freire, 1970a, 1970b) gained traction in the United States. In the 1980s, multiple U.S. and Canadian scholars at the beginning of their careers, including Peter McLaren, Henry Giroux, Antonia Darder, Donaldo Macedo, Myles Horton, and Ira Shor, took up Freire's work in U.S. and Canadian contexts. Critical pedagogy became an integral part of education discourse.

Freire and others, however, did not intend critical pedagogy to be a method or a set of tenets to be applied universally to different contexts (Dale & Hyslop-Margison, 2010, p. 73). Freire put forward critical pedagogy as fluid; however, educators often employ critical pedagogy as a method:

> Many of Freire's ideas . . . have been reduced to slogans and technical approaches. He would probably quite correctly scoff at the notion that another person's pedagogy could be reconstructed or reconstituted in another time or another place. Freire and Macedo (1998) recall Freire's request of teachers choosing to pursue his objectives: 'I don't want to be imported or exported. It is impossible to export pedagogical practices without reinventing them. Please tell your fellow American educators not to import me. Ask them to re-create and rewrite my ideas.'
> (Dale & Hyslop-Margison, 2010, p. 74 citing Freire & Macedo, 1998, p. 6)

Reinventing critical pedagogy for specific contexts becomes important when engaging Freirian concepts. In the early to mid-2000s, critical pedagogy became a focus for some in music education. Rooted in critical theory, the praxial turn in music education (see for example Bowman, 2002a, 2002b; Elliott,1995; Regelski, 1996, 1998) created possibilities for engaging with critical pedagogy in music education—a path taken shortly thereafter by Frank Abrahams (2005a, 2005b, 2006, 2007) and Patrick Schmidt (2001, 2005) in particular. Both scholars engaged critical pedagogy in ways that considered what Freire's work might offer music education, although Abrahams' work seems to "ask what critical pedagogy can do for music education . . . rather than how music education, through critical pedagogy, can reclaim its moral purpose of fostering needed changes" (Gowan, 2016, p. 23). The next section explores how music educators have taken up Freirian concepts and responded to critical pedagogy.

Critical Pedagogy and Music Education

Music education scholars engage concepts from critical pedagogy in multiple ways. Examining concepts from Freirian praxis as initially presented, this section explores how music educators have taken up these same ideas, drawing upon literature in both music education and literacy education, as many literacy scholars engage music in critical pedagogy. Moreover, as music educators look to students' music to drive the curriculum, literature on culturally responsive teaching (Gay, 2018; Lind & McKoy, 2016) also becomes pertinent.

In considering praxis as a process of reflection toward action and transformation, the manner in which music education scholars have taken up Freirian ideas in different capacities informs any enactment of critical pedagogy for activist music education. Music education has a long history of discussions of praxis and praxialism. Rooted firmly in ethics, scholars including Regelski (1998), Bowman (2002a, 2002b), Elliott (1995), and Elliott and Silverman (2015) base their discussions on Aristotelian philosophy. Regelski and Bowman specifically differentiate between what Aristotle calls *techne*—technical, skills-based knowledge—and praxis rooted in *phronesis*—"an ethic concerned with right action in the variable and unpredictable realm of human interactions" (Bowman, 2002b, p. 69). Rather than being universal or deterministic, "right action" is determined by context and by the people involved. Educators, guided by ethics, work to determine with students the "right action" for given populations in specific situations. This focus on right results for students honors what they want for themselves. Accounting for the ethical basis for praxis in music education provides a foundation for considering Freirian ideals from critical pedagogy and the manner in which music educators have examined what it might mean to create the conditions for critical pedagogy, engage in reflection, and move from reflection toward action and transformation.

Creating the Conditions for Critical Pedagogy in Music Education: Honoring Lived Experiences and Fostering Mutuality between Students and Teachers

In considering the conditions necessary to enact a critical pedagogy in music education, I return to Freirian notions of honoring students' lived experiences and developing mutuality between students and teachers in the classroom community. In music education, scholars typically account for and honor youth's lived experiences through culturally responsive teaching. Scholarship on culturally relevant pedagogy (Ladson-Billings, 1995, 2009, 2015), culturally responsive teaching (Gay, 2018), and culturally sustaining pedagogy (Paris & Alim, 2014, 2017) calls upon educators to attend to and honor youth's experiences and make them an important aspect of classroom culture. Current discourse in music education urges these same pedagogical moves to honor both students' identities and their musical choices, as they intersect in unique ways (Gurgel, 2016; Hess, 2014, 2015b; Hoffman, 2012; Koza, 2006; Lind & McKoy, 2016; Martignetti et al., 2013). Importantly, this body of literature acknowledges the strengths that youth bring to the classroom—what Yosso (2005) terms "community cultural wealth"—and refuses the deficit framing of students, particularly youth of color, so prevalent in common discourse (Castagno, 2014; Delpit, 2006/1995, 2012; Howard, 2013; Vass, 2013).

Some music educators also value mutuality between students and teachers. Martignetti, Talbot, Clauhs, Hawkins, and Niknafs (2013) describe the ways that they work in their varied contexts to create learning communities based upon mutual respect and understanding (p. 15). Abrahams (2005a, 2006, 2009) similarly asks four crucial questions: "Who am I? Who are my students? What might they become? What might we become together?" These questions center students in classroom pedagogy and indicate a commitment on the part of teachers to working alongside students toward common goals. Abrahams (2005a) further notes that what he calls "Critical Pedagogy for Music Education" (CPME) advocates for "a shift in the power relationships within the music classroom by suggesting that teachers and students teach each other" (p. 14). Abrahams (2006) and Martignetti et al. (2013) prioritize recognizing what students bring to the classroom.

Early feminist scholarship in music education (see for example Gould, 1994, 1996; Koza, 1994a, 1994b, 1994c, 1994d; Lamb, 1987, 1994a, 1994b, 1996; O'Toole, 1994a, 1994b, 1997, 1998) often intentionally unsettled dominant power dynamics. In a direct challenge to the lack of mutuality in director-ensemble relations, for example, O'Toole (1994a) critiques hierarchies in typical choir settings. She argues that ensembles (choirs) often erase what individual singers bring to the experience, instead privileging the knowledge and authority of the conductor. Her doctoral thesis (O'Toole, 1994b) explores different ways to center and honor choristers' knowledge in ensemble settings and shift the unidirectional hierarchies of the ensemble toward more mutual constructions.

Allsup (2016) similarly argues for an "open" philosophy of music education, in which teachers work alongside students as "fellow adventurers," in opposition to what he calls the Master-apprentice model that remains pervasive in music education. The commitment to honor the lived experiences of students through culturally responsive pedagogy, simultaneously considering what it might mean to work collaboratively with youth both musically and on problems they identify, sets the conditions for critical pedagogy in music education.

Processes of Reflection in Music Education: Conscientization and Problem-Posing Education

Music education scholars have also taken up Freirian processes of reflection, including conscientization and problem-posing education. Congruent with Freire's work, these integrated mechanisms for reflection provide the basis for ethically-guided action. In music education, Abrahams conceptualizes Freirian conscientization in terms of students "knowing that they know" (Abrahams, 2005a, 2006), developing awareness of their knowledge. In raising questions about curriculum and privileging critique, Schmidt (2005) draws on Macedo's (1994) definition of conscientization—"the process of becoming critically conscious of the socio-historical world in which one intervenes or pretends to intervene politically" (p. xi). Spruce (2015) similarly describes conscientization in terms of students' awareness of "power relationships that impact their lives and those of others" (p. 299). Beyond music education, literacy education scholars encourage exploring hip-hop lyrics to facilitate Freirian conscientization (Akom, 2009; Alim, 2007; Williams, 2007). Conscientization in music education, then, similarly focuses on critique, knowing, questioning, and awareness of power—critical reflective processes in the movement toward action.

As a second important facet of the reflective process, music educators often take up problem-posing education as questioning (Gowan, 2016; Narita & Green, 2016). Problem-posing education, Narita and Green write, involves "questioning and attempting to understand the world we inhabit, in relation to the transformations that are needed to ensure the right of being active subjects in control of our choices" (p. 303). Gowan (2016) argues that developing questioning skills "would undoubtedly transcend the classroom and lead students to rethink previously 'deposited' knowledge and understandings" (p. 24). Moreover, Colwell (2005) explores the use of both skepticism and doubt in relation to any material presented as practices in critical pedagogy. I conceptualize these ideas following what Giroux and Giroux (2004) call a "culture of questioning" (p. 123), a direct contrast to the "banking education" that Freire (2000/1970) criticized. These reflective processes privilege questioning and skepticism in relation to the situations encountered. Drawing on Goulet (1996), Regelski (2005a) critically contrasts problem-posing with problem-solving:

> Problematizing is the antithesis of the technocrat's problem-solving stance. In the latter approach, an expert takes some distance from reality, analyzes it into component parts, devises means for resolving difficulties in the most efficient way, and then dictates a strategy of policy. Such problem solving, according to Freire, distorts the totality of human experience by reducing it to those dimensions which are amenable to treatment as mere difficulties to be solved. But to problematize in his sense is to . . . generate critical consciousness and empower [people] to alter their relations with nature and social forces.
> (Goulet, 1996, p. ix, as cited in Regelski, 2005a, p. 14)

Following Regelski, I view problem-posing education as a practice of generating inquiry and thinking critically about the world. Conscientization and problem-posing education provide important reflective mechanisms in music education through which to consider lived conditions.

Reflection toward Action and Transformation in Music Education: Naming the World, Dialogue, and the Imperative of Dreaming

In moving from reflection to action toward transformation, music education scholars also take up interrelated processes of naming the world, dialogue, and the importance of dreaming. Naming the world becomes an important point of departure for music education in this volume. For multiple music educators, *naming the world* translates to identifying inequities in order to work against them. Vaugeois (2009) suggests that as music educators, we need to ask questions that point to systemic injustices alongside striving for social justice, a point with which Bowman (2007b) concurs in his discussion of the difficulties of social justice as the latest "trend" of music education. Tools to address injustice allow us to locate ourselves historically, which includes acknowledging our own complicity in injustice.

Given music's expressive potential, naming the world in music education contexts potentially provides opportunities for creative expression. Schmidt (2005) conceptualizes interplay between critique and emotion:

> Freire (1986) suggests that education is more rewarding when it stimulates the development of "this radical, human need for expression." Such a need for expression has for too long in our field been connected to the ineffable, the emotional. Education can only be effective if learning is associated with creative acts that see expression not only as connecting to the emotional but most importantly as a critical understanding of the relationship between word and world.
> (Schmidt, 2005, p. 4)

Coupling critique and expression has interesting implications for engaging music to name the world. Much of the early literature in music education on critical pedagogy seems to focus on critiques of music and music education (Abrahams, 2005a, 2005b, 2006, 2007; Schmidt, 2005). Grounded in the perspectives of activist-musicians, this book engages critical pedagogy within music education to examine larger local, national, and global contexts that move beyond the critiques of music and music education characteristic of earlier critical pedagogy scholarship in music education. As such, this volume aligns more with the music education scholarship of Gaztambide-Fernández (2008) and Kaschub (2009), who consider music as a means to engage the world. Gaztambide-Fernández' (2008) discussion of the artist, for example, positions critical pedagogy as a means to encourage youth to embrace their artist selves as border crossers, thereby challenging the boundaries that shape their lives, engaging critically with the prescribed techniques and styles of histories and institutions (Gaztambide-Fernández, 2008, p. 254). Kaschub's (2009) work actualizes Gaztambide-Fernández' ideas. She explores a project she calls "critical pedagogy for creative artists"—a course in which high school youth explore socially conscious music, identify issues of import to their lives, and ultimately create music about these issues. Some of these youth, for example, musicked about child abuse, the situation in Darfur, and being an immigrant. Gaztambide-Fernández' and Kaschub's efforts to engage the world through music resonate with the ideas of activist-musicians in this volume.

While music education literature on critical pedagogy often focuses on musical practices, this book draws upon music to challenge conditions that shape the lives of youth. As such, I look to literacy scholars, many of whom center music—particularly hip-hop—in their scholarship. Literacy scholars, for example, connect critical pedagogy (Freire, 2000/1970) with hip-hop to formulate critical hip-hop pedagogy (Akom, 2009; Alim, 2007; Williams, 2007), which facilitates Freirian conscientization or critical consciousness through analysis of hip-hop lyrics. Other academics observe that hip-hop can serve as a site of identity development, as well as supporting youth in articulating social issues (Petchauer, 2009; Söderman & Folkestad, 2004; Turner, 2012). While literacy educators regularly engage hip-hop to consider the world, this body of literature tends to consider music as a text and focuses on listening and responding, rather than on the performance- or creativity-based approaches one might see in music education. Hill and Petchauer (2013) note that much of the hip-hop literature focuses on lyrics rather than musical analysis. At this point, little literacy education scholarship focuses on creating music in response to critical analysis (Fiore, 2015; Hallman, 2009; Hess, Watson, & Deroo, 2019).

Notions of Freirian dialogue in music education typically manifest in discourses of democracy and what that might mean for the music classroom (see for example Gould, 2007, 2008; Schmidt, 2008; Woodford, 2005). Critical ideas about democracy in music education validate dissensus—the ability to disagree with or dissent from material or discussion both inside and outside of the classroom. Schmidt (2008) advocates for a music education ripe with conflict and dissensus. Bowman (2002a) argues that where disputes threaten discourse, it is important that rivals be able to assess their respective positions by their own standards, but using their rivals' characterizations. The ability to state a rival's view in terms acceptable to her or him would thus seem a minimum condition for entering into a conversational exchange.

(p. 21)

Gould (2008) further challenges democratic principles that involve allowing students to make decisions. She argues that employing such principles fails to change structural and material power relations. Instead, she calls upon music educators to engage the Other in terms of her anger. Rather than enabling student voice that is effectively disempowered, she suggests opening the floor to what needs to be said—to make room for marginalized students to name not only the world but their terms of engagement. A critical music education, then, involves a process of dialogue through which youth may dissent from dominant discourse on their own terms.

As an important aspect of moving to action and transformation in music education, dreaming allows for creative envisioning. Allsup (2003b) argues that praxis is "not simply the capacity to imagine alternative scenarios but is instead the slow burning fuse of possibility *and* action" (p. 157). Allsup centers ethics and empathy and draws upon Freire (1998b, 2000, 2000/1970) and Greene (1978, 1982, 2000, 2001) to privilege the dreaming and imagining that critical pedagogues identify as crucial to transformation. The three Freirian processes of naming the world, dialogue, and dreaming shift critical pedagogy from thoughtful reflection to reflective action toward transformation.

Liberation, Empowerment, and Coming to Voice in Music Education: What Critical Pedagogy Makes Possible

As conceptualized by Freire, the interrelated processes of reflection and action striving toward transformation can result in liberation, empowerment, and coming to voice. Music educators also engage with these concepts, although the conceptualization of these ideas in music often focuses on music-specific goals. Abrahams (2005b), for example, argues that "Fundamental to [a critical pedagogical] approach is a view of music education that empowers musicianship and transforms both the students and their teachers" (p. 2). He thus explicitly likens empowerment with developing musicianship and aims to transform students and teachers, rather than taking aim at broader systems of oppression. Later, however, he argues that empowering students "to be informed and critical thinkers, active creators and caring makers of their own cultural history" involves looking "to both the implicit *and* explicit; the internal *and* external understandings, meanings and practices of music in education" (Abrahams, 2007, p. 231). This later perspective, while still focused on music education, likens empowerment to fostering critical thinking, creativity, and care. Schmidt (2016) argues for a balance between musicianship and questioning:

> In music education this might mean considering that pedagogies that build up, empowering individuals to become excellent technicians and interpreters, might need to be balanced at times by pedagogy that builds down, helping learners to disinvest from authority, to risk their way into music making that is self-directed, innovative, non-prescriptive, and open.
>
> (p. 21)

Schmidt's notion of "building down" resonates with the questioning so crucial to problem-posing education. Beyond music education, Akom (2009), a hip-hop education scholar, argues that engaging hip-hop and participating in a deep critical analysis of lyrics may empower youth who resonate with these lyrics to "solve everyday problems by interrogating how [their] findings impact social theory" (p. 55). I assert that engaging with critical pedagogy in a manner that facilitates empowerment, liberation, and coming to voice extends beyond conceptions of musical empowerment to focus attention on lived realities.

While many have lauded critical pedagogy as an approach to help youth develop a critical approach to the world, others raise serious concerns about the potential for critical pedagogy to reinscribe oppressive relations. In the next section, I review critiques leveled against critical pedagogy. Enacting critical pedagogy mindfully for music education requires remaining cognizant of any power dynamics exacerbated by this approach.

Critiquing Critical Pedagogy

While the tenets of critical pedagogy and the manner in which music educators have taken up these ideas provides a helpful mechanism for thinking about education, many scholars have challenged and criticized critical pedagogy, dating back to its inception. Critiques leveled against critical pedagogy often focus on the manner in which critical pedagogy can exacerbate power hierarchies between teachers and students, as well as reinforce systems of domination, including colonialism, patriarchy, and racism. Given the potential to reinforce unhelpful (and possibly oppressive) power relations, I urge music educators to avoid any dogmatic implementation of critical pedagogy. As Freire and Macedo (1998) note, we must reinvent our pedagogy for specific contexts. In doing so, we have the opportunity to guard against oppressive power relations. Following Lather (1998), I urge us toward uncertainty in our implementation—a praxis of "not being so sure" (p. 488). Ellsworth (1997) argues that critical pedagogy may reinscribe the narrative of the "one who knows" or "the One with the 'Right' Story" (p. 137). In putting forward ideas of critical pedagogy in this volume, following Freire, I reject the possibility of a "right" or "correct" pedagogy. Refusing to be educators with the "Right Story" may allow us to avoid reinscribing oppressive power relations through critical pedagogy. Certainty when implementing critical pedagogy has the potential to produce an opposite effect from the emancipatory ideal imagined by Freire. Attending to potentially hierarchical and oppressive relations informs our re-envisioning of critical pedagogy for activist music education, reminding us, as educators, of the importance of uncertainty and humility when enacting critical pedagogy.

Hierarchical Relationships between Students and Teachers

Critical pedagogy may exacerbate the hierarchy between teachers and students through multiple mechanisms, including implementing problem-posing education, aiming for conscientization, and working toward empowerment. Problem-posing education raises questions of who poses or identifies the problems, as well who has knowledge about particular situations. Conscientization entails "coming to consciousness." Conceptually, then, conscientization involves a tacit assumption that one "does not know" before this process. Similarly, *empowerment* implies that a teacher has the power to empower the "unempowered." In order to counteract or ameliorate these implications, a pedagogy that allows for uncertainty may help educators navigate hierarchies that inherently weave through concepts of problem-posing education, conscientization, and empowerment.

In *Pedagogy of the Oppressed* (Freire, 2000/1970), Freire elaborates on problem-posing education as a process in which students and teacher identify issues in the students' lives and codify them into representations familiar to the students. The teacher then re-presents these situations back to the people as "problems." Problem-posing education may exacerbate teacher-student hierarchies, first, through the implicit assumption that people are not capable of identifying problems in their own lives or addressing them without the help of an outsider; second, that the teacher knows what will be good for the students; third, that the teacher can more clearly see the challenges that the people face; and fourth, that it is appropriate for someone external to a situation to determine circumstances of oppression for groups or individuals. Teachers who act without awareness of these assumptions potentially negate the agency of students to identify for themselves any challenges and oppressions they face and instead grant the teacher the authority to speak to the lived experiences of students. When educators impose their own perspectives on what might ameliorate the conditions of Others, they reinstall the hierarchy between student and teacher.

Freire (1998b) himself, however, cautions that

> The role of the progressive educator, which neither can nor ought to be omitted, in offering her or his "reading of the world," is to bring out the fact that there are other "readings of the world," different from

the one being offered as the educator's own, and at times antagonistic to it.

(pp. 102–103)

He thus encourages educators to share their perspective of the world and position it as one perspective. Given the issues of authority and power dynamics inherent in all classrooms, remaining less than certain may enable teachers to value students' readings of the world alongside their own. Freire deliberately conceptualizes a process rooted in mutuality between students-teachers and teacher-student. Entering into problem-posing education with humility may help educators enact a more a mutual process.

Conscientization may also exacerbate the hierarchy between students and teacher; "coming to consciousness" can imply a lack of an already-present consciousness or less-than state among students whom Freirian educators may identify as "oppressed." Taking critiques of his work into account, Freire regularly engaged in the reflection for which he so seriously advocated. As such, Freire (1998b) critiqued his earlier thinking for suggesting that one person has a critical consciousness while others do not (Mato, 2004, p. 674). Freire (2000/1970), in fact, notes that "attempting to liberate the oppressed without their reflective participation in the act of liberation is to treat them as objects that must be saved from a burning building" (p. 63). He thus acknowledges the imperative of students' participation in their own liberation. Approaching conscientization with uncertainty may help educators enact critical education in a way that honors the full humanity of students rather than taking a deficit perspective.

Power relations also thread through questions of "empowerment"—a Freirian ideal in critical pedagogy. *Empowerment* implies a power relationship between teacher and students in which the teacher "empowers" the students (Ellsworth, 1989). Ellsworth argues that Freire fails to account for asymmetrical power relations between students and teacher (pp. 314–315). Centering "empowerment" as a key principle or goal of critical pedagogy may assume that students lack agency and that teachers facilitate "empowerment," rather than students empowering themselves. Ellsworth (1989) contends that Freire's (2000/1970) connection of "student voice," or the articulation of oppressive situations, to "empowerment" both assumes that when students do not speak in class, they are not empowered, and fails to recognize any reasons rooted in structural power relations that may encourage students not to speak. While it is a lofty ideal, approaching "empowerment" tenuously in enacting critical pedagogy for music education will help avoid reifying unhelpful power dynamics.

Freirian notions of problem-posing education, conscientization, and empowerment may all potentially reinscribe hierarchies between teacher and students. Implementing activist music education with a degree of uncertainty may allow us to both better navigate the potential to exacerbate power hierarchies and re-center the mutuality that Freire proposes. Prioritizing mutuality, then, creates a process in which teachers work alongside students to address issues identified by youth.

The Potential for Colonialism

Critical pedagogy has also been criticized for its potential to exacerbate colonial relations. Dei (2006) defines *colonialism* as anything "imposed and dominating rather than that which is simply foreign and alien" (p. 3). Concepts of problem-posing education, conscientization, and empowerment may create the conditions for educators to impose their own perspectives or readings of the world on students. Ellsworth (1997) fears that critical pedagogy may allow teachers to perform themselves as "the One with the Right Story" (p. 137). This potential for imposing an outsider perspective becomes more complex when considering what may occur when a Western educator or an educator who has internalized oppression teaches students with personal and/or familial experiences of oppression that may include colonialism. Reflecting upon the structural power imbalance and history of colonialism alongside teacher-student relations in critical pedagogy reveals a possible colonial undercurrent in Freire's (2000/1970) conceptualization. Accounting for the history of colonialism alongside the already-uneven power relationship between teachers and students requires a degree of uncertainty to avoid or at least remain aware of the possibility of reinscribing a colonial dynamic.

Critical pedagogues should further consider the cognitive emphasis of the primary mechanism employed in critical pedagogy for conscientization: critical reflection. Privileging critical reflection perhaps unintentionally devalues different epistemological perspectives (Bejarano, 2005), as it remains only one way of engaging the world. Its cognitive focus may unwittingly negate other ways of knowing. For example, critics of critical pedagogy worry that critical educators may marginalize Indigenous knowledge or themes or problems important to communities when implementing critical pedagogy (see for example Siddhartha, 2005).

In employing critical pedagogy, remaining cognizant of the potential to reinscribe colonial relations and privilege Western knowledges and epistemologies allows educators to resist colonialism and ethnocentrism. Grande's (2010) *Red Pedagogy*, for example, puts forward a response to critical pedagogy rooted in Indigenous knowledge and praxis. In this decolonial approach, "pedagogy is understood as inherently relational, political, cultural, spiritual, and perhaps most importantly, place based" (p. 204). Grande's work provides a way to re-center Indigenous perspectives and principles of decolonization.

Exacerbating Dominant Power Structures: Patriarchal and Race Relations in Critical Pedagogy

Critical pedagogy may also exacerbate gendered and raced power structures. The question of who speaks as a critical pedagogue often reinscribes both patriarchy and Whiteness. Darder et al. (2009) note that with few exceptions, the scholars publicly recognized for the development of critical theory and critical pedagogy have been men, causing "much suspicion and concern about the failure of critical pedagogy to engage forthrightly questions of women, anchored within the context of female experience and knowledge construction" (p. 14). Dei and Sheth (1997), moreover, note that the dominant discourse of critical pedagogy often consists of White men speaking for Others. They challenge Freire to consider whether critical pedagogy may actually silence marginalized voices. Apple (2003) cautions that

> [W]e must be on our guard to ensure that a focus on Whiteness doesn't become one more excuse to re-center dominant voices and to ignore the voices and testimony of those groups of people whose dreams, hopes, lives, and their very bodies are shattered by current relations of exploitation and domination. It becomes a monologue masquerading as a dialogue. This is something Freire was deeply concerned about, and we need to remember his insistent warnings about "fake" dialogues.
> (p. 115)

Attending to who speaks as a critical pedagogue thus involves interrogating whether those speaking reinscribe patriarchal or racist structures. These critiques also apply to the voices dominating the discourse of praxialism and critical pedagogy in music education.

Scholars also note critical pedagogy's lack of attention to women and people of color. Feminist critiques of critical pedagogy point to the ways in which the "universal subject" striving for liberation is male (Brady, 1994; Weiler, 1994), a point Freire (1998b) himself concedes and moves to correct. Given the early inattention to women, the manner in which Freire constitutes "oppression" in individuals and groups in his earlier work does not necessarily account for the unique forms of oppression particular to women's experiences. Further to these feminist critiques of critical pedagogy, critical race scholar Ladson-Billings (1997) contends that critical pedagogy fails to address the question of race, thus conceptualizing the universal subject not only as male, but as White, and calls instead for a critical race theory, putting forward culturally relevant pedagogy for the classroom. Enacting critical pedagogy, then, ethically requires an intersectional approach (Crenshaw, 1995) to avoid perpetuating patriarchy and racism. Approaching critical pedagogy with uncertainty and a keen awareness of the potential to perpetuate oppression may prompt educators to consider our actions in relation to possible minoritization resulting from institutional

Moving Forward: A Critical Lens on Critical Pedagogy

While activist-musicians' assertions often resonate with the primary themes of critical pedagogy, I raise these critiques to guard against the ways critical pedagogy may reinscribe power hierarchies between teacher and students, and further exacerbate colonial, patriarchal, and racist systems of oppression. In enacting a critical pedagogy for music education, I purposely look for ways that activist music education might similarly reinscribe dominant power relations. As pedagogues, remaining uncertain and refusing to be "the One with the 'Right' Story" (Ellsworth, 1997, p. 137) may assist us in navigating the possible reinforcement of unhelpful power dynamics. Lather (1998) deems critical pedagogy impossible; yet despite this impossibility, she finds a way forward through "stuck places," "ruptures, failures, breaks, and refusals" (p. 495). Lather's assertions remind us of the importance of humility and urge us not to "figure out" one right or "correct" pedagogy—to choose problem-posing over problem-solving. Yancy (2008) describes what he calls the "White ambush"—a phenomenon in critical race work. He argues that the moment in which White individuals believe we[4] have come to understand the ways that we are complicit in racism and White privilege is the same moment in which we will be unseated by new knowledge. The same idea applies to critical pedagogy. I argue for attentiveness to the potential to reinscribe problematic power relations in tandem with Lather's (1998) call for vigilance against certainty. We[5] are obliged as critical pedagogues to continually "second-guess" ourselves. The work of critical pedagogy, when not undertaken with awareness of these negative possibilities, can be detrimental, if not oppressive. We must, therefore, enter into critical pedagogy fully conscious of this potential and the fraught nature of the pedagogy. Going in with the full knowledge of the potential for harm may help us avoid reinforcing the same oppressive structures we seek to disrupt. We must also be prepared to slip. Drawing upon the tenets of critical pedagogy, I urge readers to engage in a "praxis of not being so sure" (Lather, 1998, p. 488), to consider the critiques, and question whether these dynamics operate in any enactment of critical pedagogy in music education.

Actualizing Tenets of Critical Pedagogy for Music Education

Acknowledging both the manner in which music education scholars have taken up critical pedagogy and these critiques, in this section, I reintroduce the tenets of critical pedagogy outlined previously and explain the ways in which the critiques and the perspectives of activist-musicians inform my enactment of Freirian ideas across subsequent chapters. These tenets comprise the theoretical underpinnings of the book, but in exploring possibilities for a practical enactment of critical pedagogy for music education, I aim to utilize both the critiques raised in the previous section and the (music) education literature to propose a critical pedagogy for today's music education. In the spirit of uncertainty, I present this reactualization as highly flexible and fluid.

In this book, I adhere to the rich concept of praxis put forward by Freire (2000/1970) and consider praxis as the integration of thoughtful reflection and action toward possibility (Allsup, 2003b). Relying on *phronesis* and an ethical approach to action that produces "right results" specific to each classroom population (Bowman, 2002b), I look to underpin a pedagogical praxis of music education through the framework of critical pedagogy and through my reflections on music education, in conjunction with the perspectives of activist-musicians, rooted in their particular lived experiences.

Creating the Conditions for Critical Pedagogy in Activist Music Education: Honoring Lived Experiences and Fostering Mutuality between Students and Teachers

Honoring lived experiences and creating mutuality in classroom relations represent important considerations in setting the conditions for critical pedagogy in activist music education. Throughout their interviews, activist-musicians continually underscored the importance of honoring and sharing lived experiences through music and music education. They further suggested several ways to center lived experiences in music education. Critical pedagogy adamantly centers lived experiences: all education emerges from the experiences of individuals and groups. In music education, considering lived experiences involves understanding musicking as a fundamentally ever-evolving human practice. Following the music education emphasis on cultural responsiveness, activist-musicians suggested a place-based education rooted in the experiences of youth in their local communities. In actualizing the critical pedagogical focus on lived realities, this book centers the humanity inherent in musical practices and the quotidian experiences of youth. The further prioritizing of mutuality between students and teachers follows Freire's conceptions with careful attention to power hierarchies between students and teachers. Activist-musicians similarly emphasized horizontal relationships. Focusing on mutuality requires dialogue and a deep valuing of all participants in education.

Processes of Reflection in Activist Music Education: Conscientization and Problem-Posing Education

The interrelated processes of reflection that set the foundation for action and transformation in activist music education involve reconceptualizing both conscientization and problem-posing education. The main critique leveled against conscientization challenges its coloniality and opposes the notion that individuals somehow become more "authentically human" (Kirylo, 2011, p. 149) through coming to consciousness, an inherent assumption that participants in education somehow lack consciousness or humanity. Following from ideas gleaned from the activist-musicians, I conceptualize *conscientization* as a practice of noticing and attending to representations, ideologies, and discourses. Rather than assuming any deficit or lack in the student population that needs amelioration through "coming to consciousness," I instead foreground the ways in which youth can develop their astute abilities to critique and challenge the world around them through activist music education.

Critics challenge the complexities of problem-posing education wherein educators help participants in education identify issues in their lives and re-present these challenges to students to solve, perhaps privileging the role of the teacher. I take up Freire's challenge to eschew a passive "banking" education and conceptualize "problem-posing education" as an education in which youth actively construct and make meaning of the world around them for themselves, drawing on their knowledge and strengths. They thus play an active role in their own education, forging connections between materials and their worlds and practicing critique. Darder (2017) notes that "a revolutionary praxis of education begins with the view that all human beings participate actively in producing meaning and thus reinforces a dialectical and contextual view knowledge" (p. 117). Activist-musicians pointed on many occasions to the importance of such meaning construction. As such, I reconceptualize problem-posing education as a process of active meaning-making. This subtle re-envisioning of both conscientization and problem-posing education similarly foregrounds mechanisms for reflection.

Reflection toward Action and Transformation in Activist Music Education: Naming the World, Dialogue, and the Imperative of Dreaming

Integrated processes of naming the world, dialogue, and dreaming inform the shift from reflection toward action and transformation in activist music education. As noted, naming the world involves identifying the conditions that negatively affect the lives of groups and individuals in order to transform them. In considering the process of naming the world and the larger dialogical cycle of reflection, naming, action, and further reflection (Darder, 2017; Freire, 2000/1970) in the context of activist music education, youth agency remains at the center. Educators may facilitate identifying difficult conditions, but youth themselves drive the process of any reflection, naming, and action that occurs. Given this book's focus on music education, the process of naming lived conditions involves musicking about them in some capacity, and activist-musicians offer multiple possibilities for enacting this practice.

Following Freire (1998b), I position hope and imagining as crucial to activist music education. Activist-musicians repeatedly spoke to the power of imagining and collective envisioning, and these ideas also permeate Kuntz' (2015) discussion of activism (shared in the introduction). Activist-musicians' thoughts about creative imagining resonate with Freire's ideas and center the role of music and the arts in such envisioning. Keeping in mind critiques leveled against critical pedagogy, in actualizing critical pedagogy for music education, I intentionally remain uncertain, explicitly center power dynamics, and challenge oppressive, hierarchical, and colonial relations.

Liberation, Empowerment, and Coming to Voice in Activist Music Education: What Critical Pedagogy Makes Possible

Enacting these processes of action and reflection built on the foundation of honoring the lived experiences of all members of the classroom community may result in Freirian processes of empowerment, liberation, and/or coming to voice. The primary criticism of these concepts focuses an understanding that all three ideals involve the intervention of a critical pedagogue to empower students, which may reinscribe the hierarchy between teachers and students and negate participants' agency, despite the intention of horizontal power relations. The notion of coming to voice emerged as important to many of the activist-musicians interviewed. In this book, coming to voice centers youth agency. Rather than a teacher-centered notion of empowerment or coming to voice, the music education put forward by activist-musicians outlines a process of coming to voice that involves youth asserting their experiences in the world musically, if they so choose. This student-driven approach to empowerment aligns with other approaches to active learning.

It bears reiterating that critical pedagogy is not a method. While many of the ideas the participants in this study put forward for an activist music education resonate with themes in critical pedagogy, in sharing their ideas, I maintain that such a music education is deeply contextual. Enacting critical pedagogy further requires uncertainty. In exploring possibilities for an activist music education, I do not suggest the application of these ideas across contexts, but rather, like Freire, call for music educators to "re-create and re-write" these ideas for their particular contexts and locales. Such enactments of activist music education, then, serve their specific communities in ways that forward equity and justice toward transformation. Moreover, remaining open to slippages and refusing to "figure it out" may allow us to navigate the impossibility of engaging critical pedagogy in schools (Lather, 1998).

Outlining the Chapters through a Critical Pedagogical Lens

In the Introduction to this book, I provided an outline of the chapters. Having explored and critiqued the tenets of critical pedagogy and reimagined the ideas for music education, I now briefly introduce how the ideas discussed in this chapter underpin the chapters to follow. Chapter 2 examines what activist-musicians perceived as the role of (their) musicking in the world. Chapter 2 is not explicitly pedagogical. I argue, however, that the concepts of critical pedagogy present in activist-musicians' descriptions of the potential for music set the conditions for a critical education, as explored in subsequent chapters. In considering music as connective, their ideas speak to both the idea of music as a human practice rooted in lived experiences and the necessity of active meaning-making in musicking. They also point to the ways in which music can facilitate storytelling and the expression of emotions in ways that center lived experiences while prioritizing coming to voice and naming the world. Their explicit assertion that music is inherently political points to the potential of music to foster a practice of noticing (a creative reimagining of conscientization) and naming the world. The notion that music can also be dangerous recalls the quality of the critiques of critical pedagogy offered in this chapter and serves as a reminder to guard against colonial, oppressive, and hierarchical relations. Chapter 2 underpins all subsequent chapters.

Chapter 3 explores the ways in which music education fosters connections through building community, linking musics to their histories, and connecting youth to people unfamiliar to them through musical practices. The practice of building community encourages youth to understand music as a human practice rooted in lived experiences, as well as to assert their own unique contributions. Connecting musics to their histories and situating them as emerging from groups of people similarly recognizes the humanity in musical practices while also encouraging youth to actively make meaning of their musical encounters.

Discussions about honoring lived experiences underpin Chapter 4; the activist-musicians advocate for a place-based education—an education rooted in the local context. The second component of the chapter explores ways to encourage youth to assert their experiences through songwriting—a process that involves facilitating youth to name their worlds and assert their voices drawing upon their own agency. Ultimately, that chapter considers possible consequences for sharing lived experiences. Chapter 5 positions music education as political and explores activist-musicians' ideas about fostering critical thinking through music education. This process involves naming the world and coming to voice alongside a practice of active meaning-making. Chapters 4 and 5 also draw upon the imperatives of dreaming and imagining. In Chapter 6, I explore possible dangers that may emerge in enacting this type of activist music education. This chapter draws upon the critiques leveled against critical pedagogy to consider potential power dynamics at play in educational pedagogy. Dangers related to implementation of this pedagogy are addressed in the Afterword. The Conclusion puts forward a tri-faceted pedagogy for an activist music education that includes fostering connection, honoring and sharing lived experiences, and engaging in critical thinking. This tri-faceted pedagogy draws together the elements of critical pedagogy as actualized in Chapters 3, 4, 5, and 6 to create a praxis for music education.

Notes

1 Freire later collaborated with Donaldo Macedo on a book with that title in 1987 (Freire & Macedo, 1987).
2 While I situate my discussion of praxis in the writing of Freire, I note that Elliott (1995), Elliott & Silverman (2015), and Regelski's (1996, 2005a, 2005b) work conceptualizing a praxial music education connects well to Freirian praxis. Elliott, Silverman, and Regelski all prioritize reflection in their process of active music making.
3 By *internalized oppression*, I identify the process that occurs when the oppressed come to understand themselves through the perspectives of the oppressor.
4 I use the word *we* here because I am White, and I include myself in this commentary.
5 I use the word *we* throughout the text, with the exception of the previous note, to identify the collective of music educators, noting that this group is not homogenous but rather encompasses many interests and identities.

2 The Potential of Music

TAIYO: Life is bread. In life, you need bread, but it's music and art that leavens it. [Music] helps get you up in the morning. It helps you run faster when you're running. I think of music as something that's very much tied to what people did in the ancient ways. Work songs that helped them get through the day working better. And because they were participating in a chorus or a lyric or a song that was with other people that they would all get behind. It's music and art that helps heal when people have passed, and that there is this death that is inevitable. But music and art helps us. It helps us depart physically from these folks and helps us to remember. Music and art play all of these ceremonial and communal functions, and, without a doubt, spiritual functions that lift us.

Taiyo Na points to music's role in many facets of life, including work, leisure, exercise, healing, ceremony, remembering, and spirituality. A 31-year-old hip-hop artist, Taiyo described himself as an Asian American male from New York City. He centered community in his work and explored identity in his music. His education focused on African and Asian Pacific American Studies and, subsequently, inclusive education. At the time of the study, Taiyo performed regularly and taught high school English in New York City.

Taiyo's words underscore the inherently social nature of music. Music is an intrinsically human practice. Small (1998) contends that meaning in music is derived relationally. Musical meaning, he critiques, does not reside solely in musical objects. Similarly, Nattiez (1990) and Shepherd (1991) both eschew an immanent view of music. Nattiez (1990) asserts that the processes through which people create, interpret, and perceive music remain vital to deriving meaning. Indeed, Elliott and Silverman (Elliott, 1995; Elliott & Silverman, 2015) describe music as a diverse human practice encompassing many practices, styles, activities, and functions.

Taiyo highlights many possible functions of music and alludes to the immeasurable qualities art adds to our lives—not as an aesthetic object, but rather as a human practice. Engaging with music may allow us to reinforce our values (Small, 1998) or explore our emotions (Campbell, Connell, & Beegle, 2007; Davis, 2007; DeNora, 2000; Lundqvist, Carlsson, Hilmersson, & Juslin, 2009; Meyer, 1956; North, Hargreaves, & O'Neill, 2000), challenge our political views (Berger, 2000; Brooks, 2015; Rosenthal, 2001), provide a vehicle to tell our stories (Baker, Wigram, Stott, & McFerran, 2008; DeNora, 2000; Williams, 2012), or facilitate coming to know ourselves (Frith, 1996). These functions of music—communication, expression, identity exploration, and reinforcing or challenging our values—point to the relational nature of music. It remains impossible to extract music from its context; rather, understanding music as a situated human practice and a lived experience allows us to consider different social functions of music.

Music educators often position music making as intrinsically invaluable (Davis, 2007; Jorgensen, 1995), thus celebrating music as an art form for musical qualities alone, and perhaps situating it as an aesthetic object. Music educators frequently describe "non-musical" qualities of music as *extramusical*—the social, emotional, and political qualities that musicking engages (Reimer, 1970, 1989, 2003).[1] Following others (see for example Elliott, 1995; Elliott & Silverman, 2015; Nattiez, 1990; Shepherd, 1991; Small, 1998), I assert that, in fact, all elements that musicking engages—the social, emotional, political, and expressive qualities—remain intrinsic to the practice itself. The immense potential of musicking to help us move through our everyday lives (DeNora, 2000), to both reinforce and challenge our values, to support us in difficult times, and to help us work more effectively makes musicking exceptional. In considering the multifaceted nature of musical practices, we can understand its social qualities not as extramusical, but inherently musical. The manner in which musicking can play a role in social justice work (Benedict, Schmidt, Spruce, & Woodford, 2015; Gould et al., 2009) remains innate to musical engagement.

Activist-musicians' perspectives facilitate considering music's social functions. Drawing on their own musicking practices, activist-musicians pointed specifically to music's connective, communicative, expressive, and political potential. They further recognized musicking as a profound means to foster learning. Participants also identified more dangerous social possibilities of musicking—the manner in which it may reinscribe the status quo, further fascistic tendencies, or incite violence. The perspectives that activist-musicians shared make claims about musicking. The diverse perspectives across identities and musical practices and their agreement on certain potentialities of engaging with music make these claims valuable. Moreover, the inherently social possibilities for musicking that they identify offer important implications for constructing activist music education.

In this chapter, I focus on activist-musicians' perspectives on music and musicking rather than (music) education. As such, given its educational aims, critical pedagogy plays a supporting role in this discussion. Many ideas expressed by activist-musicians about musicking underscore the reflective, action-oriented, and transformative themes of critical pedagogy. They point

42　*The Potential of Music*

to ways that musicking involves active meaning-making, the consideration and centrality of lived experiences, the process of naming the world, and a practice of noticing I liken to conscientization. Activist-musicians' attentiveness to the dangers of musicking further highlights the need to attend to critiques. While pedagogy plays a secondary role in this chapter, the alignment of aspects of musicking with the tenets of critical pedagogy set the conditions for activist music education and for actualizing critical pedagogy in subsequent chapters. It also further emphasizes musicking's potential for critical pedagogy.

Musicking as Connection

Activist-musicians viewed engagement with music as profoundly connective, underscoring the nature of music as a human practice and a social phenomenon. Musicking, they argued, allows participants to create community and build relationships. Musical engagement also potentially connects us to people outside our immediate communities. We may draw upon music to connect our personal experiences to larger narratives, as well as to histories and past struggles. Enacting musicking as connective, activist-musicians centered lived experiences and recognized music as a human practice about human relationships. They further identified meaning-making processes inherent in forging connections.

Connecting to Others and Building Community

> NOBUKO: Music and dance can be a community-building tool that brings people together. In those instances that we're together, it reminds us that we are a community. It reminds us that we are connected.

Musicking in any capacity—whether performing, listening, creating, producing, or dancing—potentially creates relationships and community between participants and sometimes with more distant Others. Nobuko Miyamoto, a third-generation Japanese American born in 1939, was a child of the Japanese relocation camps (Burton, Roosevelt, & Cohen, 2002). Nobuko transitioned from musical theatre to activism through music in the late 1960s. In 1978, she founded *Great Leap*, a multicultural arts organization that "uses art as both performance and creative practice to deepen relations among people of diverse cultures and faiths and to transform how we live on the earth."[2] Nobuko argues that musicking brings us together. Other activist-musicians suggest that this coming together may occur through shared emotion, through using music to build bridges between people, through intentionally placing people together, through learning when to assert one's voice musically and when to support others, and through engaging with unfamiliar music.

Bryan DePuy felt that music's emotional potential builds connections between people. At the time of the interview, Bryan was a 31-year-old punk musician in a post-hardcore punk band called Spoils. He described himself as "a White, cis, queer guy [from an] upper middle-class family . . . outside of Washington, D.C." His academic work focused on women and gender studies. Exposure to the punk scene in Washington, D.C., as a preteen inspired Bryan to connect politics to music. Activist work played a significant role in his life. He noted that

> [Music is] a powerful site of connection between people and potentially a powerful site of community building and organizing people. Songs that invoke a particular emotion can galvanize people around an idea, almost irrelevant of the content of the song in some cases, but just the feeling. If a song invokes a similar feeling in a bunch of people and they all share that, then the song kind of becomes more about the connection between those people.

If musical engagement can galvanize individuals around ideas or emotions, people may potentially connect across barriers and differences. That type of transcendence points more directly to what musicking might do for humanity. In bringing us together around a common feeling, musicking might also provide a means to understand and honor different identities and foster community formation.

Chucky Kim, a 29-year-old producer, worked across musical styles, including hip-hop, to bring out the unique voices of the Asian American artists he produced. Born in California, he described himself as Korean American. His graduate work at Harvard blended philosophy, religion, and art. Chucky shared that

> My focus was always on how you form communities, and how you understand community formation through the vehicle of the arts, and through deeper understandings of self and community, and the Other. How music becomes a bridge [across] different identities and contexts.[3]

Chucky viewed musicking as a bridge that may facilitate understanding both self and community and further deconstruct barriers between individuals and groups. Thinking about community formation allowed Chucky to consider arrangement and composition as "not just something on a page, but a way of placing people together, as a way of writing for specific people so that they can tell an even bigger story." His ideas about arranging point to the intention and thoughtfulness required to bring people together. Chucky's words underscore the idea of musicking as an inherently human practice that encourages relationships and honors individuals' and groups' lived experiences.

Taiyo described a similar perspective on creating community musically:

> Jamming, vibing, and improv[is]ing with a group of people musically, theatrically—that's the practice of community. You have to listen to each other and make sure that people have their solo space or lecturing space, but at the same time, fall back and listen to places where everybody can participate.

If musicking can teach us both to value our own voices and to recognize that, at times, listening to others' voices takes precedence, then music as a practice of community teaches us to honor the contributions of both self and others (Lashbrook & Mantie, 2009).[4] Participating in music in this way shows us how to be together. Activist-musicians' perspectives suggest that engagement in musicking in any capacity may encourage individuals to value the voices of others, build relationships between individuals and groups, and further generate common feelings.

While musicking may connect individuals to each other locally, it may also help individuals connect to people more distant from their realities. Jason Hwang, age 58 at the time of the interview, described himself as an independent artist, violinist, and composer. A Chinese American originally from Illinois and living in New Jersey, Jason wrote and performed jazz, "new," and "world" music. His music fused Western and Eastern sounds, drawing innovatively upon traditional Chinese instruments. He worked regularly in schools as a teaching artist. While familiar stories may validate musickers' own realities, Jason suggested that engaging with unfamiliar musics potentially fosters open-mindedness:

> At the end [of my high school workshop], I play a mixtape of singers. All types of sounds—from Tuvan to Motown, to artists that they know. And I ask them to guess who's singing. It's kind of a game, but I say, "The more music you are open to, the more people you will be open to" . . . Music can have that function in education. Over the years, more sounds and more people make you a more open person.

Encountering unfamiliar musics may encourage open-mindedness—an element of what Bradley (2006a, 2006b) terms "multicultural human subjectivity"—a cosmopolitan sensibility one develops through participating in "global song." Experiencing and engaging in different musics' potentially both encourages a more global sensibility and connects individuals to people distant from their realities while honoring their lived experiences. Whether through shared emotion, intentional work to build bridges and place people together, opportunities to both lead and support, or open-minded encounters with the musics of others, engaging with music can facilitate building community; it connects us.

Connecting to Larger Narratives and Histories

Music's connective role extends beyond connecting people; musicking can also link personal experiences to larger narratives, including political movements, past struggles, and rich histories—a process that requires intentional meaning-making. SKIM articulated that

> I definitely started [as a musician] from a space of needing to express all these bottled up things for the past 20 years of my life. My whole life. The rawest, rawest feelings, stories, and experiences. I feel like we're about always connecting personal stories to larger political movements. In the beginning, it was a [means] to process the history of this country, war, and the reality of prison, politics, and racism that I needed to speak out on.

SKIM identified as a second-generation Korean American who was originally from the East Coast. In their[5] thirties at the time of the interview, SKIM wove fluidly between hip-hop and Korean folk drumming. Their bio proclaims that SKIM "bends genders and genres through singing, rapping, and Korean folk drumming. They began drumming in 2002, writing and performing in 2004, released 'For Every Tear' in 2006, and continued touring nationally until 2011."[6] SKIM's work began as a means to consider their own experience; they later connected their experiences to social movements that resonated with their politics. Beyond connecting individuals, musicking provides opportunities to link individual experiences to larger narratives and social movements.

Musicking may also foster connections to past struggles and varied histories and experiences. SKIM, for example, interacted with their personal history through music:

> My grandmother's generation was under Japanese imperialism. Korean traditional music was banned, so that carried into my folks' generation . . . My folks found it funny that I started wanting to drum. But I know what they're feeling is, "Wow. That's something you're interested in?" And so this kind of education happened through connect[ing] to the drum—where I come from, where my family comes from.

SKIM connected deeply with their family's past through musicking—finding a way to access their history and explore it, reclaiming music previously suppressed by imperialism. SKIM further noted that engaging with music provides a means to reflect on societal structures over time:

> [In music,] we can hear how long that same struggle has been going on and also find the space to let that frustration go and be encouraged.

When artists musically explore the trajectory of a struggle, they can contextualize it historically. As SKIM remarked, historicizing struggle is not necessarily discouraging, but may rather initiate movement forward. In moments of connectivity, the past weaves through the present toward a different possible future.

CHUCKY: So much of artistry is concerned with expressing your own story. [That] can be an empowering experience, but also very insular, [because] you become very concerned with what you've gone through. The role of a producer, in my case, is to create context for people. Whether that's a musical context of bringing in different forms and open[ing] up creative avenues, or a political and social context of like, "These are the kinds of questions that are [being asked] in the world. These are the things that are happening. How do you connect or relate what you've gone through to these other things?"

Chucky found that when he encouraged artists to connect their stories to larger narratives, the experience of creating became transformative. What might it mean for individuals grappling with their own stories to musically explore where their stories weave in and out of existential questions and structural issues? What might it mean for listeners to know that stories similar to theirs connect to larger structural issues and that systemic challenges have faces?

Musicking as Connective: Summary

Inherently connective, musicking can build community locally, provide a medium to connect to unfamiliar Others, link personal narratives to larger social movements, and connect to histories. Considering the connective potential of musical engagement allows musickers to honor lived experiences and make meaning to understand musical practices in their larger sociopolitical and sociohistorical contexts.

Musicking as Communication and Expression

People may engage music, as an expressive, social medium, to communicate ideas, stories, and emotions (Berger, 2000; Cross, 2014; Davis, 2007; Lundqvist et al., 2009). Individuals or groups may use music to tell a story (Baker, 2015; Baker et al., 2008; Williams, 2012) or express themselves (Baker, 2015). Activist-musicians all identified communicative and expressive potential in musicking practices. Indeed, musicking allows artists to speak to conditions that affect them (Berger, 2000; Brooks, 2015; Rosenthal, 2001). Listeners may also recognize themselves and others in their chosen musics. All facets of musicking—performing, creating, listening, dancing, producing—may facilitate communication and expression. Engaging in music as a means to tell stories or express emotions, moreover, encourages coming to voice and naming the world. Coming to voice and naming the world involve a three-part reflective and action-oriented process: exploring identity, asserting one's experience, and learning to value others' assertions.

Telling Stories

Chucky argued that musicking gives "tools to people to help better tell their stories," underscoring the possibilities of conveying human experiences through engagement with music. Activist-musicians, who considered themselves political to varying degrees, found that musicking presented a way to communicate stories, including underrepresented narratives, and explore identity politics (Hess, 2019). Indeed, the Freirian process of coming to voice frequently involves storytelling or reckoning with past experiences.[7] Taiyo noted, "[Music is] really about community and bring [ing] stories that are underrepresented out there in the music."

Musicking provided a means, for example, for Dan Matthews to grapple with complex issues of identity and assert an underrepresented narrative— his own story as an Asian American adoptee. Dan, a 29-year-old, self-described "1.5 generation" Korean American adoptee, lived in Los Angeles at the time of the interview. A prominent hip-hop artist, DANakaDAN's music often focused on identity politics—race politics, being adopted, and what it means to be "Asian in America,"

> how it is, as an adoptee, feeling Asian, but also feeling White. Never feeling accepted by the Asian people, but never feeling accepted by the White people. What does it mean to be Asian with White parents? Does that mean I have White privilege or do I have a weird combination of White privilege, but also not because I'm still a minority?

Dan's (DANakaDAN's) song "Is There Anybody Out There"[8] wonders if there are others with similar adoption stories. What might it mean for young Asian American adoptees to listen to a song that grapples with issues they also face? Hearing this song may allow for the expression or exploration of the complexity of belonging and not belonging.

Casey Mecija, a 32-year-old Filipino Canadian multidisciplinary artist, lived in Toronto, Ontario, Canada, at the time of the interview. The former vocalist and songwriter of the Canadian orchestral pop band Ohbijou, a filmmaker, and the host of a Canadian Broadcasting Corporation radio show called *The Doc Project*, Casey's music spanned multiple styles, including indie pop, folk, and bluegrass. A Ph.D. student at the time of interview, Casey's academic work focused on art, media, and cultural studies in relation to immigration and multiculturalism. Casey's song "Balikbayan" presented personal family history intertwined with the Filipino diaspora.

> We have a song called "Balikbayan" that talked about Filipino diaspora and the impacts of migration. I'm really proud [of that song] because it was inspired by my family, and I never used to think about incorporating my family and the story of my family in my music in such an

upfront way—and was scared to—like was unsure how that would be received.

Through "Balikbayan," Casey gave these issues voice. When someone tells a difficult story that represents the experiences of many, that story may validate people with similar stories. "Balikbayan" allowed Casey to explore identity, context, and history, and assert it into public discourse, naming the world. Musicking facilitates communicating such stories.

Musicking as Emotional Expression

DAN: I think that a lot of musicians use [music] as a way to communicate their feelings about life and their struggle and what they're going through.

Musical storytelling provided a mechanism for Dan to express feelings about life. Engaging with music can be therapeutic (Adamek & Darrow, 2010; Baker, 2015; Baker et al., 2008; Dalton & Krout, 2006; Rhodes & Schechter, 2014). Musicking can help people process trauma and grief and provide emotional support (Bradley, 2012b; DeNora, 2013; Hill, 2009; Kinney, 2012; Rhodes & Schechter, 2014) and may also facilitate exploring the human condition. Bryan noted that

> I always associated music really strongly with accessing feelings in a form that is not as bound to material experience. And it may invoke a memory of an experience or an expected experience, but I feel like it's a raw form of feeling feelings . . . One of the main things music does is provide a space to process emotions, however unconsciously or consciously.

Dan and Bryan both noted that musicking helps individuals express and process emotions and experiences.

Coming to Voice and Naming the World: Exploring and Expressing Identity

The Freirian processes of coming to voice and naming the world inform the manner in which youth engage music to tell stories and express emotions. I conceptualize coming to voice and naming the world in three parts consistent with the reflective and action-oriented goals of praxis: exploring identity, finding one's voice and learning to assert it in the world, and valuing the voices and contributions of others. The stories activist-musicians shared in their music often necessitated careful consideration of identity before any creating (Hess, 2019)—the reflective facet of the process. People may participate in musicking to explore their musical identities (O'Neill,

2002), their positionalities (MacDonald, Hargreaves, & Miell, 2002), their ethnic, cultural, and national identities (Folkestad, 2002; Frith, 1996; Stokes, 1997), and/or catalogue their personal life experiences (DeNora, 2000). Frith (1996) argues that identity formation related to music relies on two premises: "first, that identity is *mobile*, a process, not a thing, a becoming not a being; second that our experience of music—of music making and music listening—is best understood as an experience of this *self-in-process*" (p. 109, emphasis in original). Musicking allows us to explore ourselves as in-process—an important first reflective step in coming to voice.

After exploring identity, we may subsequently develop and assert our voices through musicking, engaging the action-oriented process of naming the world. Theresa Vu (tvu), a 32-year-old Vietnamese American, grew up on the West Coast. A computer programmer and hip-hop artist in New York City, her group, Magnetic North, created the album *Home:Word* to explore issues of Asian American identity in the 21st century. tvu saw music as a way to educate listeners on political issues and organized benefit concerts to raise awareness and funds for issues affecting Asian American populations in particular. She shared that

> At the end of the day, music is meant to say something. And trying to teach people [at a songwriting workshop] how to say it, how to articulate it, but also trying to figure out what they want to say is really the hard part. When I first started, I was just emulating people. It took a long time to find the voice.

This second phase in coming to voice, then, involves finding one's own voice—to shift from emulating others, as tvu noted, to developing and honoring one's own perspective. The second aspect of this phase involves asserting one's voice by articulating one's experiences or musically naming the world, if one chooses. Jason valued individual voices deeply in his work and argued that musicking fundamentally involves recognizing individuals' unique contributions—the final phase in coming to voice and naming the world, an important element of Freirian dialogue:

> In jazz, it's probably the concept of improvisation—of spontaneous language that is your own—that is [the] most graphic.

Learning to value the contributions that we, as individuals, put out into the world is, as Jason later noted, "an extraordinarily political act." Jason's words connect to Taiyo's "practice of community"—a space where individuals listen carefully to others and learn when to assert their voices and when to support others' contributions. This three-part process of coming to voice and naming the world allows musickers to explore their identities, assert their voices, and value the voices of others. Coming to voice, as an interrelated process of reflection and action, ultimately facilitates both telling stories and expressing emotions.

Music's Potential for Communicating Difficult Truths

In positioning musicking as a medium to share personal stories, express emotions, and name the world, grappling with the content of music may prove difficult for listeners. tvu noted that music may communicate difficult themes more easily than other media:

> Sometimes it's like Mary Poppins saying medicine needs sugar. Sometimes messages need these flowing beautiful instrumentals to get through to you. It can be a lot to take in, but music can kind of be that sugar to just open up your mind.

Drawing on a metaphor from a musical, tvu articulated why music may impart ideas more effectively than speech. Indeed, music may help us hear difficult truths. When it comes to issues of race, for example, Applebaum (2010) argues that when some White students encounter topics that name their complicity in oppressive structures, they enact "White indignation"—defensiveness against the violation of their understandings of themselves as "good." Magnetic North's song "Fukushima"[9] speaks to natural and human-perpetuated tragedies in a manner perhaps easier to hear than a news channel delivering similar information. While students may shut down defensively when they encounter difficult issues, music creates opportunities to present these same issues "with sugar."

Musicking as Communicative and Expressive: Summary

Intrinsically expressive, musicking provides a vehicle to tell stories, share experiences, name the world, process emotions, and develop and assert one's unique voice. Listeners may also receive difficult messages more easily when they grapple with these ideas through musical encounters. Inherently social and relational, music's communicative and expressive potential creates opportunities to engage in processes of coming to voice, naming the world, and honoring and expressing lived experiences within music education.

Musicking as Political

An inherently political force, music acts; it is never neutral. Activist-musicians suggested that while musicking can potentially generate change that challenges the status quo, it can also reinscribe it. They argued that music provides a mechanism to critique various conditions and identify issues affecting groups or individuals—what Freire (2000/1970) calls naming the world. Activist-musicians and musickers may also use music to organize social movements (see Eyerman & Jamison, 1998; Roy, 2010 for examples). The potential for music education lies in music's ability to name the world and engage in a practice of noticing ideologies, discourses, and power structures (a re-actualization of conscientization).

Music to Generate Change

LEE: I'm a huge believer in the power of the arts to change hearts and minds. . . . The TV show *24* had an African American president before we had Barack Obama. I think it carries a lot of weight in shifting and shaping—sometimes shape-shifting—perceptions. I have high hopes. We're all in it because we really think that the work has the power to touch people. Perhaps our hope [as artists] is it will make [audiences] feel empathy.

Activist-musicians note that, as an inherently social phenomenon, musicking can generate change and create possibilities. Lee Phenner, a White woman of Western European descent, described herself as "far left politically." Raised in Western Massachusetts, she moved to Boston in 1994. Age 51 at the time of interview, Lee worked as a professional writer. She wrote the book and lyrics for the musical *A Pint of Understanding*—a show that fictionalizes the events surrounding the arrest in 2009 of Henry Louis Gates, Jr., by a White police officer at Gates' residence—in order to speak to complex issues of race in the United States. Lee hoped to facilitate critical conversations, empathy, and change through retelling the events artistically. Half of the activist-musicians spoke of music's potential to generate change. Lee's words about the Black president on *24* who predated Obama remind us that art can make the implausible seem plausible, and perhaps even naturalize it. In musicking, we may create conditions for hopeful possibilities to become realities—a powerful collective imagining.

Musickers can also purposefully envision specific changes. Nobuko shared that

> One [cultural tradition that could be useful in the environmental movement] is the tradition of "no waste" called *mottainai*. I created a music video about disposable chopsticks and how many trees are cut down for disposable chopsticks. I created another video called "Mottainai"[10] which talks about different ways that we cannot waste. [This is] a way of giving messages that are fun, that are engaging. The environment is the scariest proposition. People say, "There's not going to be anything left for our children." So, people feel overwhelmed instead of saying, "We can make small changes. We can do this personally and then we can look at our institutions and begin making changes there."

52 *The Potential of Music*

Music can generate change. While Lee's commentary on *24* focused on the power of the arts to create possibilities, Nobuko offered practical and actionable strategies. Global challenges—terrifying environmental issues, systemic oppression that ends in fatalities, class and racial divisions that become more pronounced daily, and other outwardly immovable systems and structures—can seem monumental. Nobuko described how she engaged music to suggest implementable strategies against structures that overwhelm individuals. Musickers, then, potentially both facilitate small shifts against oppressive structures and immobilizing problems and provide a medium to consider and discuss difficult issues.

Challenging the Status Quo: Enacting Social Justice through Music

In *Musicking*, Small (1998) argues that we engage in music to reinforce our values. His illustration of the symphony demonstrates how this affirmation of values may reinforce the status quo. White, middle-class symphony attendees, for example, see White, middle-class values reflected at the symphony. While artists may position music to reinscribe oppressive structures, they may also musically critique dominant systems; hip-hop artists, for example, can challenge racism and racist societal structures (Au, 2005; Ladson-Billings, 2015). Critiquing dominant structures challenges the status quo. When I interviewed the activist-musicians, I asked them to speak about the potential of engaging with music to either reinscribe or subvert the status quo. Most activist-musicians felt strongly that music could do both.

SKIM: Music can be used for anything that one intends. It has become boxed into that commercial machine, so it's used to sell alcohol or the American capitalist machine. Or war. But every day, it's [also] used to deal with the traumas these injustices bring. There's so many activists and artists and people that don't even use those terms that do workshops with young people who are incarcerated or start conversations about some of the traumas in people's lives. We see how crucial it is; someone could be 16 or 60 years old and never put thoughts on paper and read it aloud. Even heard their voice. Or shared that with somebody.

Engaging with music can both reinscribe and disrupt the status quo. Artists can position music to reinforce capitalism, war, and other dominant discourses through lyrics and representations valorizing wealth, violence, and oppression. SKIM, however, articulated how artists may engage music to address traumas and injustices and facilitate individuals' ability to insert their own voices strongly into the world—processes of both coming to voice and naming the world (Freire, 2000/1970). Musicking may help people counter dominant deficit narratives (Hess, 2018a). Casey pointed, for example, to A Tribe Called Red, a band in Canada that troubles "what is inherently understood as Canadian music" and speaks out on Indigenous issues. In doing so, they oppose settler colonial narratives. Musickers who provide counter-narratives to dominant discourses create space for different imaginaries.

Representations through media and music can create similar possibilities. tvu's song "New Love" with her band, Magnetic North, for example, represented queer love lyrically and visually with images of tvu and a partner in the video.[11] People who identify as LGBTQQIA may experience marginalization in society, and "New Love" worked against such marginalization through presenting queer love as beautiful. Artistic representations across identities can humanize unfamiliar groups and create understandings of lived experiences outside of one's personal scope.[12] As such, purposeful musicking may facilitate valuing and legitimizing lives deemed not valuable—or worse, disposable, and/or unlivable (Foucault, 1994).

For people whose identities have historically been underrepresented in certain roles, taking on such roles can challenge the status quo. Age 37 at the time of the interview, L'Oqenz (El), a Toronto-based deejay, collaborated with multiple artists. A Canadian with roots in Guyana and Barbados, she worked across multiple styles that included hip-hop, rock, funk, soul, house, and reggae. El noted that she grew up with "a blend of the arts and activism." Magali Meagher, a White woman with French and Canadian heritage, grew up in Guelph, Ontario. She was 38 at the time of the interview. The frontliner for an indie rock group called The Phonemes, multi-instrumentalist and singer Magali also co-directed Girls Rock Camp in Toronto, a program in which teenage girls learn instruments and enact musical practices that resonate with their identities. As members of underrepresented populations, tvu, Magali, and El all spoke of representing when they emceed, sang, played, and deejayed across genres of hip-hop and rock:

> TVU: When I started performing in college, it was great to have women come up afterwards and say how great it was to see a female emcee up there that wasn't a 16-bar in a love song. That was something other than a foil to the guy on a rap. And I think that really cemented it in me how important it was to, so cliché, but to represent.

Centering minoritized identities in key musical roles sends the message that it is possible to participate in music in ways previously unimagined. In this case, when women see tvu emcee, Magali sing rock and play drums and guitar, and El deejay, those musical practices become possibilities for the women watching. Would-be musicians sometimes need to see themselves represented before they feel they can participate.[13]

Music as a Medium to Critique and Name the World

Artists can also deliberately engage oppressive structures with their music—a practice of noticing. At the time of the interview, Pete Shungu, a 33-year-old hip-hop/soul/jazz/funk musician, emceed and played trumpet in the Afro D All Starz.[14] Originally from New Jersey, he identified as multiracial and Black. He studied international relations and education, taught in classroom settings, and worked with youth through uAspire.[15]

> I wrote this spoken word piece about the "B" word[16] and why I choose not to use that word. I've been in classrooms where I'm sharing [that poem] and there [are] young men in that classroom who are like: "Oh, I never thought about that before. I'm not going to use that word." And to me that's powerful. I had a young woman thank me after I shared that poem one time, and say that she had been in an abusive relationship and hearing those words helped her to see that there were people out there who . . . get it, and don't think domestic violence is acceptable.

Pete artistically challenged using the "B" word. Audiences who heard him perform this spoken-word piece either considered the inherent patriarchy of the word or let his words affirm them. This anti-oppressive musical critique created awareness of oppressive language and allowed Pete to name the world (Freire, 2000/1970). Engaging with music can make us aware of conditions that shape our lives; it can also help us interrogate language structures and the way our actions unintentionally reinscribe oppressive systems (see Hess, 2017).

Patrick Huang (DJ Phatrick), a 32-year-old second-generation Chinese American, lived in California at the time of the interview. A prominent hip-hop deejay, he deejayed for multiple artists, including Bambu—a Filipino American emcee. A youth educator in a community hip-hop program in California, DJ Phatrick asserted that youth can become aware of conditions that affect them through musical engagement:

> [As an educator,] you break down a song like "The Message" by Grandmaster Flash and Furious Five, which talks about growing up in the projects—broken glass everywhere. You take these themes and analyze why these themes are so prevalent in hip-hop music. Then you start talking about class. You start talking about racism. You start talking about history. Because the population of youth I predominantly work with are from the same background as the folks who are making the music in terms of class, neighborhoods, and what they're experiencing, that's the self-reflection aspect. 'Cause social justice is also about internal social justice. You're figuring out why you are the way you are, why the neighborhoods you live in are the way they are, why the police act the way they do in your neighborhoods.

Patrick spoke of musicking as a means to think about structures that shape individuals' lives. In this case, youth and other listeners can name their worlds (Freire, 2000/1970) through music. Musicking provides a means for individuals to identify systemic issues.

Musicking as Political: Summary

Musical engagement potentially generates change. It may reinscribe or subvert the status quo, and also provides a medium to critique dominant and oppressive narratives and name the world (Freire, 2000/1970). Because of its connection to emotion (Berger, 2000; Hill, 2009; Lundqvist et al., 2009; Meyer, 1956), music as an inherently human practice may facilitate the rich communication of stories, experiences, and ideas. The manner in which activist-musicians describe the political and critical potential of musicking has implications for enacting similar ideas in music education.

Musicking as Dangerous

> Pied Pipers are still playing their tunes in many places and trying to entrance people through the transforming power of music. Perhaps Adorno's most powerful advice is: To resist the myth of the entrancing power of music is to make the world a better place.
>
> (Kertz-Welzel, 2005, p. 10)

Amidst the possibilities musicking offers, we may forget its dangerous potential—the manner in which people may engage the "entrancing power of music" to mobilize unthinking masses and, on some occasions, create fascistic experiences or reinscribe oppression. As SKIM asserted, "Music can be used for anything that one intends." Artists can position music to reinforce the status quo, affirm violence, and replicate oppressive relations (Bradley, 2009b; Turino, 2008). In music education, attending to these possibilities will help educators and artists guard against musicking's entrancing potential. These possibilities remind us to proceed with both caution and uncertainty when enacting critical pedagogy.

In exploring music's dangerous possibilities, observing how musickers can reinscribe oppression becomes important. Artists may engage music to propagate stereotypes and violence and replicate oppressive relations. Small's (1998) work affirms that musical experiences may reinforce values aligned with the status quo. Pete asserts that music can easily go in any direction:

> I think there's a lot of music out there that does reinforce the status quo, and does perpetuate the same stereotypes, and I think the industry is set up to monetarily reward a lot of music that does reinforce that. It takes guts to go against that, but there's definitely music out there that pushes to make change.

Pete's words underscore the need to vigilantly consider the political potential of musicking. Artists may engage music to reinscribe oppression through perpetuating stereotypes, and the industry routinely celebrates such music (hooks, 2008/1994). As this chapter argues, music is never neutral; attentiveness involves interrogating the political intentions inherent in all music encountered—a practice of noticing ideologies.

El's thoughts on vibrations further complicate this discussion:

> I respect what my son wants to listen to because I was his age and I did the same thing. But I also have the same conversation with him that my mother did, 'cause I get it now: "Please listen to the words. Listen to what's being said and be conscious of that." . . . It becomes a part of your inner conversation. It's a vibration. It's a frequency. It's an affirmation.

If musickers do not deliberately interrogate the music they encounter, it may integrate into their thinking (American Academy of Pediatrics, 2009; Anderson, Carnagey, & Eubanks, 2003; Wass et al., 1989/1988). Music that reinscribes oppression and/or reinforces stereotypes may easily become part of what El calls our "inner conversation." When individuals critique what they hear, they can challenge or affirm the content before it enters their bodies and minds. In engaging music politically, then, particularly in the classroom, educators and activist-musicians alike must remain mindful of its "dangerous" potential.

Music may also propagate violence. El cautions that while music can bring people together, it can also divide people:

> [Music] can pull people apart. If I'm hearing a lot of gun music and it's saying a certain message then, depending on my circumstances, I can fall into that frequency and that becomes my reality.

We must critique music we encounter lest violence and oppression become part of our "inner conversation" (American Academy of Pediatrics, 2009; Anderson, Carnagey, & Eubanks, 2003; Wass et al., 1989/1988).

This entrancing power of music can further lend itself to fascist agendas. Bryan argued that "songs that invoke a particular emotion can galvanize people around an idea, almost irrelevant of the content of the song in some cases, but just the feeling." Organizing music toward specific social ends has historical roots. Turino (2008), for example, considers how Nazi Germany and the U.S. Civil Rights Movement both employed music to shape people's perspectives of political issues (also see Kertz-Welzel, 2005). Becoming aware of the motivations of artists, production companies, and political movements for producing music remain crucial in considering how to navigate the music we encounter. Uniting people across a common feeling may well result in an unthinking mass or, worse, a mob mentality. Scholars point to music as powerful (see for example Hebert & Kertz-Welzel, 2012; Kertz-Welzel, 2012; Southcott, 2012), citing, for example, the power of music to bring people together and convene individuals around a common idea (Abril, 2012; Dairianathan & Lum, 2012). Lamm and Silani (2014) argue that musicking can galvanize groups around shared affective experiences:

> This lack of self-awareness and self/other distinction is one putative mechanism of collective affective experiences such as the high synchrony between individuals that occurs during mass phenomena, such as at music concerts or at political demonstrations. There, the individual becomes part of a larger crowd, and loses his or her ability for self-awareness and self/other distinction.
>
> (p. 73)

Bradley (2009b) refers to the "magic feeling" that musicking can create when a perfect constellation of conditions comes together, perhaps limiting any possibility of dissent. Creating room for dissent must legitimize possible opposition rather than result in ostracization. In imagining the collectives that musicking can facilitate, I aim to consider the possibility of thinking, fully engaged individuals *within* collectives, rather than unthinking masses.

To provide an example, tvu's community gathered to support a benefit concert for Aid to Children Without Parents (ACWP), an organization that builds vocational schools to help youth sold into the sex industry learn skills to make a living outside of the industry.

> ["Home for the Holla! Days"] was such an eye-opening experience to think of music as a conduit, vs. just as background noise, or something to feel good. And seeing how it affected the audience that was there too. Seeing how it energized people. How it got the community together. There was such power in bringing people together and aligning them to a message that was so palpable, and really made me believe that the music had to say something worthwhile.

In reading her words, the danger is audible. A "palpable message," "the power in bringing people together," "aligning [people] to a message"—as a social phenomenon, music facilitates "palpable" feelings. In this case, the fundraiser supported an organization providing crucial interventions. As Bradley (2009b) argues, however, governments, groups, organizations, or institutions may use these palpable feelings for other ends entirely. Given the ubiquity of music, attending to and challenging the messages it communicates presents us with choices about the ideas with which we align.

Activist-musicians identified musicking's dangerous potential, noting the manner in which groups may use it to mobilize unthinking masses and promote a fascist agenda. Artists may also position music to further oppression through reinforcing stereotypes, promoting violence, and reinscribing the status quo. Given these possibilities, resisting the "entrancing power of music is to make the world a better place" (Kertz-Welzel, 2005, p. 10).

Musicking as a Learning Site

In this chapter, I focused on activist-musicians' perspectives on the role of music in society. That their words resonate with themes in critical pedagogy has implications for music education that I begin to examine in Chapter 3. It therefore becomes important to note that half of the activist-musicians explicitly named the educative potential of musicking. Pete noted that

> Playing a version of the South African National Anthem for students and then talking about the history of apartheid [lets me] introduce those concepts and talk about how music can represent different things for different people. There are people who hear the South African National Anthem and associate it with oppression because it's the anthem of this country that has this problematic racial history.[17] There are other people who hear it and see the liberation beyond that. . . . It doesn't always mean the same thing to different people.

Encountering different musics within their historical contexts allows participants in music to consider music and its complexities. This example demonstrates specific instances in which engaging with music can serve as a vehicle to explore issues of power, equity, sociohistorical and sociopolitical context, and justice (see for example Bradley, 2006b; Hess, 2013b, 2014, 2015b, 2016; Morton, 1994; Schmidt, 2005; Vaugeois, 2009).

Music can also communicate complex information in a way that people can perhaps more easily receive and respond to:

PATRICK: I deejay for an artist named Bambu. He's a Filipino American artist. You could call him a revolutionary, politically conscious artist. He deals with complex issues of police oppression, of class warfare, of colonialism, and neo-colonialism in a song. In one verse. And not only is it in a verse, he's doing it in a way that's, for lack of a better word, that's cool. 'Cause his music is fun to listen to and it doesn't sound like a lecture. Some rappers are definitely lecturers. Some rappers, you listen and they're preaching to you or they're lecturing to you. Bam can tell a story about a meth addict in the Philippines and you don't know it, but he's really teaching you about feudalism and what it leads to.

Patrick (DJ Phatrick) speaks to Bambu's ability to communicate information in an accessible manner. His listeners and participants might learn about complex issues through a relatable story he emcees. Engaging with music not only enables learning; it actually facilitates understanding highly complicated systems, structures, and issues.

To conclude, I draw again on Taiyo's ideas:

That pie-in-the-sky concert is the pie-in-the-sky class. Last year, I went to see Stevie Wonder at Central Park. He's going through all his hits and he's got an amazing band, and everybody's up and dancing. Everybody's involved, everybody's singing. Not just the band, but everybody in the audience is singing. And three-quarters in, he starts playing the chords of John Lennon's "Imagine" and he's like, "This was written by my friend John Lennon who died a few blocks away, right in this park. By a mentally disabled man who had access to guns. We need to do something serious about gun control in this country." This was just when the country was in uproar about Trayvon Martin. And then, within the song, when he's singing "Imagine," he starts singing Marvin Gaye "What's Going On." He sung that for a little bit and comes back to "Imagine." So right then and there, he wove together Trayvon Martin, John Lennon, Marvin Gaye, gun control, mental health, altogether in one song, one moment, one critical moment. Everybody's moved. Everybody. So many of us are just in tears, but everybody was up just enjoying themselves and singing. That to me was a profoundly educational moment as well as a cultural moment, and that's the pie-in-the-sky for me. When I'm designing an ideal class, everybody should be up and participating, singing, dancing, whatever it is. It should be multi-modal. They're visually interacting, the band is playing, and there's a lot happening, sensory-wise. And then there's something really critical of the moment that is engaging with the past, present, and the future. That's an ideal curriculum to me. That's pie-in-the-sky. A pie-in-the-sky class to me is like what you would find in a pie-in-the-sky show. Concert. Cultural event.

This concert was the epitome of a learning experience for Taiyo. It involved participation, addressed and wove together multiple significant issues, and connected past, present, and future. As Chapter 3 pivots from music to focus on music education, music educators might consider ways to intertwine issues important to the youth we teach in a manner that is multi-modal and inherently participatory (Keil & Feld, 2005; Turino, 2008).[18]

Summary

The activist-musicians identified the connective, expressive, and communicative potential of musicking practices. They further noted the manner in which artists engage music politically. Music is never neutral; recognizing the ways in which artists position all musics remains crucial to learning to think critically and challenge assumptions. Musical engagement can also be dangerous. Musicking's inherently political nature requires participants (including listeners) to precisely interrogate which movements and frameworks their chosen music serves. Finally, and perhaps most importantly for our purposes, musicking presents opportunities for learning. Whether participating in a concert, listening to lyrics, analyzing the political context of a complex song, or imagining new possibilities, musickers can learn through music. Activist-musicians' ideas further resonate with the tenets of critical pedagogy and identify ways that musicking involves reflective and action-oriented processes that include active meaning-making, honoring lived experiences, naming the world, coming to voice, and engaging in a practice of noticing. The presence of critical pedagogy in a discussion of music underscores musicking's critical pedagogical potential and underpins subsequent chapters. The next chapter examines music education as connection and explores the ways in which music education can connect individuals to others in their community, link musics to their histories, and connect youth to unfamiliar Others.

Notes

1 Reimer (1970, 1989, 2003) typically identifies the social aspects of musical experiences as *extramusical*.
2 See www.greatleap.org for more details on the organization.
3 In Hess (2019), I present a discussion of identity politics that draws upon Chucky's words and other participants' contributions in this chapter.
4 Lashbrook and Mantie (2009) explore the way that educators in the One World Youth Arts Project explicitly worked to value the "subjugated knowledges" and experiences of youth in the program.
5 "They" is SKIM's preferred pronoun.
6 See http://conference.advancingjustice.org/2013/speaker-lineup/saeun-skim-kim/
7 In considering unrepresented narratives, I utilize the concept of *coming to voice* in critical pedagogy to contextualize such stories. I note, however, the importance of the concept of *counterstorytelling* within Critical Race Theory. Counterstories consist of stories or narratives that highlight the perspectives of subjugated voices in order to subvert or interrupt dominant narratives and oppressive power structures (Delgado, 2000; Delgado & Stefancic, 2001; Ladson-Billings, 1998). "Powerfully written stories and narratives may begin a process of adjustment in our system of beliefs and categories by calling attention to neglected evidence and reminding readers of our common humanity" (Delgado & Stefancic, 2001, p. 43). Taiyo's emphasis on privileging underrepresented voices aligns with the notion of the counterstory, and we can understand his work through a critical race framework.
8 See "Is There Anybody Out There": www.youtube.com/watch?v=c_PcFDoOihY
9 See "Fukushima": www.youtube.com/watch?v=kgVEfCnqtmk
10 See "Mottanai—Don't Waste What Nature Gives You . . .": www.youtube.com/watch?v=TrMLqbxL0E0
11 See "New Love": www.youtube.com/watch?v=vTfQ1M-v9gk.
12 Importantly, representations can also powerfully communicate and reinforce stereotypes about groups of people (Hall, 1997; hooks, 1992).
13 A number of feminist music education scholars point to the importance of the representation of women in varied musical activities (Gould, 1992, 1996; Grant, 2000; Koza, 1992b, 1994c, 1994d; Lamb, 1987). Critical race scholars similarly advocate the representation of people of color across musicking pursuits (Bradley, 2006a, 2006b; Hess, 2013b; Lind & McKoy, 2016). Representations play an important role across all identity categories.

14 See the Afro D All Starz' album *Strength in Numbers*: https://afrodallstarz.bandcamp.com
15 uAspire is an organization that "works to ensure that all young people have the financial information and resources necessary to find an affordable path to—and through—a postsecondary education." See www.uaspire.org/about/mission
16 See "The 'B' word": www.youtube.com/watch?v=mAOVeck0vbo
17 "N'kosi Sikele" became the anthem of South Africa in 1994 after apartheid fell and Mandela was elected. As a symbol of the anti-apartheid movement, the song was suppressed during apartheid (Hirsch, 2002).
18 Participatory musical culture in this context embraces all facets of musicking identified by Small (1998) and beyond—performing, creating, listening, dancing, production, and otherwise facilitating musical happenings (p. 9).

3 Music Education as Connection

Activist-musicians identified the connective nature of music as a quality they deeply valued, pointing to the ways in which musicking builds community and connects us to people distant from our own experiences and to histories and past struggles. They similarly identified the connective potential of music education, understanding musicking as an inherently relational and situated human practice rich with humanizing potential. Musicking, Small (1998) argues, is a human encounter. Recognizing the humanity embedded in our diverse musicking practices further connects us to each other by acknowledging the shared mechanism for expression. Activist-musicians elucidated the value of building connections between youth in the classroom community, between musics and their human contexts, and between youth and unfamiliar Others by including a broad range of musics in the classroom.

Each section of this chapter describes practices intrinsic to enacting music education as connective in this manner—becoming an able facilitator, developing rich contextual knowledge, and building knowledge of multiple traditions. In alignment with critical pedagogy, choosing to understand music education as inherently connective emphasizes the nature of music as a human practice—a lived experience—and encourages coming to voice and ethical action within that human connection. Connecting music to its sociocultural and sociohistorical context further calls upon participants in education to make meaning of their encounters—a reactualization of problem-posing education in opposition to passive education (Freire, 2000/1970).

"The Practice of Community": Building Community in the Classroom

In considering music education's connective qualities, activist-musicians underscored the importance of building community in the classroom and emphasized the relational nature of musicking. They identified three interrelated practices to foster relationships based on mutual respect in classroom communities: teaching ensemble as togetherness, creating mutually supportive spaces, and giving youth important responsibilities. Choosing to understand music education as intrinsically connective encourages classroom relationships. Music educators, recognizing musicking as an inherently human practice, facilitate experiences that connect youth to each other and foster community, potentially encouraging them to come to voice (Freire, 2000/1970) and assert their unique musical and personal contributions in the classroom community.

Teaching Ensemble as Togetherness

A number of activist-musicians advocated for actively teaching ensemble. *Ensemble* means "together" in French; coming together is thus intrinsic to the concept of ensemble. The practice of ensemble creates opportunities to build relationships. Dale and Hyslop-Margison (2010) assert that enacting critical pedagogy involves fostering dialogue in ways that create

> open and trusting relationships between two or more people; monologues, too often the dominant discourse in schools, are closed relationships that demand centralized epistemic authority. One important aspect of dialogue is its ability to build social and emotionally caring relationships between people.
>
> (p. 4)

Jason argued that musicking fundamentally involves human relationships:

> When an ensemble of people from diverse backgrounds make music, it is the most ideal set of human relationships you can imagine. . . . One musician spontaneously offers initiative, and then another musician spontaneously supports that initiative. This dynamic exchange becomes fluid throughout the ensemble. When [people] hear that interaction—this empathy that is required to make music—they're experiencing this wonderful set of human relationships that I think will inspire them to open and deepen their societal and political relationships.

Jason identifies the manner in which music allows people to share their unique voices with their communities in collaboration with others. Small (1998) similarly points to the relational nature of music and the ideal relationships musicking makes possible: "we bring into existence a set of relationships that model the relationships of our world, not as they are but as we would wish them to be" (p. 50). Ensemble enacted as togetherness fosters interaction, human relationships, and what Turino (2008) calls "social synchrony" (pp. 41–44). These dialogical interactions communicate the inherent value of all participants in musicking and underscore their important contributions—a significant Freirian theme (Kirylo, 2011). Ensemble as the practice of community teaches youth to value others' contributions and assert their own voices when appropriate, enacting music as an intrinsically human practice rooted in lived experiences that encourages coming to voice (Freire, 2000/1970).

Musicking provides a means to engage in supportive relationships and participate in valuable experiences. As Taiyo suggested in Chapter 2,

> Jamming, vibing, and improv[is]ing with a group of people musically, theatrically—that's the practice of community. You have to listen to each other and make sure that people have their solo space or lecturing space, but at the same time, fall back and listen to places where everybody can participate.

Taiyo identified the reciprocal and collaborative nature of participating in a musical community. Ensemble, in this sense, is not director- or conductor-centered (Bartel, 2004, pp. xii–xiii; Hess, 2013b) or particularly hierarchical (O'Toole, 1994b; Small, 1998), as frequently enacted in bands, orchestras, and choirs. This type of ensemble honors all members' contributions and encourages them to listen to and for each other and take up different roles when appropriate—a type of coming to voice (Freire, 2000/1970). Dialogic ensembles and Western classical ensembles, however, are not necessarily mutually exclusive. Literature on democratic music education often points to ways that educators can facilitate dialogic relations in (classical) ensemble contexts (Allsup, 2002, 2003a; Benedict, 2007; Tan, 2014).

Creating Mutually Supportive Spaces

To create ensemble, activist-musicians advocated for fostering supportive learning environments in music education that cultivated respect, encouragement, and mutual acknowledgement among all classroom community members. For Griffin, fostering mutual respect in classroom contexts included intentionally opposing any shaming that youth faced:

> Make a mutually-supportive space to the best of your ability in a non-mutually-supportive world, but make a mutually-supportive space where kids can make music and get encouragement from other kids, as opposed to shame from other kids. You start creating a space for mutual appreciation and mutual acknowledgment of people's creativity, and musical output, before they have totally internalized the ideas of "good" and "bad" music and "right" and "wrong" people to make it.

At the time of the interview, Griffin Epstein was a 30-year-old punk musician in bands called Spoils and Griffin & the True Believers. They[1] identified as a "White settler and an Ashkenazi Jew." Originally from New York City, Griffin moved to Toronto and completed a doctorate in sociology and equity studies in education.[2] Griffin taught at a community college in Toronto and engaged in education, community organizing, and formal front-line social service provision.

Creating activist music education involves fostering positive learning spaces. Similar to critical pedagogy, such spaces facilitate relationships and dialogue between classroom community members. Noddings (2013) and O'Brien (2011) advocate for an "ethic of care" in critical education. This ethic of care resonates in Griffin's call to create mutually-supportive spaces for creating and further extends to all musicking practices. For Griffin, creating a mutually-supportive space requires a twofold effort: encouraging mutual respect while simultaneously opposing oppressive discourses and practices that may restrict the participation of particular students. Drawing on their own experience, Griffin highlights gendered conceptions of who might make different musics. Girls, for example, receive influential messages about musics and instruments that societal norms dictate may not be appropriate for their use (Abeles, 2009; Conway, 2000; Koza, 1992a; Sinsabaugh, 2005). Gendered norms also restrict boys to particular instruments and certain musics (Kennedy, 2002; Koza, 1992a, 1993, 1994b), lest they receive ridicule for choosing musics and instruments gendered as feminine. Griffin argued that when music educators foster supportive environments that denounce oppressive discourses, practices, and representations, gendered norms may exert less influence. Fostering such spaces and prioritizing an ethic of care (Noddings, 2013; O'Brien, 2011) in music education extends to supporting intersectional identities. Griffin pointed to the necessity of mutually-supportive spaces specifically for creating, underscoring the importance of classroom environment in asserting unique contributions.

Giving Youth Responsibilities

Activist-musicians further noted that trusting youth and giving them responsibilities also helped foster positive learning spaces—a third facet of building community. Magali offered an example:

> Darren O'Donnell started this group Mammalian Diving Reflex,[3] and they do a bunch of projects with kids and youth. One of them is free haircuts by children. Getting a haircut is something that we don't put into the hands of anyone. [The] kids train in community-based salons and they learn how to cut hair. On Saturday, they open up this shop and people come in for a free haircut by kids. So you're trusting young people to do something. . . . And then we did this project in the Grade 8 string class. A couple of bands from Blocks Recording Club, this record label I am a part of, went in, and taught the kids a song, and they worked towards backing up the bands. And they did a big show at the Gladstone.[4]

Magali identified times when adults in the community gave youth significant responsibilities: providing haircuts and backing professional bands. The latter example speaks specifically to musical possibilities. Magali insinuates that youth feel empowered when adults in their lives trust them with important tasks. Letting youth know that their teachers, communities, and schools deeply value both their persons and their contributions potentially bolsters their self-image (Hess, 2013b) and encourages them to respect themselves and others.

Activist-musicians thus identified three elements of building community in classroom contexts. Creating connections between youth includes teaching ensemble as a practice of community through which youth learn to value the contributions of others and assert their own voices. Educators may also consider ways to create mutually-supportive spaces that simultaneously foster mutual respect and counter oppressive norms and restrictions on musicking. Activist-musicians further suggested that trusting youth with significant responsibilities communicates to them the value of their contributions. This type of education positions youth as crucial participants in present and future society and urges educators to foster dialogical education (Freire, 2000/1970), employing a strong ethic of care (Noddings, 2013; O'Brien, 2011) to encourage youth to assert their voices strongly in the world.

Teacher as Facilitator

Building a practice of community requires educators to develop skills as facilitators. Facilitating dialogue and respect may assist in building community and encourage youth to assert their unique contributions or come to voice (Freire, 2000/1970). Taiyo asserted that able teachers-as-facilitators foster communication between vastly different groups and individuals:

> So much of what I do as an artist and as an educator is trying to bring people together—bring people on the same page and to a critical consciousness. . . . I went to a very exclusive private school [in New York City] where the majority of students were upper class and White and the students of color were scholarship students. I was a scholarship student, but I would hang out with everybody. . . . Since then, I've been a kind of communicator between different groups. So much of what I do as an artist and as an educator is to get different people talking to one another and making sure that we really communicate and that cooler heads prevail—the dialogic sense of communication.

For Taiyo, teachers-as-facilitators foster communication between groups and individuals and work toward critical consciousness (Freire, 2000/1970). He identified critical pedagogy as a crucial discourse for music educators and underscored the importance of dialogue as an outcome of successful facilitation (Freire, 2000/1970). Practicing reflective listening (Ferrara & LaMeau, 2015), taking time to learn about youth's lived experiences, and drawing upon youth's expertise on their lives (Greene, Burke, & McKenna, 2013; Roberts, Bell, & Murphy, 2008) may assist educators in building a community of trust in classrooms where youth feel valued.

Chucky advocated for educators to share their own stories:

> The curriculum, in my mind, at the very beginning, needs to be set in a way where you talk about what [students are] doing with you—open up your own story and your personal journey of why these things matter to you particularly.

Chucky wanted educators to reveal their motivations for introducing particular topics, musics, and ideas. Openly sharing one's own lived experiences perhaps leads to a willingness among students to share their own stories and motivations, creating a classroom community (Hill, 2009). Chucky further argued that teachers who model interest in classroom topics and share their journey with students create an exemplar for youth to shape the pursuit of their own interests. Rather than a hidden curriculum (Apple, 2004), Chucky moreover wanted educators to disclose their reasons for enacting curriculum in particular ways, a pedagogical move that allows youth access to the information required to make decisions about how they will participate. Chucky also envisioned teachers providing exemplars of artistic praxis to encourage youth to explore their passions and perhaps share their musicking with their communities.

Activist-musicians identified facilitation as critical to building community among youth in music classrooms. Being a facilitator does not entail dominating the class, but rather mediating dialogue and helping youth to be in conversation with each other. Facilitation centers youth in the classroom space and considers relationships. It also involves educators sharing their own experiences and revealing their motivations for curricular choices. Prioritizing facilitation that values the contributions of all assists the process of building community and creating mutually supportive spaces. Giving youth important responsibilities potentially further facilitates their sense of self-worth in the classroom community and their willingness to share their own contributions.

Connecting to Histories: Music as a Situated Human Practice

BRYAN: All music emerges from a moment in time, and a person, and a community, and a society, and if we don't acknowledge those connections, we're not going to be able to appreciate the substance of these songs. Not that there isn't something to be said for aesthetic pleasure but establishing that connection between people and music and the inextricable link between what music makes us feel, what the people who wrote it were feeling when they made it, and why they were feeling those things [is important].

As a human practice, music always emerges from a context. Considering what it might mean to situate and contextualize musics studied in schools allows us to acknowledge the humanity present in all musical practices. Activist-musicians adamantly supported contextualizing all school musics—drawing explicit relationships between musics studied and their histories to encourage meaning-making. Contextualization helps youth understand the social, political, and material contexts of musics they encounter, perhaps exposing them to perspectives beyond their own experiences and enabling them to recognize common humanity across musical practices. Freire asserts that all academic subjects are situated:

> I cannot put history and social conditions in parenthesis and then teach biology exclusively. My question is how to make clear to the students that there is no such a thing named *biology* in itself. If the teacher of biology does that and the teacher of physics does that and so on, then the students end up by gaining the critical understanding that biology and all the disciplines are not isolated from the social life.
> (Horton & Freire, 1990, p. 108, emphasis added)

Freire later clarifies:

> And let it not be said that, if I am a biology teacher, I must not "go off into other considerations"—that I must only teach biology, as if the phenomenon of life could be understood apart from its historico-social, cultural, and political framework.
> (Freire, 1998b, p. 68)

Placing music in parentheses from its lived context proves equally impossible. Activist-musicians offered specific suggestions for enacting a pedagogical practice of contextualization that encourages meaning-making and honors music as a human practice. Because music is inherently situated, they argued that grappling with contexts involves considering sociohistorical and sociopolitical contexts of individuals and groups making music, instruments, and language.

As music educators, we can further encourage youth to consider the typical contexts of musics studied:

CASEY: There's a lot of focus on the practice of music—the playing of instruments, the physicality of music. History is such an important part of contextualizing the music that you're playing: questioning where its roots are from and who were the people who were playing that music before 15 teenagers started playing it in some type of ensemble. Giving it a context might change the way that people engage in the music and ultimately create a better performance, and a better understanding, or a better communication of that music to an audience.

Casey called upon educators to consider "the people who were playing that music before 15 teenagers started playing it in some type of ensemble." When community music becomes school music, it often undergoes significant changes. Accounting for this recontextualization of community music, educators can mindfully engage any changes that occur in conversation with students. Grappling with community and individual contexts, instruments, and languages in musicking allows us to consider music as a human practice. Further identifying any changes that occur as *music* becomes *school music* acknowledges both its community context and the types of changes deemed "necessary" to engage that same music in schools. Examining these changes communicates what various stakeholders in education deem "appropriate" for school and for youth, as well as the assumptions different societies make about youth's capabilities. Contemplating the rationales for such changes may provoke fruitful discussions about power and different ideologies.

Considering Communities and Individuals

In acknowledging music as a human practice, considering community and individual contexts may allow us to situate classroom musics. Bryan emphasized the importance of understanding the role music plays in communities:

> Knowing more about different ceremonies where people played different songs, or knowing a song is a song that would only be played at a funeral, or a wedding, or at a certain time of year, would be helpful.

Understanding on which occasions and in which locations musicking typically occurs potentially informs engaging with the music in school contexts. In acknowledging the typical context, however, I do not advocate for any romanticized notion of "authenticity." In his discussion of context, Schippers (2010) places "recontextualization" at the opposite end of a continuum from "original context." Musickers continually recontextualize musics, placing them in new contexts with different participants. My consideration of typical musicking contexts seeks to inform school practices rather than replicate community musicking. Youth gain valuable experiences from participating in different musicking practices. Understanding how musical practices look and sound in the community alongside the specifics of appropriate or typical performance context informs musicking in music education and encourages youth to connect music to human practices, recognizing commonalities across musicking practices.

James Dumlao's work as a secondary music educator offers an example of what it might mean to grapple with community music contexts in school. He purposefully connected music and social movements in curriculum. James described himself as an indie–hip-hop–soul musician. Age 28 at the time of interview, he identified as "a first generation Filipino American, an educator, musician, multi-instrumentalist, and activist." He played trumpet and drums and sang in a California band called Dirty Boots. James taught at a project-based continuation high school for youth who needed to obtain their diplomas. Each project at the school emphasized a different medium or subject. James taught the "core"[5] subjects through his emphasis—music. He shared that

> I'm teaching social movements. . . . This past semester, we've been appreciating the music that [accompanies] the social movements we've been studying. We've studied the Occupy Movement, we've studied the American Indian movement. I started the semester with Mike Brown[6] and issues of police brutality. And we listened to all the songs that deal with police brutality. We listened to all the songs that had to do with the Occupy Movement—the songs that had to do with financial inequality, songs that had to do with the American Indian Movement, music that had to do with the United Farm Workers. We're going to be studying the LGBTQ Movement and Women's Liberation Movement, and we're going to keep listening to music that accompanied all of these movements.

James intentionally linked music to social movements to educate youth about contemporary issues that are both familiar and foreign to their lived realities. Music often plays a role in social movements (Eyerman & Jamison, 1998; Roy, 2010), and exploring music in tandem with social movements allows musickers to recognize the ways in which people employ music to further equity and justice in the world. From there, youth can create music to speak to their own realities, as I explore in Chapter 4. Purposefully engaging with the contexts and communities from which music emerges allows youth to acknowledge the humanity present in all musics by considering the conditions through which groups created specific musics.

While James focused specifically on social movements that produced particular musics, as music educators, we may also choose to grapple with contexts by focusing on specific people or artists and considering their circumstances. Griffin suggested that contextualization could involve studying individuals' lives:

> One of the things that was really helpful for me was writing biography reports when I was a kid—learning about individuals, or learning about spaces, and having to deal with the complexity of another human

being's life. [Asking] questions like: Where did this person grow up and what was the political situation for that person? Can you find out what it was like to grow up learning how to play music in that place? What did it mean for this person to play music?

Griffin spoke about what it means to grapple with the complexity of a human life. They discussed studying specific musicians and connecting music contextually to different topics:

> I'm pretty people-focused in general, so for me as a kid, looking at people was good. It creates empathy and feelings of intimacy. You can have slightly older kids write a report about Lead Belly, for example, and how Lead Belly was used. Made beautiful music, but was used by White folks, basically. You can [ask]: What does it mean to consume certain kinds of music? Or Elizabeth Cotten and Pete Seeger. What does it mean that this person was "discovered" by this White guy as part of the Smithsonian music? . . . Even though it is inherently individualizing in some ways, having kids look at a single person's life, and look at it as a node connected to others in a matrix of social relations is really helpful. When they're really small, kids are coming to a sense of themselves as individuals in a node of social relations. . . . Kids have a really strong sense of unfairness. When you show kids that things are "unfair," you give them something they like, like a piece of music, and then look at the unfair conditions.

Whereas in Chapter 2, SKIM suggested connecting music to larger social relations, Griffin argued that youth can experience that sense of connection through studying individuals and the sociopolitical conditions they encounter.

Karl Buechner similarly centered individual artists when discussing possibilities for education. Karl was the vocalist in Earth Crisis, a metalcore band that focused on communicating themes about animal rights, ecodefense, environmental justice, and veganism. Age 43 at the time of interview, Karl lived in central New York. He described his heritage as German and Irish. Karl suggested selecting musics that illustrate how artists responded to contexts such as South African apartheid, the Vietnam War, and the Civil Rights Movement:

> [In choosing music for study, teachers may think about how] this artist during this era addressed this social problem, and it had this outcome or it drew this attention, or it shined this light on this specific thing that was going on. I bet it caused a lot of problems for a lot of those [artists].

Karl suggested centering artists and considering their contexts as a classroom activity. I take up his final note about personal risks to artists in Chapter 4.

In considering music as a human practice, grappling with context involves recognizing any risks artists assumed in communicating their messages.

In bringing community musics into schools, melodies and rhythms of musics may undergo changes. Composers, educators, and publishers may alter (or "whiten") rhythms for classroom use (Gustafson, 2009; Hess, 2018c; Trinka, 1987)[7] and adapt or arrange music for ensembles distinct from the instruments or voices originally intended. Examining how the music education industry transforms music for classroom use could foster interesting discussions about "straightening" and "whitening" rhythms and the simplification of melodies and their transformation into diatonic tonal structures. This conversation could help youth to develop skills to critique school materials and look for their equivalents in the world. In selecting music for classroom use, we might also look for highly syncopated and rhythmically complex music to better facilitate an experience of the music chosen. Moreover, relying on aural transmission practices privileges the ear in highly syncopated music, rather than trying to represent or decode these rhythms through a complex series of dots, double dots, and thirty-second notes on the page. When we examine the context of an ensemble piece, we may enhance the performance through our understanding and communicate the importance and relevance of the music to our audiences, as Casey noted.

Considering Instruments

We also might consider how the instruments typically used for different musics teach us about the situated nature of music. Bryan noted that

> If you're playing a certain instrument in music class, talk about where that instrument comes from. How people first made this instrument. I remember vaguely in elementary school learning about instruments—you'd scrape something along the jawbone of an animal. We had some synthetic form of that in class, but I remember the teacher mentioning, "Traditionally people would have the jawbone of a whatever—a donkey—and they would drag this stick along it and make a percussive sound." And that was all we got.

Bryan encouraged educators to situate instruments within human practices. In school music, when we encounter the synthetic versions of instruments typically used or Western classical ensemble instruments, considering the instruments typically used in a musical practice may, as Casey noted earlier, allow us to better understand the contexts of the musics studied. Materials used to create instruments for various musics may teach us about the value of specific products in society, as well as the types of sounds that particular groups value. We might consider, for example, how different tuning systems operate or the manner in which some mbira players, for example, may attach bottle caps to their instruments to add a percussive element to its melodic sounds. The way that specific groups construct instruments and the sound possibilities these instruments create teach us what "sounds good" to particular groups and further remind us that what "sounds good" differs vastly from group to group. Rather than hierarchizing sounds, perhaps such recognition will allow us to develop respect for a multiplicity of sounds and recognize that different musical systems are neither superior nor inferior to each other. Considering any practices that surround particular instruments—such as specific rituals, blessing of instruments for first usage, rules surrounding when, where, and by whom instruments can be played—provides further insights into the contexts and values of different communities.

Youth may encounter instrumentation changes when community music becomes school music. Casey pointed to Western classical school ensembles performing different styles of music. Composers frequently arrange "folk music" for classroom use, which often entails shifting instrumentation to Western classical instruments. A change in instruments may necessitate a change in tuning systems. Most classical instruments, at a beginning level, cannot account for microtones or tuning that may value variations in unison. Classical music typically deems such variations as "out of tune," presenting a distinct value system associated with specific instrumentation. Students may further encounter synthetic versions of instruments typically used in different musicking practices. Drums with animal skin heads, for example, often deteriorate in colder climates, unlike the synthetic drums commonly used in schools. Engaging students in conversation about both changes that may occur in music to account for classical instruments and distinctions in synthetic versions of various instruments creates possibilities for interesting discussions about what particular instruments make possible and what they limit sonically. Further considering whether traditions surrounding where, when, and by whom particular instruments can be played may provoke conversations about ways to maintain the integrity of the rules that govern various instrument use.

A Question of Language

Grappling with the languages of the musics studied may also provide a window into the human qualities and contexts of different musics. Bryan advocated for translation:

> Any time you encounter a song that's in a non-, whatever the language at the school is, if it's in a different language, translating it, and saying, "These are the lyrics to this song. It's not just sounds to memorize, it's words that mean something."

Without translation, musickers may approximate sounds and syllables devoid of meaning. A translation for a song may reveal a narrated story that provides insight into others' lives and experiences. It may also offer some insight into the manner in which different cultures draw on metaphors to signify varied challenges or situations. A song that draws on proverbs also creates an interesting opportunity to learn about different cultural values. Language itself provides a glimpse into values. Different languages may combine or separate concepts in distinct ways. In Ewe (a Ghanaian language), for example, the word *vu* means "drumming, dancing, and singing," reflecting their inseparability in that context. The separation of these same ideas in English elucidates that these practices often occur as distinct in English-speaking musical cultures. Translation, and engaging with language in the process, enriches musical experiences and fosters meaning-making. In its own way, grappling with language facilitates connecting to the communities from which different musics emerge.

Language use may change significantly in school contexts. As youth continue to value hip-hop in their musicking practices (Aidi, 2014; Williams, 2007), many music educators wonder how to include hip-hop in the classroom, often citing "inappropriate" (misogynistic, racialized, or profane) language as an excuse for exclusion. Educators raise questions of engaging with "clean versions" or critically engaging oppressive language issues to address concerns about inappropriate language, but once we alter language for school use, we must further respond to questions of whether school hip-hop becomes what I call elsewhere the *"not quite" edition* (Hess, 2014, p. 235)—a coopted version of community music sanctioned for school use. We then might wonder whether, when we change the language and adapt the music for school, engaging with hip-hop remains satisfying for students.

Language may also become an issue in translation. During my undergraduate education, I learned a song called "Mama Paquita" from a book entitled *An Orff Mosaic from Canada* (Birkenshaw-Fleming, 1996, pp. 177–178). The book noted the song's Brazilian origin, but presented it transcribed with English lyrics without the Portuguese text. The English lyrics were innocuous. Years later, upon hearing the song, a colleague from Brazil alerted me to the sexual nature of the original lyrics—a connotation erased from the book. Translation without including the original text may erase context. While English versions of lyrics that exclude original text occur far less frequently than at the beginning of the multicultural movement in music education, seeking out original lyrics may foster a better understanding of any song chosen for the classroom.

Both of these examples point to the type of language deemed appropriate for youth. The erasure of racialized, sexual, misogynistic, and/or profane language for classroom music elucidates what dominant groups deem appropriate. Considering that students encounter these texts beyond school music contexts, engaging with such language in the classroom purposefully, after clear communication with the school community about the intentions to do so, may equip youth to better grapple and critique these complex ideas. Moreover, discussing with youth the type of content deemed inappropriate for their consumption may prompt conversation about societal stereotypes regarding their capabilities and depth of understanding.

Developing Contextual Knowledge

In order to richly situate classroom material, grapple with context, and encourage youth to forge connections between the music they encounter and the world around them, educators thus require contextual knowledge of a range of musics. Vaugeois (2009) offers a series of questions to reveal what she calls "musical life histories." These critical questions offer a starting point for uncovering the contexts of various musics and any embedded power relations:

1. Who engages in this music? Who does not? (Male, female, cross-gendered [sic], Black, White, Native, rich, poor, middle class, formally/informally trained?)
2. What venues are used? (Why here and not somewhere else? How is access to music-making venues controlled? How much do they cost? Are these spaces policed?)
3. What instruments are used? Why these and not others?
4. Are there restrictions on when and where this music is allowed to be performed and who can perform it? Has it ever been outlawed? If so, where, when, why and by whom was it forbidden? Did it go underground? If so, what conditions have led to its reemergence?
5. Who is the audience? Who is not? How is attendance regulated? Are there people who would not be welcome in this audience?
6. How is this music learned? (Orally, through notation, through master/pupil relationships, through peer exchanges, through listening?)
7. How do race, class, and gender locations influence who learns this music?
8. Are lyrics significant to this music? What languages are used? Why these languages and not others? What are the lyrics about? How are genders, races, classes represented? Why are genders, races, classes present or absent?
9. Do available technologies intersect with the production of this music in any way?
10. What else is going on politically at the same time?
11. Who earns money from this music and through what processes?
12. What forms of interaction produce this kind of music? (Is it led from above—like bands, symphonies, and choirs, based on notated musical texts; led from within—like jazz combos, garage bands, free improvisation groups, based on lead sheets or oral transmission; led by a single artist with the support of "sidemen"?)
13. How was/is this music disseminated? (Through word of mouth, advertising, radio, the internet? What resources were/are available

to support its dissemination? Does the power to disseminate something widely affect earnings or what musics become familiar?)
14   What kind of social capital is associated with this music? Where does music learning intersect with concepts of child-rearing, success, and community values?
15   What kind of physical comportment is expected or allowed? (Is dancing present? What kind of dancing? What kind of clothing is worn? What expressions of physicality are expected? What expressions of sexuality and gender are possible? Are drugs and alcohol part of the experience? How are behaviours constrained in each setting?)

(pp. 9–10)

Vaugeois created these questions to provide a way to critique and analyze musics encountered through education. Asking these questions offers a mechanism for considering the embedded power relations and political contexts of any music. Teachers may explore these questions with youth in ways that encourage them to consider not only which populations participate in various musics, but which populations do not. The way Vaugeois poses these questions challenges musickers to examine the conditions that produce the current and historical incarnations of the music they appreciate. The questions require considering any exclusions perpetuated by music—the groups disenfranchised by the mechanisms that produce particular musics. In education contexts, asking these questions creates a practice of critique within which youth can learn to question the sociopolitical and sociohistorical conditions that shape the musics and other media they consume.

Summary: Considering Music as a Situated Human Practice

Considering music as a situated human practice involves grappling with communities, individuals, instruments, and language, as well as examining changes made to music in its classroom incarnation and asking questions that reveal power relations. This deep contextualization accounts for the sociohistorical and sociopolitical contexts in which music occurs and connects all musics richly to their social contexts. Such contextualization situates music meaningfully in the lives of the youth we teach, connecting them to history and calling upon youth to forge connections between what they encounter in music education and the world beyond the classroom. Accounting for music's situated nature accounts for the emphasis placed on lived experiences in critical pedagogy. McLaren (2000) argues,

> If I teach Portuguese, I must teach the use of accents, subject-verb agreement, the syntax of verbs, noun case, the use of pronouns, the personal infinitive. However, as I teach the Portuguese language, I must not postpone dealing with issues of language that relate to social class. I must not avoid the issue of *class* syntax, grammar, semantics, and

spelling. Hoping that the teaching of content, in and of itself, will generate tomorrow a radical intelligence of reality is to take on a controlled position rather than a critical one.

(p. 156, emphasis in original)

Fostering activist music education similarly requires engaging musics in their political contexts—to acknowledge their situatedness and their relationships to others, to relations of power both past and present, and to all participants in the educational process. Moreover, recognizing our common humanity in our diverse musicking practices connects us across our commonalities while valuing our differences.

Expanding Youth's Worlds: Connecting to Others

The majority of activist-musicians advocated for expanding youth's worlds by selecting a broad range of musics for the music classroom, connecting youth to Others through introducing different musics, and acknowledging music as a fundamentally human practice. When youth encounter musics of Others, as Jason noted in Chapter 2, they may become more open-minded about both people and musics. Activist-musicians asserted that youth need to both see themselves represented in the curriculum in a way that honors their lived experiences—a point I take up in Chapter 4—and encounter musics beyond those that are already familiar.

Engaging with unfamiliar musics potentially has larger implications. The majority of atrocities committed across history occurred through processes of dehumanization—marking particular groups as less-than-human in order to justify inhumane treatment. We might look, for example, at the one-drop rule (Davis, 2001), the Jim Crow laws (Klarman, 2004), and the three-fifths clause of the U.S. Constitution (Goldwin & Kaufman, 1988). Oppressors, Freire (2000/1970) argues, see the oppressed as less than fully human and thus not entitled to the same rights and freedoms they themselves enjoy. In response to Freire's call for humanization through dialogical praxis, O'Brien (2011) draws upon feminist scholarship on care and relationality:

> Emotional connection and responsiveness are central to human morality, and to the ability to connect with, and reach out, to act in the interests of another, and to fostering the capacity to care about our world and ourselves, in Freire's terms, to humanization, to becoming more human.
>
> (p. 24, citing Nussbaum, 2001)

Music education may present an opportunity for humanizing amidst ongoing dehumanization. When we encounter different groups through studying multiple musical practices, perhaps we can find a way to encounter Others "in such a way, in a *better* way, that allows something to give" (Ahmed, 2000, p. 154, emphasis in original). As we consider what it might mean to teach for connection, introducing musics that allow students to encounter people beyond those with whom they typically interact, we create a mechanism for tangibly humanizing different groups.

In considering how to facilitate music education through which youth can encounter both familiar and unfamiliar musics and the groups who practice them, Lise pointed to Style's 1996 article expounding upon this idea:

> The article "[Curriculum as] Window and Mirror" is a simple concept—that kids need to see themselves, so that's the mirror, and you want that mirror to be something that's life-affirming for them, but you also want to open up the world.

According to Style (1996), youth need to see themselves represented in the curriculum, but also need the curriculum to show them different possibilities. This chapter focuses on the "window" to the world to consider how music may facilitate youth's connections to Others through their musical practices, potentially leading to a process of humanization, whereas in Chapter 4, I examine the "mirror." I note here the importance of grounding youth in their own experiences (the "mirror") before turning them toward the "window."

Pete emphasized the value of travel and experiencing diverse perspectives:

> One thing that's critical is giving people the opportunity to travel to other places. I recognize that travel is a privilege but seeing the world and learning about the world around you can have such a profound impact. . . . I've learned so much from going to different parts of the world and that's also made me a better musician. Those [experiences] inspire that curiosity and that passion to move beyond perceived boundaries—whether it's in terms of physical space or other boundaries.

While Pete acknowledged that travel is a privilege, it is possible in the music classroom to create experiences and possible encounters that allow youth to experience perspectives distinct from their own and make meaning of these experiences. Music educators may reconfigure the classroom space into what Pratt (1991) calls a "contact zone"—a social space "where disparate cultures meet, clash, and grapple with each other, often in highly asymmetrical relations of power" (p. 4). Educators might consider classroom spaces as places of possibility wherein youth can experience diverse world views that both coincide with and differ from their own and can recognize the humanity present across all perspectives.

Activist-musicians considered exposing youth to a broad range of musics fundamental to activist music education. James participated in multiple world music ensembles throughout his undergraduate music education degree—an experience he found immensely valuable:

> In the Afro-Cuban ensemble, we would play salsa, merengue—a wide variety of Latino music. And jazz too, because I was in jazz ensembles. I participated in world music ensembles. It was interesting. Hard to describe. You would come into this setting [with any instrument] and the professor guided us. We either created our own music or we would play covers of world music—like the music of many countries melded altogether. The ensemble was very diverse; we had an Indian tabla player. We had Latino vocalists. I was a Filipino trumpet player. We also had a Filipino Kulintang player. We combined all of our cultures' music and made it our own.

Much like Pratt's (1991) "contact zone," in James' world music ensembles, music students encountered different traditions and came together through the experience. These world music ensembles provided a "window" into other musical practices and experiences, connecting participants to unfamiliar Others and acknowledging their value. Encountering music in this capacity creates the possibility for youth to recognize disparate worldviews and epistemologies held and utilized by different groups (Hess, 2013b, 2018b). In recognizing diverse musical epistemologies, teachers set the conditions for youth to understand that different people operate through different epistemologies that are no more or less valuable than their own. Educators then call upon youth to recognize Others' humanity and perhaps acquire "multicultural human subjectivity" (Bradley, 2006a, 2006b)—a sensibility that includes open-mindedness toward Others.

When including a wide range of musics, however, educators must simultaneously remain mindful of potential appropriation:

BRYAN: A multicultural education is a precarious thing because it can easily become: "Let's appropriate something from everyone and throw it into a mish-mash with no context." I think properly centering the curriculum or a set of performances around a non-European tradition would be pretty cool.

Bryan elucidated an important caveat about including a range of musics in the classroom. He reminds educators to contextualize classroom musics and examine relationships between musics in order to honor a range of musical traditions. When educators diversify the curriculum to include multiple musics, mindful contextualization minimizes the possibility of students drawing upon already-present stereotypes when engaging with different musics (Bradley, 2003, 2006b; Meiners, 2001) or creating a stereotype (Vaugeois, 2009). I address the risks related to stereotyping more fully in Chapter 6.

Griffin pointed to youth's sense of justice (Kelly & Brooks, 2009) and suggested that they can grapple with issues of cultural appropriation:

> [In an activist school music program,] there would be a combination of trying to teach kids about lots of different music traditions from lots of different places, and simultaneously teach kids about cultural appropriation, cultural suppression, and cultural genocide. And cultivating in kids a love for various kinds of music and an understanding of the contexts out of which music comes. So, taking kids to see various kinds of music, listen to various kinds of music. Getting kids to understand the stories behind [it]—the cultural, economic, contextual relations in the production of music and how this music came to be in this way.

Griffin prioritized focusing on appropriation in music—considering, for example, the manner in which musicians may "borrow" the musics of individuals from different groups. Casey tempered acknowledging the appropriative side of music with the importance of generating a love for and commitment to music and its many contexts. She suggested that focusing on appropriation could be done gently:

> I think there are ways of [having a conversation about cultural appropriation] that are still playful. Like: "This is where this music is from. Here's what this person looked like." Without being too didactic about it. "This is where they lived. This is what the instrument was made out of." Or: "This is where the beat originated. This is how it came to be." I like to learn about where things start or and how they got to where they're at. And then that history is still important in some way. You wipe out the history of so many people by cutting it up and sampling it. It gets to a point where the person, or people, or the community of people who were behind that music aren't even there anymore.

Centering the histories and contexts of musics helps to reclaim appropriated music and honor any erased history. Contextualization and situating music within human practices can involve acknowledging the appropriative side of music through reclaiming rather than shaming. Engaging cultural appropriation in music education supports reclaiming appropriated materials and further calls upon youth to challenge and critique music they encounter.

Encountering Others through musicking may also offer nuanced understandings of privilege, particularly among populations segregated by race and class in a school system that is theoretically no longer segregated.[8] Casey pointed to ways that a "window" into the experiences of Others may influence White, middle-class youth:

> I wanted [youth at Girls Rock Camp] to imagine the world in a way that maybe they weren't seeing in the safety of their neighborhood.

How we can grow their imaginations to consider other people in their [lives]—where they're from or what sort of things may make it difficult for people to access music.

Girls Rock Camp in Toronto provided a funded, intensive summer opportunity for young women aged 8 to 16 to come together to create and produce rock music. Casey looked for ways that youth's experiences in the camp might allow them to see perspectives that differed from their middle-class experiences. When groups segregated by privilege and groups marginalized on the basis of identity encounter different groups' realities, exposure to these perspectives may help them to consider and challenge privilege and oppression in a manner that may encourage open-mindedness (Hess, 2013b).

Activist music education engages a broad range of musics both relevant to youth (Lind & McKoy, 2016) and beyond the scope of the familiar (Hess, 2013b). Including multiple musics helps youth not only to see themselves, but also to connect to others who are both distant and not so distant from their realities while simultaneously recognizing the humanity present in all people and intrinsic to all musical practices. Offering rich contextualization for these musics limits the use of stereotypes and appropriation as the basis for these connections. Drawing upon youth's lived experiences—the foundation of critical pedagogy (Freire, 2000/1970; Freire & Macedo, 1987)—activist-musicians advocated for honoring youth's musical experiences and extending them to other traditions. These musical experiences and encounters may take place within the classroom space as a "contact zone" (Pratt, 1991) or in the community. Activist-musicians shared Style's (1996) perspective of curriculum as both window and mirror. I focused in this chapter on the window.

Introducing youth to such a diverse range of musics while avoiding appropriation requires knowledge of multiple traditions. Including many musics in the classroom may serve to humanize unfamiliar groups by considering the humanity intrinsic to all musicking practices. El discussed her desire as a young person for explicit instruction in deejaying:

> We taught [a] deejaying 101 type thing. . . . Youth would come in and learn a couple things on the turntables. I think the reason I got involved in that kind of work is because I remember thinking to myself that if someone had showed me this—I remember wishing and praying that someone would show up and show me how to do this. If someone had showed me how to do it, I could be so much further along.

El provided deejaying education to youth in the Toronto community. Her words remind educators of the importance of fluency across multiple musics relevant to youth, as well as musics beyond their scopes. Hip-hop, while increasingly named as a possibility for music education (Gustafson, 2009;

Kruse, 2016; Söderman & Folkestad, 2004), is not a musicking practice with which many music teachers are familiar.

Developing knowledge across multiple musical traditions may seem like an insurmountable task. Allsup (2016), however, suggests working alongside students across multiple musical traditions. We continue, as music educators, to develop our knowledge in multiple traditions, recognizing the humanity present in these musical practices. Engaging in this ongoing process, openly learning alongside the students we teach while asking critical questions like those offered by Vaugeois (2009), allows for critical engagement with multiple musics.

Difficulties with Relationality: Navigating Potential for Re-Experiencing Trauma

Situating all musics in human practices involves recognizing that many musics emerge from traumatic contexts and carry histories of struggle and pain. In considering music as a human practice, re-experiencing trauma becomes possible when situating musics in their lived contexts. As we include the sociohistorical and sociopolitical human contexts of music in music education and aim to move students beyond familiar musics, we must also be aware of any traumatic or triggering potential. Lise Vaugeois was a 58-year-old musician, scholar, composer, educator, and activist living in Thunder Bay, Ontario, at the time of the interview. She self-identified as a White, Canadian with Italian and French heritage. Her doctoral work in music education focused on colonization and Indigeneity in Canada and Western classical music's complicity in colonial violence (Vaugeois, 2013). Lise described possible ways to discuss injustices against the Indigenous community in Canada in the classroom:

> I think that you have to always be careful. You don't want to traumatize the kids in the classroom or create a vulnerability by talking about [traumatic issues]. How you do it is really important. One teacher I've been working with has two children's books—one called *Shi-shi-etko*, (Campbell & LaFave, 2005) and another one about the experience of going to residential school. And they're written for children. The first one's not so scary; [it's] more about the anticipation of going, and the nervousness and sadness of leaving your family. The second one has more of the loneliness and hardship. And that speaks to children on an emotional level and on a level they can understand. And you don't want to traumatize the non-Aboriginal kids in the class, either.

Lise routinely taught about Indigenous issues in the Canadian context in her community in Thunder Bay, Ontario. She described a delicate balance. Engaging musics with traumatic histories in the classroom involves educating youth who do not have these experiences about different struggles in the world while also assuring youth who live these experiences daily that they are not alone—that they have community. In balancing these issues in the classroom, we risk re-traumatizing youth who live these experiences personally and perhaps frightening youth unaware of these struggles. Education about oppression, however, is a way to create a different possible future—particularly when youth with significant privilege encounter injustices and oppression and begin to resist them in their lives. Facilitating conversations about traumatic issues both inside and beyond classroom contexts carries the potential to shut down conversation instead of creating space for youth to dialogue and encounter different experiences. Lise's colleague offered a mechanism to foster discussion with relatable children's books—a strategy echoed by a teacher in Kelly and Brooks' (2009) study who also drew on Campbell and LaFave's (2005) *Shi-shi-etko* (pp. 208–209) as a springboard for critical and courageous conversations (Singleton & Linton, 2006).

It is a delicate balance for educators: if we pursue difficult content, youth with privilege may become defensive and refuse to hear profound histories of oppression (Applebaum, 2010; DiAngelo, 2011). As we integrate the complex human histories of multiple musics into classrooms, remaining mindful of the potential for trauma may help us to better navigate difficult material. I address these concerns in greater depth in Chapter 6.

Summary

This chapter explored the connective potential of music education. Enacting music education as connection includes fostering relationships between youth in the classroom through building community, situating musics within their histories and political contexts, and creating connections between music education participants and unfamiliar Others through the exploration of multiple musical traditions. Understanding music education as inherently connective recognizes the humanity present in all musical practices and further encourages youth to make meaning of musics they encounter, connecting them to their histories and asking critical questions—a reconceptualization of Freire's (2000/ 1970) problem-posing education and an intentional honoring of lived experiences. In encouraging relationality, however, educators must carefully navigate the potential for re-traumatization through musical encounters. Enacting music education as a practice of community that honors the contributions of all may embolden youth to assert their own voices in the world, enacting a process of coming to voice (Freire, 2000/1970). In Chapter 4, I explore what it might mean to both honor and share lived experiences in music education.

Notes

1 "They" is Griffin's preferred pronoun.
2 Griffin's doctorate was in progress at the time of interview.

3 See http://mammalian.ca/about/ for more details about Mammalian Diving Reflex.
4 The Gladstone Hotel is a concert venue in Toronto (www.gladstonehotel.com).
5 "Core subjects" typically include language arts, mathematics, science, geography, or history. The No Child Left Behind Act (NCLB) in the United States emphasized these subjects to the exclusion of the arts for the purposes of standardized testing. The Every Student Succeeds Act (ESSA), conversely, passed in December 2015, emphasizes a "well-rounded education" that includes music (Walker, 2016).
6 James refers to the murder of 18-year-old Michael Brown, a Black youth in Ferguson, MO, on August 9, 2014 by White police officer Darren Wilson.
7 Trinka (1987) found that textbooks simplified and stereotyped melodies in Anglo and African American folk music in such a way that limited connections to social and cultural traditions.
8 Apple (2004), Lareau (2011), and Anyon (1981) all note that school serves as a site of social reproduction to maintain the status quo in terms of raced and classed subject positions.

4 Honoring and Sharing Lived Experiences in Music Education

Activist-musicians emphasized music's communicative and expressive potential (as explored in Chapter 2) and noted that music serves as a vehicle to share stories and experiences. Pivoting in this chapter from music to music education necessitates a semantic shift from telling stories to valuing youth's stories and lived experiences. When educators honor students' realities in schools, it may become possible for them to assert their experiences musically. The first part of this chapter focuses on activist-musicians' perspectives on fostering place-based education. In place-based education, educators consider the community context and the needs of youth in the classroom in a manner that honors students' experiences. This centering of lived experiences aligns with Freirian tenets of critical pedagogy. Activist-musicians emphasized facilitating creative work in the classroom. The second section thus explores practical ways that educators can support youth to share these stories through musicking—a process that both honors lived experiences and encourages youth to come to voice and name the world (Freire, 2000/1970). I ultimately consider the possible implications for youth who may share their experiences musically in order to process and reflect upon oppression, but who, in doing so, may face consequences, particularly when the stories they choose to share emerge from trauma.

Place-Based Education

Activist-musicians considered place-based education fundamental to activist music education. Practically, place-based education encourages educators to align their curricula with specific community contexts—an endeavor that involves the ideals of critical pedagogy (Freire, 2000/1970; Freire & Macedo, 1987), culturally relevant pedagogy (Koza, 2006; Ladson-Billings, 1995, 2009), culturally responsive teaching (Gay, 2018; Lind & McKoy, 2016), and culturally sustaining pedagogy (Paris & Alim, 2014, 2017). Implementing place-based education attempts to ensure that youth see themselves reflected in their school programs in a manner that honors their experiences and encourages them to assert their voices. Freire adamantly opposed any possibility of a standardized curriculum, affirming the importance of honoring specific contexts (Dale & Hyslop-Margison, 2010). Recalling the concept of curriculum as window and mirror (Style, 1996) from Chapter 3, place-based education prioritizes the mirror—reflecting youth back to themselves in a way that honors their lived experiences.

Aligning Education with Context: Critical Pedagogy and Culturally Responsive Teaching

Activist-musicians asserted that school music curricula ought to draw on youth's context and experiences. They advocated for a student-driven curriculum that reflected youth's realities. Critical pedagogy must be contextual; Freire and Macedo (1987) suggest that teachers adapt their pedagogy for their unique situations (p. 92; see also Kincheloe, 2009, p. 110). Freire's (2000/1970) problem-posing education, for example, draws material directly from students' experiences to address collaboratively in the classroom. Moreover, Freire and Macedo's (1987) work on literacy urges educators to draw vocabulary directly from the issues students face in the world. Rooting curriculum in youth's realities honors the experiences they bring to the classroom. The issues youth face may differ across different identities and personal circumstances. Even in perceptibly homogeneous communities, students' experiences will likely vastly differ. In a classroom of students with diverse identities and experiences, implementing place-based education requires attention to the nuances of the challenges youth encounter.

Literature on culturally relevant or responsive pedagogy in education (Delpit, 2006/1995, 2012; Gay, 2018; Ladson-Billings, 1995, 2009) and in music education (Abril, 2010; Countryman, 2009; Gurgel, 2016; Hess, 2014, 2015a; Hoffman, 2012; Koza, 2006; Lind & McKoy, 2016) similarly supports curricula rooted in youth's lived realities. Magali, for example, argued for catering curriculum to context. Two months after White police officer Darren Wilson killed 18-year-old Michael Brown, a young Black man in Ferguson, Missouri, on August 9, 2014, Magali noted that Ferguson youth needed their experiences since the shooting acknowledged in schools. In light of those experiences, she contended that what might be relevant to youth in one part of the country may be far removed from youth's realities elsewhere. A "one-size-fits-all" curriculum thus remains impossible. Freire insisted that critical pedagogy was not a methodology (Dale & Hyslop-Margison, 2010); every school population is vastly different. Lind and McKoy (2016) argue that youth must have "opportunities to engage with music in ways that are congruent with their own lived cultural experiences with music" (p. 72). When educators provide such opportunities, they honor youth's lived realities.

Reflecting and Validating Youth in School Programs

Youth may respond positively when they see themselves reflected in school programs—the *mirror* of Style's (1996) *window and mirror* and a fundamental aspect of place-based education. Freire (1998a) wonders, "Why not establish an 'intimate' connection between knowledge considered basic to any school curriculum and knowledge that is the fruit of the lived experience of these students as individuals?" (p. 36). Music educators often take up reflecting students' realities as an issue of representation. Multiple music education scholars assert that students must see themselves represented in their music class, whether that means providing role models who share students' identities engaged in various musicking activities (Gould, 1996; Grant, 2000; Koza, 1992b, 1994c; Lind & McKoy, 2016), studying musics related to students' identities and affinities (Bradley, 2006b; Green, 2008; Hess, 2013b; Lind & McKoy, 2016; Schippers, 2010), considering different musical epistemologies (Countryman, 2009; Hess, 2013b), or using resources that purposefully represent many identities (a discussion that has primarily focused on gender and race) (Gustafson, 2009; Koza, 1992b, 1994c; Lind & McKoy, 2016). Representation can play an important role in place-based education.

As a teaching artist, Jason extends reflection beyond representation. He worked with second, third, and fourth grade youth at under-resourced schools without music programs in Harlem, New York City. He created chants for the youth:

> There's a mantra-like potential in giving them chants—positive thoughts. The lyrics were repetitive and simple, but it was a good message. I thought, "Well, that'd be nice if that idea was running through their heads out of music class." One song was a blues [song] called "We Speak Two Languages" and how great that is. Another was a rap [called] "We Are Here and We Know Who We Are in This Land."

Jason considered the experiences of youth he taught and created affirming texts to validate their identities. While U.S. society often criticizes individuals for not speaking English and some anti-bilingual education movements exist (Caldas, 2006), Jason provided a chant that valued multilingualism. Jason used music to position multilingualism as a source of pride, assessing the student populations and centering their experiences in the curriculum. Educators can select musics that affirm youth's experiences by choosing musics congruent with their realities or focusing on texts that resonate with and reflect youth's lives. Jason's lyrics validated the students he taught and reflected their experiences in the curriculum.

Valuing youth's voices and experiences in the curriculum prioritizes recognition. In securing a place for students' perspectives, we must also ensure that we validate them. Horton and Freire (1990) argue that "[y]ou can't *say* you respect people and not respect their experiences" (pp. 177–178, emphasis in original). Recognition and acknowledgement in place-based education communicate to youth the value of their knowledge and experiences. Taiyo noted,

> People are going to make music. Young folks are going to make music, whether it's beats on their phone or YouTube videos, or SoundCloud, or whatever it is, they're going to make music. It's whether or not everybody else—especially the adults—acknowledge that and see some humanity and beauty in that.

Taiyo's recognition of the humanity and beauty in what youth produce emphasized the importance of valuing what they bring to the classroom. Upon including many experiences and perspectives in the curriculum, educators can find ways to honor and acknowledge youth's contributions and communicate their inherent value. When youth see themselves reflected in their schooling, their experiences in education affirm them.

Student-Centered Curricula in Music Education

Educators might also encourage youth to participate in constructing classroom curricula in a way that centers their perspectives so that they see themselves reflected in their schooling. Critical pedagogy centers lived experiences in the curriculum. Freire and Macedo (1987) note that,

> In the case of Black Americans, for example, educators must respect Black English. It is possible to codify and decodify Black English with the same ease as standard American English. The difference is that Black Americans will find it infinitely easier to codify and decodify the dialect of their own authorship. The legitimation of Black English as an educational tool does not, however, preclude the need to acquire proficiency in the linguistic code of the dominant group.
>
> (p. 88)

Freire and Macedo underscore the importance of honoring and centering students' own frameworks and knowledges, while looking to extend them, reflecting youth first in the mirror before urging them toward the window (Style, 1996).

Pete's history class centered African history and African knowledges, eschewing Eurocentricity in a way that attempted to make history more relevant for the many Black youth in the program. Reframing the curriculum through students' perspectives potentially validates their lived realities. The arts school where Pete taught served a population of approximately 60% Black and Latino youth. Pete described his Afrocentric history program:

> I [taught] African history to ninth graders, and incorporated learning to read primary sources, and other aspects of history and humanities. I was able to incorporate some of my own art—perform a couple of times for the students myself, bring in other artists, as well as encourage students to incorporate their own art.

This Afrocentric history program made school a place where youth's experiences and perspectives drove the curriculum, potentially validating them in the process. This affirming approach to schooling stands in stark contrast to a school where "students are reacting to a curriculum and other material conditions in schools that negate their histories, cultures, and day-to-day experiences" (Freire & Macedo, 1987, p. 85).

Moving Beyond Reflection: Reflecting and Extending Worlds

Lise concurred that curriculum should reflect youth's experiences but also underscored the importance for youth to encounter music and people beyond their everyday realities:

> Students need to see themselves reflected in a positive way, but they also need to see that the world is bigger than themselves. Every teacher has to look around [their] room and see who's there. At the same time, I've talked to teachers at exclusive private, White schools of diplomats in Latin America and at upper-class private schools. If you want to reflect [those students] back to themselves, then you reflect back whatever music they happen to have grown up with, and that's the end of the story. Or is it? If I'm teaching a song, let's say, that comes out of the slave tradition, how do I present that? I want to frame that in the sense of rebellion and resistance. So that there is a strength for students to take away from the music that we share in the classroom.

Lise articulated the importance of validating youth's lived experiences. She also emphasized the value of moving youth beyond their own realities, toward the window (Style, 1996) into others' experiences, as taken up in Chapter 3. She identified a flaw in place-based education: when such education reflects privileged populations back to themselves without unsettling their privilege, place-based education fails to alter conditions of oppression or dominant power structures. The window *and* the mirror thus work together in anti-oppressive education. Lise also specifically sought ways to validate the experiences of minoritized youth, not only through including related music, but by framing these musics as musics that emerged from oppression, strength, and struggle. Lise cautioned educators who encouraged youth to participate in musics beyond their lived experiences to emphasize the resistance and strength inherent in music rooted in oppression, as well as the resiliency of the group represented. Privileging strength and resistance may validate the experiences of youth with personal connections to the music studied.

Summary: Place-Based Education in Activist Music Education

Orienting activist music education that both relies on the cultural backgrounds of youth and creates a space where youth's experiences are intrinsic to curricula generates a context-specific music education. Activist-musicians asserted that curricular construction and implementation must honor youth's lived experiences—the mirror that reflects and validates youth (Style, 1996). Music education that privileges youth's voices honors the community as integral to education. Many youth have significant community cultural wealth upon which they can draw (Yosso, 2005). Place-based education encourages educators to recognize youth's strengths and help them shape their school music programs, potentially resulting in multi-faceted, cross-cultural, strengths-based curricula. Extending place-based education among dominant groups to include musics that emerge from oppression further facilitates the connective education described in Chapter 3.

From Honoring to Sharing Lived Experiences: Naming the World as Creative Curriculum

The practical manifestation of honoring lived experiences in music education involves sharing these stories musically—an idea that draws upon music's communicative and expressive potential, as explored in Chapter 2. Music education provides a mechanism for youth to come to voice and name their world (Freire, 2000/1970). Through music, we can create spaces for youth to productively respond to local realities as well as realities far removed. To consider what inviting students to name their world musically might entail, I return to the three-part process of coming to voice and naming the world identified in Chapter 2. Coming to voice and naming the world involve exploring identity, asserting one's experiences, and learning to value others' assertions of their experiences. In this chapter, I add a fourth phase to this process: intentional movement toward transformation. These integrated processes of reflection and action toward transformation provide a means for youth to consider and identify the conditions that affect them and to potentially imagine a different way forward. Freire (2000/1970) asserts that

> To exist, humanly, is to *name* the world, to change it. Once named, the world in its turn reappears to the namers as a problem and requires of them a new *naming*. Human beings are not built in silence, but in word, in work, in action-reflection.
>
> (p. 88)

Many activist-musicians shared their stories or named the world through their artistic practice. They thus advocated for school music curricula to include both creating and performing possibilities, following purposive listening (Green, 2001). This section explores their perspectives on what naming the world or sharing lived experiences musically might mean for creating, performing, and listening practices in schools. When youth share their experiences artistically, then music expresses a diversity of lived experiences. I explore activist-musicians' perspectives as they align with the four-part process of coming to voice and naming the world and consider what it might mean to facilitate creative work in school music in a manner that helps youth identify their experiences musically, through action-reflection, toward transformation.

Exploring Identity

Coming to voice and naming the world first involve exploring identity. As noted in Chapter 2, musicking may allow individuals to examine and express issues that interweave with identity, including, for example, the complexities of international and cross-cultural adoption, as Dan explored in "Is There Anybody Out There" and as in the stories of immigration that Casey shared in "Balikbayan."[1] While activist-musicians have established a strong sense of identity, youth's identities are emerging and in-process (Frith, 1996). Purposeful exploration of identity in music class may create opportunities for youth to reflect upon their experiences and their values. This process may begin with active listening in order to provide youth with ideas of what they might explore with their music before working to discover what one's musical voice and language may be for expressing these issues, ideas, and emotions.

Active Music Listening

Given the diversity of experiences present among any group of students, facilitating identity exploration may prove difficult. Guided questions for reflection likely will not resonate with all students. I instead propose that active listening may provide a helpful starting place to consider the types of issues, experiences, and emotions explored in the musics that students value. In centering listening, we can encourage youth to explore musics they find significant and encourage them to engage with others' selected musics as well—another practice of reflecting youth's interests in the mirror before moving toward the window (Style, 1996). Listening can serve as a cornerstone of exploring identity.

In James' school music program exploring social movements, students listened to the music of various social movements before considering what they themselves might like to express.[2] When educators encourage youth to assert their lived experiences through music, students require examples of others doing such work. Purposive listening (Green, 2001)—a process through which youth listen to music in order to subsequently put their listening to use—may help them shape their own work. Youth may listen to music that shares experiences in order to explore what they might like to express in their own music. Purposive listening, then, involves listening in order to ultimately assert one's experiences as well as to see what resonates with one's own voice and lived reality.

Liz Sunde, the founder of Music2Life: Soundtrack for Social Change,[3] worked to connect music explicitly to social change and activist work and engaged artists to speak to different political issues. Age 49 at the time of the interview, Liz identified as a White woman living in Vermont. The daughter of Paul Stookey from Peter, Paul & Mary, Liz grew up watching her father perform. She noted that "growing up in the shadow of a folk icon opens your eyes to the larger meaning of music and impact." Listening was a crucial part of her childhood. She shared,

> We would sit and listen. I think that was the big difference for us. Music was never background. Never . . . We would be listening to it. Or we'd be writing it.

Liz described "attentive listening" (Green, 2001)—listening with the same level of attention as with purposive listening without subsequently putting the listening to use. Both purposive and attentive listening allow youth to critically analyze music that results from individuals sharing their experiences in order to explore what they might wish to assert musically.

"Messing Around" and Improvising

Given that students will ultimately music about their experience, exploring identity also involves considering what one's musical voice and language might be. Providing opportunities for youth to "mess around"—to experiment with instruments and sounds and try out musical ideas (Kennedy, 2004)—may help them decide which "language is their own," as Jason noted in Chapter 2. Dan contended that

> Having instruments in the classroom and giving kids time to be able to play music or to be creative and bang drums or do something like that is incredibly important.

Play can facilitate meaning-making in the arts (Connery, John-Steiner, & Marjanovic-Shane, 2010) and can help youth shape their musical voices. This exploratory "play" or "mess around" time can be valuable (Burnard, 2000).

Youth can also explore their musical ideas through improvisation. Jason created opportunities for youth in New York schools to experiment musically and improvise:

> There would be choral breaks and between, there would be jam sessions and slide whistles, solos, duos, ensembles. They learned how to do riffs.[4] I would assign a group to listen to this person, assign a leader, and they would create a riff. Which is basically what would happen in a blues band, but without the conducting. So someone would riff and someone else would solo. I tried to open the space like a Parliament Funkadelic session, so that kids who wanted to dance would choreograph the song. And kids that had their own rap would be given space

so they might have my chant, a soloist, and then a kid would say his rap. And then it would be an ensemble slide whistle thing and then it would be a dance break. It would be a duo between dancers and two slide whistles. We would jam for 40 minutes without stopping.

Jason chose slide whistles as a medium for youth in New York schools because of their accessibility and minimal cost. He found slide whistles highly expressive because of their range and potential for glissando. Youth in Jason's program could improvise freely and explore their strengths and ideas in a mutually-supportive space, allowing them to develop their musical voices. Music education literature often positions improvisation as important to musical engagement (Elliott, 1995; Elliott & Silverman, 2015; Sarath, 2002, 2013); similarly, most activist-musicians prioritized learning by ear, improvisation, and composition when fostering creativity in school.

Youth might also consider which instruments or musical media may facilitate their voices. Activist-musicians advocated exposing students to different instruments, both from the Western classical tradition and from different global musics:

PETE: I [went] to summer camp at a local community college, where kids were able to take "college" classes. One of them was called "Meet the Instruments," and it was about try[ing] out different instruments. That was the first time that I tried playing trumpet. . . . A lot of times, young people, when they do take up instruments, it's not really their choice. Like they're told, "We need a bassoon player. You're gonna play bassoon." Or their parent says, "I think you should play the piano." [Instead of] engaging with different instruments and finding out what you like. And how to speak through those instruments.

We can extend Pete's words to include instruments from many traditions. His note about speaking through these instruments is significant. When Pete plays the trumpet, he clearly communicates and tells a story through his playing. Facilitating opportunities for youth to experiment and experience different instruments allows them to discover which instrument(s) might best enable them to tell their own stories and assert their own voices.

Looking for Larger Narratives

When exploring identity, educators can also help youth look for societal narratives related to their work in order to help them think about their experiences in relation to those of others and present their experiences in a way that may resonate with individuals with different experiences. In Chapter 2, SKIM described connecting their own experiences to larger systems of power in order to understand some of the forces that have shaped their life. Exploring identity, then, also involves considering where one's

94 *Honoring and Sharing Lived Experiences*

own experience connects to the experiences of different groups. When youth share their stories musically, educators facilitate making connections to societal narratives or social movements that resonate across identities.

Summary: Exploring Identity

Exploring identity, as the first phase of coming to voice and naming the world, involves reflective processes. These processes encompass both broad and exploratory listening practices and intentional analysis of where the experiences and emotions that youth identify may weave into larger societal narratives. To assert one's stories and ideas musically further requires exploring one's musical voice through improvisation, play, and experimenting with different instruments.

Asserting One's Experiences: Musicking to Share Stories

The second phase of coming to voice and naming the world involves asserting one's experiences through musicking. Activist-musicians unequivocally supported facilitating opportunities for youth to practice songwriting and use music as a vehicle to express their stories and emotions. To music about one's experience can involve songwriting, lyric writing, mixing musics creatively, or finding ways to express experiences sonically without words. These creative practices ultimately culminate in performance. As performing musicians, most activist-musicians supported performance as the mechanism for sharing experiences.

Songwriting as Curriculum

Facilitating songwriting in schools as both coming to voice and naming the world (Freire, 2000/1970) becomes the cornerstone of any activist music curriculum—the communicative and expressive element that activist-musicians identified as intrinsic to music.

NOBUKO: Giving children and young people the experience of exploring how to create their own songs is another great thing. I would love to see that. They're telling their own stories. What are their dreams? What are their visions? What are their problems?[5]

Songwriting can help youth tell their stories. In music education, songwriting literature often focuses on legitimizing songwriting as a classroom practice (Kratus, 2013, 2016; Williams, 2011). Several music education scholars call for robust songwriting programs in school settings, citing the centrality of songs in youth's musical lives (Kratus, 2013) and the potential of songwriting to promote musical autonomy and independence (Kaschub & Smith, 2013). Hickey (1997) notes that using technology in songwriting may help youth realize their creative potential. Psychologically, songwriting also potentially provides a medium to work through emotional issues, offering a means to cope with grief, trauma, and other difficulties (Baker, 2013, 2015; Baker & Krout, 2012; Dalton & Krout, 2006; Riley, 2012). Songwriting may also help youth build self-esteem (Baker et al., 2008; Draves, 2008). Importantly for this book, songwriting may also facilitate critical pedagogy (Kaschub, 2009) and counter deficit discourses (Hess, 2018a).

Cruz' (2012) work on *testimonios* (Beverley, 1993) informs enacting songwriting as naming the world. *Testimonio*, she argues, "is a storytelling that challenges larger political and historic discourses and undermines other official knowledge meant to silence or erase local histories of resistance" (p. 461). *Testimonio* involves speaking back to dominant discourses.[6] In centering songwriting practices, music as *testimonio* may emerge within youth's processes of coming to voice and naming the world.

Activist-musicians suggested multiple ways to structure songwriting activities to help youth understand themselves as creators and producers of music. These strategies included purposefully demystifying music. tvu considered how music educators could break down popular music in order to make creating accessible:

> I would start by breaking away some of the mysteries of music. You know that moment where you find out that all pop music comes from pretty much the same chord progressions? Whenever I point that out to my cousins, ages 8, 9, or 10, they're like, "No way! They sound like completely different songs." And it takes away—in a good way—some of the mystique of music and makes them think, "I can do this too." It's not some rocket science. It's based on these very accessible building blocks. It makes them break down: "Why does this sound different? What about it makes it so different and rich?" It makes you think about music in a more tangible way vs. "That's so awesome. I could never recreate or do that."

Breaking down pop chord progressions makes music accessible; it becomes something youth can create. When tvu considered music education, she began with pop music because of its accessibility and because "you have to break away this idea that it's hard." When educators demystify popular music and demonstrate how possible it is to create within that model, we help youth understand themselves as creators of music as well as consumers and performers. Presenting the creation of music as a genuine possibility perhaps becomes the first facet of enabling youth to share their experiences musically.

Patrick, a hip-hop deejay and producer, offered a structured digital curriculum in his grassroots hip-hop recording program:

> We do digital recording. We do digital music production. And we do deejaying. During the school year, we work on a mixtape. We recruit youth who are either emcees or singers—or nowadays, what's very popular with kids is the whole beats scene, where it's all based around a beatmaker and it's just them; there's no vocalist. With the goal of making this mixtape, we teach all the skills [that youth need]. We teach beatmaking, we teach folks how to record themselves, how to write a song, how to structure a song. What a verse is, what a bar is. What a tempo is. We teach basic musical theory—basic rhythm. It gives them structure.

Like tvu, Patrick advocates for explicitly teaching the form and structure of music to promote accessibility. The hip-hop program he directs in California teaches all aspects of digital music production, helping youth gain the skills they need to make their music.

At his alternative school, James takes a similar approach with acoustic instruments:

> At the beginning of the semester, we start off with music workshops, so we have students learning guitar, learning drums. We hired a piano teacher. We hired a bass teacher and vocal teacher. Maybe a month into it, as soon as they developed on their instruments, we created [student] bands.

Magali and Casey offer a similar program at the Girls Rock Camp in Toronto. While James' program ran for a semester, Girls Rock Camp was a one-week program. Their approaches align in some ways to Green's (2008) work facilitating popular music in the classroom. Both approaches place youth in bands to create music. While Green's Musical Futures program does not offer explicit instrumental instruction, but rather allows youth to figure out the instruments, James, Magali, and Casey offered some instruction. Youth in both programs may be beginners on any chosen instrument. Instructors assume that interest will drive the motivation to improve, a philosophy similar to Green's assumption that if youth want to learn an instrument, they will teach themselves, as popular musicians often do (Green, 2001, 2008). Making the creation of music accessible to youth gives them another medium to name their worlds and speak to their realities. Activist-musicians noted that offering explicit instruction on both instruments and musical form would provide tangible structures to youth wishing to create.

Writing Lyrics

Activist-musicians identified writing lyrics as a mechanism for youth to name the world:

> CASEY: I heard from [Girls Rock Camp] facilitators that some of the songs that kids were writing were saying things like, "We should all have the

chance to play." Like really political songs. I don't think the kids are intending them as being activist. They're just saying what they [feel]. Like: "We don't want to go to school because it doesn't feel fair to sit." It's just really honest and true about their experience.

The adolescents who participated in Girls Rock Camp named their worlds (Freire, 2000/1970). Youth may further find the words to be expressive and vulnerable, to speak to the pain and hurt they navigate daily. Because youth may choose to address abuse and injustices they experience in their lives, facilitating songwriting in school as an institution may become complicated. If issues of personal abuse emerge through songwriting, the school system obliges teachers to file a mandatory report—an issue I take up in depth later in this chapter.

JULIET: If you were [leading a songwriting workshop], are there limits to what you would have [youth] explore topically if they were writing songs?

CASEY: I guess that's where that tension is when you put something like a practice or the idea that music is just supposed to be something that, I think, at its core, used as a way of expressing yourself, your whole self. When it comes to rub against the institution, then there is that tension there that prevents being able to fully do that, but I get why those things are in place—to keep kids safer and stuff like that, but . . .

In inviting youth to speak to their realities in music class, schools may restrict content. These limitations may curtail what youth have to say. As music educators, then, we must not only create mutually-supportive environments, but also spaces in which difficult truths can be spoken without fear of reprisal, noting that in cases of abuse and safety, legislation mandates institutional action—reporting of abuse to children's protective agencies. Naming the world (Freire, 2000/1970) lyrically becomes complex in institutional contexts. Most activist-musicians, however, identified the process as fundamental to activist school music education.

Creative Mixing of Music

Employing technologies facilitates strategies beyond songwriting to create music that communicates meaning. Youth may be able to name their worlds through creatively mixing musics:

TVU: So you know the whole mash-up/remix thing going on right now? I actually love it when you have two contradictory things coming together. Jay-Z over classical. *The Little Mermaid* mixed up into EDM style. It's so creative. And I love when people do covers when they change the meaning of the song too. That shows so much in terms of context. So Cyndi Lauper's "Girls Just Wanna Have Fun," I heard this heartbreaking version about someone whose heart was broken by a girl who just wanted to have fun. So that song in that context—so different, right? And it's totally done in a singer-songwriter brooding sense. It changed the song completely from this "party whatever" to "there's this woman who is, for some reason, emotionally stunted and incapable of having a real relationship. She just wants to have fun."

Remix and mash-up culture may provide a means for youth to construct music that speaks to their realities. Drawing on music that resonates with them may allow them to manipulate it to tell their own stories, simultaneously teaching them that music can be used. This practice shifts music from "untouchable" to accessible, allowing youth to understand that art is meant to communicate and that they can construct it so it speaks for and to them.

Telling Stories Without Lyrics

Educators can also facilitate telling stories and naming experiences without lyrics. In her late 50s at the time of interview, Laura Kaminsky self-identified as a first-generation, White, American, lesbian concert music composer from New York City. Kaminsky's website describes her as "a New York-based composer of opera, orchestra and chamber works, and vocal and choral music. . . . Her scores often address social-political issues such as sustainability, war, and human rights."[7] As a composer, she attended to complex social issues in her music, which included sociopolitical matters and issues related to the environment and climate change. Laura provided an example as she described the *Vukovar Trio*, a piece she wrote after seeing the devastation in post-war Croatia in the 1990s:

> I was inspired to write a work, *Vukovar Trio*, which is an abstract piece in multiple sections, and I dedicated it to the victims of ethnic cleansing. The Trio was inspired by my having lived in Eastern Europe in the aftermath of the war that divided Yugoslavia and presenting a concert under Human Rights Watch protection in the devastated city of Vukovar in the Serbian Cultural Center there. It's an abstract piece, but the sections have these subtitles: "A Sky Torn Asunder," "The Shattering of Glass," "Ghost Chorale," "A River of Blood and Ice." I was giving a class on how to listen to music. I said, "I'm going to play you this piece of music. I'm not going to tell you the name. I'm not going to tell you the composer. I want you to tell me what you hear and draw your responses, whether you make pictures or you write words or you put energy fields. I want you to map the piece as you hear it and then tell me what the piece is about." And they all got it. Something cataclysmic has happened. There's a lot of fear. There's pain. There's running away from it. There's a sense of hopefulness, but there's always a question mark. And that was my piece. So then we talked about

whether abstract collections of sounds tell a story and whether they needed to know that the middle movement was called "River of Blood and Ice." They didn't, but when I told them, it grounded them.

Laura's abstract piece communicated devastation without using lyrics or imagery. As educators look for ways to help youth share their stories, we may consider the impact of sharing lived experiences without text. Laura suggested a possible classroom application:

> Track a story that's in the news for a week as it unfolds and collect reporting on that story. Then . . . let's create a sound world that expresses this story. Or let's read this story to the sound world we create. Or let's choose music that already exists in the world that reflects the sentiments of this issue.

Laura's idea of soundscape or sound-world for the classroom offers possibilities to speak sonically to experience. While she suggested following a news story, youth may choose to create a soundscape that captures their feelings about the news story or about other experiences or issues to which they wish to speak. Text may not be necessary to communicate important ideas.

Performing in School

Most activist-musicians also strongly advocated for including performing in schools. Performing in creative music education differs from performance in large ensemble-based music education because of the creative component. Programs in which activist-musicians taught youth to create their own music often culminated in performances. Performing became the culmination of creating music to express experiences and provided a means to assert one's experiences. Activist music education may involve performing original work, fusing and mixing musics, or creative cover songs. The activist-musicians who worked as teaching artists valued what performing experiences offered youth. While activist-musicians support a performance paradigm (Lewis, 2016),[8] their performance paradigm differs from the Western classical ensemble model and involves coming to voice and naming the world (Freire, 2000/1970). Moreover, in the case of digital work, performing may actually involve creating a space for sharing. Performing facilitates sharing lived experiences, drawing on the communicative and expressive potential of music explored in Chapter 2. Lise advocated for an integrated, interdisciplinary approach to musical performance:

> I'm looking for ways to create new music together so that the kids have the experience of doing research, exploring a subject area—trying to dig deeper into histories and those social relations. And they also experience working collaboratively, playing with ideas, making

decisions about what to put out in public. They also have that experience of putting their heart and soul into a performance and sharing their ideas and their performance with somebody else. You hope they take certain things away from it—maybe some trust in themselves.

Youth in the programs Lise initiated as a teaching artist wove together history, social relations, and politics in a manner that informed performances. Lise also pointed to some psychological benefits of performance, including a sense of confidence and self-worth—benefits well documented in music education literature (Adderley, Kennedy, & Berz, 2003; Baker et al., 2008; Elliott, 1995; Elliott & Silverman, 2015; Hess, 2008, 2010; Willingham, 2001). Like Taiyo's "pie-in-the-sky" concert experience from Chapter 2, Lise's concept of performance was participatory and both historically and politically informed. Context, life histories, and sociopolitical realities richly inform performance in activist music education. When performance involves sharing youth's original work, the praxis of performance becomes a meaningful articulation of their lives and the complex conditions that shape them.

Learning to Value Others' Assertions

The third phase of naming the world and coming to voice involves learning to value others' assertions. Chapter 3 includes discussion on community building that reaffirms the importance of communicating to youth their value and the significance of their experiences. Creating spaces for songwriting in classrooms involves fostering what Griffin called mutually-supportive environments before beginning the musicking. As Griffin stated, fostering such environments early, particularly with young children, may limit shaming practices on the basis of identity, acknowledging that such practices often begin quite young (Tatum, 1997). Music ensemble and theatre students are also targeted by bullies significantly more than non-arts peers (Elpus & Carter, 2016); mutually supportive spaces, then, must extend beyond the music classroom. Supportive environments are crucial for creativity. Building community and creating a practice of community, as explored in Chapter 3, require purposeful pedagogy and opportunities to experience and practice what it means to respect and support the contributions of all classroom community members.

In fostering supportive environments, educators might further consider how to address any oppressive discourse that emerges upon inviting youth to name their worlds. Creating a space that values all voices requires clear understandings of privilege and oppression. Rather than negating narratives rooted in privilege, educators can purposefully look for opportunities to discuss different experiences. Bylica (2018), for example, notes that an activity in which students created soundscapes of their neighborhoods presented interesting opportunities to discuss differences between city and suburban home surroundings. Recognizing others' contributions then entails frank discussions about identities and their intersections with oppression and privilege. Situating such discussions in systems rather than individuals further allows students to understand experiences as subject to larger systemic structures without negating any student's experience.

Moving Toward Transformation: Collective Identity and Envisioning

The final phase of coming to voice and naming the world moves from reflection and action toward transformation. Chucky spoke to collective identity and envisioning in creative work:

> [My friend's] an amazing beatboxer and deejay, but he also happens to be a scientist at MIT media lab. We were talking one night and he was like, "Yeah, the thing is that all of these great wonders of the world, they're really just mausoleums. They're really just these places that kings forwarded their wealth, and today we consider them great wonders, but think about the amount of labor and lives that went into having to build these things. And how many people were sacrificed because of these things then you see them for what they are. They're not necessarily wonders, they're ruins of empire." Imagine if each person that built those mausoleums were given agency and there was a certain amount of collective vision that went into revisioning the kinds of things that could be built to remember civilization by. How much more wonderful could that be?

That idea profoundly influenced how Chucky shaped his work. His words challenge us to reimagine what art might do when created collectively in service of the community, or humanity at large. As we imagine possibilities for creative work, we might consider how we can enact collective envisioning. Greene (1995) calls upon us to "look at things as if they could be otherwise" (p. 16). With our art—even in schools—we can create an aspirational future imaginary. Chucky continued:

> If you . . . create something out of the love of people and out of the desire to be of service to people, then the reward is so much deeper than anything monetary. The reward is truly transformation. I've seen it happen over and over again—people's lives taking a different route than what they were before because of this process.

Chucky envisioned an artistic process in the service of humanity and fostered with love. When we encourage creative work in education, we might consider artistic work as a public imaginary. When youth initiate imagining, the work they potentially produce acts to publicly shape the future. Haynes describes the artist as a visionary who "attempts to envision possible futures.

This is what it means to say that the vocation of the artist is the reclamation of the future" (Haynes, 1997, pp. 227–228). Artistic imagining holds great potential. The artist as visionary often emerges from the hybridity of the "postcolonial moment" (Hall, 2003; Walcott, 2009)—from Dei and Asgharzadeh's (2001) anti-colonial academic, discursive, and political optimism (p. 298) and Walcott's (2009) "something else possible" (p. 170). Music educators can create a space in which youth may become visionaries. This artistic envisioning extends Freire's (1998b) notion of dreaming to enact it audibly through musicking. Chucky incorporates collective envisioning and the love of humanity into every artistic process. Creating through love may prove difficult for youth grappling with traumatic experiences and difficult life conditions. As educators, however, we might model creating through love in our work in the classroom.

Jason's work with youth echoed Chucky's sentiments by providing chants that underscored the value of bilingualism and multilingualism. When Jason enacted this work with youth, they emphasized positive messaging, and, in some senses, created a future imaginary for themselves. In speaking these messages, youth asserted themselves as individuals with much to contribute when they added their unique voices to a larger composition. When we intertwine Chucky's idea of collective envisioning with Jason's work, the next step may be to ask youth to assert a future they would like for themselves and for their communities—the transformation that follows Freire's (2000/1970) imperatives to name the world and dream radically (Freire, 1998b) to transform it. When teachers encourage youth to work creatively, they can also help them envision a more hopeful future.

Summary: Naming the World through a Creative Music Curriculum

Creative music education provides a mechanism for youth to "come to voice," "name their worlds" (Freire, 2000/1970), and assert their presence through performance (Hess, Watson, & Deroo, 2019). Coming to voice and naming the world involve four integrated processes of reflection and action toward transformation. In encouraging youth to share their experiences musically, educators can first provide youth with opportunities to explore their identity through listening and experimenting with music and instruments. Youth might then share their experiences through musicking, engaging in songwriting, lyric writing, creative mixing of musics, and sonic expression through structures that aim to make creating music accessible. This creative process culminates when youth assert their stories and ideas through performance, which further necessitates having built a classroom community in which youth and educators value each other's contributions. Ultimately, youth might use their music to imagine a different possible future and move their processes of reflection and action to envision transformation. These interrelated processes center youth's lived experiences in education and honor their histories and realities—important tenets of critical pedagogy.

The Difficulties with Sharing Experiences: Practical Implications for Students

Creating music that speaks to youth's realties may help them process some of their experiences as they consider how to coherently share their stories for the effect they desire. Sharing, however, also potentially poses risks to youth. Taiyo suggested that political music facilitates the processing of emotions related to oppression or injustice:

> I think politics, more often than not, actually come out when people have some sort of pain or hurt that they're dealing with. And they need to express that and articulate that. I know that all the quiet suffering I was going through as a young person was all bottled up 'til I knew how to connect it to other people and to society—and name it for what it is. It's racism. Or abuse. It's injustice. I think that those kinds of pains are in so many kids and it's a matter of first having for them a space—an opportunity to express that and to be vulnerable. And then you can talk about it and connect it to larger issues that are going on throughout time.

Music, as explored in Chapter 2, is a force for expression. Expressing feelings of pain or isolation facilitates processing these feelings. In expressing their pain, frustrations, hopes, and dreams, youth can see themselves reflected in the larger, identity-based political movements around them. They can notice how their own struggles connect to difficulties in the world. Creating a space for political expression in the classroom may allow youth to understand that they are not alone in their experiences—a significant implication of sharing stories through music. Hill's (2009) study investigates "wounded healing" practices in a "Hip-Hop Lit" class. He asserts:

> Many of the beliefs about the world that were articulated within Hip-Hop Lit were largely shaped by painful encounters with forces of inequality and marginalization that had not been previously articulated or critically examined. The conversations that emerged from these ideological narratives were therefore not less personal but less *personalized*, because the entire class was able to use a particular narrative to challenge individual and collective worldviews within a relatively safe space.
>
> (p. 272)

Like the youth in Hill's study, activist music education creates a space for youth to connect their experiences to others' experiences, challenge dominant narratives, and develop a systemic understanding of the forces that shape their lives. A political space in the classroom that challenges oppressions potentially provides opportunities for youth to situate themselves in the world and understand their relationship to the events that surround them. The songwriting process further encourages youth to consider ways to coherently share their stories, as well as to think about the desired effect of their music. This intentionality may also help youth reflect upon their experiences—a key tenet of critical pedagogy (Freire, 2000/1970).

Asking youth to share their stories in this way, however, is also fraught—particularly when the experiences youth describe could require intervention. Youth experience trauma through abuse or oppression at alarming rates (U.S. Department of Health & Human Services, 2017).[9] In inviting youth to name their worlds, educators must be prepared and in turn prepare youth for the possible consequences of sharing: educators are mandatory reporters. As such, when students disclose abuse or thoughts of harming self or others, we must act. Fulfilling one's role as a mandatory reporter, however, often fails to account for negative possible outcomes of such reporting. Students may feel betrayed, and home situations or relationships could remain stagnant or worsen with intervention (Campbell, Cook, LaFleur, & Keenan, 2010).

In inviting youth to name their worlds through their music, educators must make clear to youth that doing so is a choice. They may choose to engage with the conditions that shape their experiences, but such engagement can never be mandatory. Students who have experienced or are experiencing trauma may not fully know the nature of their experiences because of complex psychological and physical defense mechanisms that suppress traumatic events in memory. Moreover, acknowledging these experiences and sharing them may actually make circumstances more deeply felt for youth struggling to survive, but also has the potential to alleviate distress (Kennedy-Moore & Watson, 2001). As educators, respecting the decisions that youth make about musical subject matter honors their right to maintain control of their stories. That means that youth may choose to create music that seems superficial. Opting to engage superficial topics musically may be a form of protection, and respecting this decision allows youth to trust their own instincts about what feels comfortable to share. Asking youth to engage with their experiences is deeply personal, and they must be allowed to determine which stories are for public consumption. Moreover, respecting youth's choices communicates that they have autonomy and the right to determine how they are known in the world.

When youth do choose to share stories that necessitate mandatory reporting, educators face different challenges. Students may be unaware that what they share constitutes trauma. They also may not know that, after having encouraged students to share their stories, their teachers may have to initiate an intervention. Mandatory reporting typically involves third parties (e.g. children's aid agencies, counselors, social workers, the police). Involving these parties may feel like betrayal to youth who may view sharing their experiences as fulfilling a class assignment. As educators, preparing youth for third party involvement and supporting them through interventions may prove challenging, particularly when the events that unfold may not improve the situation.

Honoring and Sharing Lived Experiences 105

Educators can let professionals know in advance if the curriculum may potentially be triggering. Understanding the curriculum content and potential triggers will help inform any subsequent responses and support required. In cases in which educators are unsure of the nature of the circumstances expressed, we may wish to involve school psychologists or social workers early. It may not be clear, for example, whether the story described in a student's music expresses that individual's experience, the reality of someone s/he knows, or is fictional or an amalgamated story. Students may also possibly "project" an experience they do not recall due to personal trauma. Teachers may be unable to make such determinations. In such cases, early consultation with experts may help educators determine appropriate action.

The complexity of these issues requires careful consideration. Asking students to name their worlds could potentially have deleterious effects on their well-being. Acknowledging that possibility further underscores the importance of ensuring that sharing is a choice that students make. Educators may further need to address students' feelings of betrayal when they complete a class assignment that discloses abuse or desire to harm self or others without awareness of the potential for third-party involvement. Students will need support during any upheaval, and remaining consistent as a caring adult throughout any intervention that follows a mandatory report becomes important, as youth may experience changes in their circumstances. Asking youth to name their worlds within the institution of school involves complexities absent from encouraging the same naming when muskers are not minors subject to regulations for their protection.

Youth daring to share their stories may also put themselves at risk politically. In Chapter 3, Karl discussed exploring how various artists addressed social issues historically and presently. He further noted that writing and performing music in support of social movements sometimes involved personal risks. Karl noted in particular the risks Neil Young took in making a reference to the Ku Klux Klan in "Southern Man." Being an artist sometimes means assuming the role of the border crosser (Gaztambide-Fernández, 2008) and challenging "boundaries, rules, and expectations and disturb-[ing] the social order to promote social transformation and 'reconstruction'" (p. 244). When artists traverse boundaries that dominant groups hold dear, however, their own realities may change. Youth who use music to speak to their realities need to not only be aware of the pressures artists faced historically and presently, but also to recognize that their music and lyrics may not always be welcome. As educators working alongside youth, part of our work, then, is carving out a space in the world to support youth's voices.

Navigating the complexities of mandatory reporting, trauma, and political pressure become important considerations in inviting youth to name their worlds. Recognizing naming the world as a process with possible negative outcomes may help educators navigate deleterious or traumatic effects as they arise. Choice becomes crucial when asking students to name their experiences. Honoring that youth have the right to control their narratives acknowledges the validity of their decisions about what to share and communicates that educators will respect their choices.

Summary

In Chapter 2, activist-musicians emphasized the communicative and expressive potential of music as a means to share experiences and stories. This chapter shifts from the communicative potential of music to examine the ways in which activist-musicians perceived that educators might honor youth's lived experiences in place-based music education and subsequently encourage youth to share their stories through musicking. Fostering such creative efforts involves a four-part process of naming the world and coming to voice (Freire, 2000/1970) that entails exploring identity, asserting one's experiences, valuing the contributions of others, and imagining different possible futures. These interrelated processes of action and reflection toward transformation involve creating spaces in which youth can explore their identities and experiment with their musical voices, create and perform their own music, and value the musics of others. Youth may also use their musical storytelling as a means to process their own experiences related to oppression. In encouraging youth to share their experiences through music, educators must acknowledge the inherent risks of such vulnerability, including the complexities of mandatory reporting, trauma, and political consequences.

Notes

1. See Chapter 2 for discussion and video links to both songs.
2. Students in Kaschub's (2009) study also listened to music that engaged with social justice issues before creating their own music.
3. Liz's organization, Music2Life: Soundtrack for Social Change, collaborates with different organizations to facilitate musical pairings with activist work. For more information, see http://music2life.org.
4. Jason credits Butch Morris for the way he practices conducted improvisations.
5. See Hess (2019) for a discussion of Nobuko's words in the context of identity politics.
6. *Testimonio* recalls the concept of the counterstory from critical race theory. Solórzano & Yosso (2002) assert that these types of stories "give voice and turn the margins into places of transformative resistance" (p. 37).
7. See www.laurakaminsky.com/ for more information.
8. Lewis (2016) distinguishes the dominant performance paradigm of music education from a paradigm that privileges listening.
9. Published in 2017, the Child Maltreatment 2015 report shows an increased number of child abuse referrals in the United States from 3.6 million to 4 million with a total of 7.2 million children involved. Child deaths that stem from abuse and neglect have also increased to 1670 in 2015.

5 Music Education as Political

Teaching is first and foremost a political act (Freire, 1993, 1998b; hooks, 1994); the assumption that education is neutral and devoid of ideologies is itself political (Apple, 2004; Anyon, 1981; Bourdieu, 1973; Lareau, 2011). Actualizing music education as political, however, entails a process quite distinct from party politics. The term *political*, in this context, involves critically considering the world—both one's immediate community context and one's community in relation to the surrounding area—the regional, national, and international contexts. To engage politically entails questioning, critiquing, and working to understand the ideologies and forces that shape one's own lived conditions and experiences and those of others. Drawing on activist-musicians' perspectives, I conceptualize political music education rooted in what Giroux and Giroux (2004) call a "culture of questioning" (p. 123) through which youth learn to notice and question the ideologies, messages, and representations they encounter. While I advocate for enacting education politically, doing so does not mean propagating a particular set of political views but rather working alongside youth to help them develop their own perspectives.

I actualize this culture of questioning in three parts, rooted in the ideas of activist-musicians. In order for youth to question, critique, and challenge the conditions that influence their lives and the lives of others, they must first notice the ideologies that shape these conditions. The first phase of the culture of questioning thus involves noticing ideologies and identifying them, while the second phase entails facilitating youth's recognition of the conditions that shape their lives and the lives of others. Both phases involve explicitly naming the world (Freire, 2000/1970). In the third phase, having noticed ideologies and any forms of oppression, youth move to action, learning to dissent and coming to voice (Freire, 2000/1970). In putting forward critique and a culture of questioning, I draw on the tradition of critical pedagogy and encourage youth to engage in a practice of critique that involves active meaning-making, naming their world, and working to transform it through tools and strategies they devise themselves (Freire, 2000/1970).

Giroux and Giroux (2004) position a culture of questioning (p. 123) as crucial to education. In fostering such a culture, educators create space for dissent and contestation of dominant ideologies. Patrick, or DJ Phatrick, pointed to the importance of questioning, both in education and in the world:

> When it comes to education or social justice, we can't have our students or our peers [unthinkingly] believe the things they believe. We need to create a pathway for them to hopefully realize certain things or be critical about certain things that we hope they can believe in. But we can't just have them believe in it. A lot of people are guilty of that—not just in education, but with activism.

Drawing on Freire's (2000/1970) work himself, Patrick challenged youth in the community hip-hop program he directed to question all messages they received in order to critically engage the world around them. He urged them to refuse to tacitly accept ideologies propagated by those with authority.

This culture of questioning, in which a process of noticing both ideologies and lived conditions gives way to some sort of action, aligns with the transformational purpose of Freirian critical thinking:

> [Critical thinking] discerns an indivisible solidarity between the world and the people and admits of no dichotomy between them—thinking which perceives reality as process, as transformation, rather than as a static entity—thinking which does not separate itself from action, but constantly immerses itself in temporality without fear of the risks involved. Critical thinking contrasts with naive thinking, which sees "historical time as a weight, a stratification of the acquisitions and experiences of the past," from which the present should emerge normalized and "well-behaved." For the naive thinker, the important thing is accommodation to this normalized "today." For the critic, the important thing is the continuing transformation of reality, on behalf of the continuing humanization of men [sic].
> (quotation from personal communication cited in Freire, 2000/1970, p. 92)

Activist-musicians encouraged critical thinking and this culture of questioning, which I actualize in three phases described in the following sections. Drawing on their unique perspectives allows consideration of how these phases operate in music education. This chapter thus explores how it may look and sound musically to identify and consider ideologies, notice lived conditions, and move to action.

Noticing Ideologies

The first phase of enacting music education as a culture of questioning involves noticing ideologies and identifying them. Because they are omnipresent, ideologies inform all discourses, actions, behaviors, and events. Activist-musicians suggested value in noticing the ideologies informing (a) the actions and discourses of authority figures including teachers, (b) the representations portrayed in various media, and (c) musical lyrics. Recognizing the ubiquitous presence of ideologies lays the foundation for developing a practice of critique.

Recognizing Ideologies among Authority Figures

Pete focused on the educator as ideologue and advocated for fostering an environment in which youth may challenge authority:

> I think wherever [teachers] individually are on the political spectrum, a lot of times, teachers want students to have the exact same views as they do. Even teachers who are really progressive or really left-leaning can unintentionally not give students much freedom, 'cause they want students to believe exactly the same thing that they do. Regardless of the political leanings of the teacher, it's important for them to teach students not to just trust someone because they're a teacher—not to just trust someone because they're older than them. That it's important to be able to question.

Pete argued that youth should develop a practice of critique and refuse to accept messages received in school without first considering them and interrogating the source. He pointed to the pressure to align thinking and actions with the ideologies of those in authority and noted that the political left does not necessarily provide more flexibility in thinking or critique than the right. Pete sought a space in which youth could question and challenge their education.

Teachers who heed Pete's words may lead youth to come to recognize the ubiquitous presence of ideologies. In encouraging youth to question authority, educators may work alongside youth to facilitate recognition that different ideologies permeate all discourses and actions. A practice of critique thus involves a process through which youth identify these ideologies and notice how they impact the discourses circulating in their lives. When youth understand that all discourses emerge from ideologies, they may also recognize the bias in all of the sources they encounter and subsequently eschew notions of objectivity.

In order to encourage youth to both recognize the ubiquity of ideologies and question authority when necessary, educators can explicitly teach with these goals in mind. When youth identify ideologies that shape the discourses they encounter, teachers can affirm the naming process and extend it further. Educators can also choose to be transparent about the ideologies that shape their own approach. Freire (1998b) notes,

> Respecting the educands, however, does not mean lying to them about my dreams, telling them in words or deeds or practices that a school

occupies a "sacred" space where one only studies, and studying has nothing to do with what goes on in the world outside; to hide my options from them, as if it were a "sin" to have a preference, to make an option, to draw the line, to decide, to dream. Respecting them means, on the one hand, testifying to them of my choice, and defending it, and on the other, it mean showing them other options, wherever I teach—no matter what it is that I teach!

(pp. 67–68)

He thus argues for a transparency in ideology.

Youth may easily identify ideologies shaping discourses and actions that connect to one aspect of their lives while missing those that affect them less directly. They may struggle to identify any ideologies or easily notice their presence throughout their encounters. Educators can purposefully help youth to deepen their understanding of ideology, to practice recognizing the manner in which ideologies inform all discourse and action. We can build upon the recognition of one ideology that shapes particular events, behaviors, actions, or discourses to help youth develop a habit of actively looking for the ideology informing any discourse, behavior, event, or action they encounter. Beginning with a practice of looking for the ideologies that inform the actions and discourses of authority figures may lead to broader recognition of the circulating ideologies that shape every societal encounter.

Analyzing Representations: Addressing Absences, Presences, Stereotypes, and Industry Demands in Musical Participation

Fostering a culture of questioning also involves critically examining representations; noticing how various media and educational resources portray different groups engaged in musicking offers insight into the ideologies that shape many of our musical choices. In music education contexts, representations of musicking often depict women in limited roles across the spectrum of musical activities. In a searing analysis of music textbooks in the 1980s and 1990s, Koza (1992b, 1994b, 1994c, 1994d) finds that exclusion, underrepresentation, and stereotyping characterize gender representations in music textbooks. Textbooks typically gender composing, conducting, and playing instruments as masculine while gendering singing as feminine. Green (2002) argues that school music education itself reproduces stereotypical notions of masculinity and femininity and reinforces gendered musical roles. She concludes that

> Girls and boys on the whole respectively tend to choose particular activities and styles that already symbolically affirm conventional discursive constructions of femininity or masculinity in the wider world outside of the school. . . . The school perpetuates subtle definitions of femininity and masculinity as connotations of different musical practices

and musical styles, in which pupils invest their desires to conform, not necessarily to the school, but to the wider social construction of gender.
(p. 142)

Youth receive strong messages that dictate acceptable instrument choices by gender (Abeles, 2009; Conway, 2000; Koza, 1992a; Sinsabaugh, 2005), associate femininity with classical music and masculinity with popular music (often conceptualized as rock; Green, 2003), and limit the creative practices (composition) of youth identifying as girls (Green, 2002, 2003). More than a decade later, men still outnumber women in instrumental conducting and music education positions (Elpus, 2015; Fitzpatrick, 2013; Sheldon & Hartley, 2012), and this representation shapes what young women view as possibilities for their musicking. Music education discourse similarly reinscribes racialized understandings of ways that youth participate in music. Lyrics and textbook illustrations often conceptualize the ideal subject as White, and curricular practices frequently minimize Indigenous and Black musics, further serving to reinscribe Whiteness (Gustafson, 2009). Whiteness remains the dominant ideology of music education (Bradley, 2006a, 2007, 2015, 2017; Gustafson, 2009; Hess, 2018e; Koza, 2008), as well as the ideology operating globally—what Mills (1997) calls global White supremacy. As Koza (2008) and others (Elpus & Abril, 2011; Vaugeois, 2009) explicate, racialized limitations placed on who can participate in music also connect intricately with classed relations. School music often operates as a middle-class endeavor (Bates, 2012; Elpus & Abril, 2011).

hooks' (2008/1994) discussion of representation similarly identifies ways that racism, White supremacy, and patriarchy operate in popular culture. She calls on us to resist these representations: "To intervene and transform those politics of representation informed by colonialism, imperialism, and White supremacy, we have to be willing to challenge mainstream culture's efforts to 'erase racism' by suggesting it does not really exist" (Kindle Locations 2837–2839). She asserts that a practice of colorblindness fails to move forward any project of transformation. hooks challenges the commodification of "underclass Black life" and its consumption by "mainstream" White audiences:

> Why . . . does so much contemporary African American literature highlight the circumstances and condition of underclass Black life in the South and in big cities when it is usually written by folks whose experiences are just the opposite? The point of raising this question is not to censor but rather to urge critical thought about a cultural marketplace wherein blackness is commodified in such a way that fictive accounts of underclass Black life in whatever setting may be more lauded, more marketable, than other visions because mainstream conservative White audiences desire these images. As rapper Dr. Dre calls it, "People in the suburbs, they can't go to the ghetto so they like to

hear about what's goin' on. Everybody wants to be down." The desire to be "down" has promoted a conservative appropriation of specific aspects of underclass Black life, whose reality is dehumanized via a process of commodification wherein no correlation is made between mainstream hedonistic consumerism and the reproduction of a social system that perpetuates and maintains an underclass.

(Kindle Locations 2372–2380).

Catering to consumerist desires for stereotypes, music can reproduce racism, patriarchy, classism, sexual stereotypes, and heterosexism. hooks further notes that dominant culture criticizes "gangsta rap" for its misogyny without recognizing the consumerist (White) supremacist culture that demands such misogyny and materially rewards young Black men who produce music that acquiesces to these demands (Kindle Locations 1917–1918).

While music education research notices how school music reproduces gender, race, and class through representation, hooks looks for the ideologies that reinscribe these same oppressive structures in popular culture. Ryan (2011) argues that "Freirean educators who seek to *critically intervene in reality* cannot remain detached from this agenda but must actively engage in dialogue pertaining to all aspects of education provision" (p. 87, emphasis in original). Examining ideologies in representations then involves facilitating at least two distinct processes with youth: (1) noticing what representations communicate about possibilities and limitations on musical participation and (2) recognizing any ideologies that shape the way artists perform themselves in order to be publicly celebrated.

First, critically engaging representations of musics and musicians offers an essential site for critique, dialogue, and new possibilities. As educators, we can encourage youth to actively look for and notice the manner in which representations place limitations on participation. I draw an example from my elementary and middle school teaching experience to point to a way that educators may challenge students to question who participates in particular musical practices and whose bodies these practices exclude.[1]

In my first year of teaching elementary and middle school music, I received a set of free posters of musicians playing Yamaha instruments. While in the process of displaying them in my classroom, I noticed that all of the musicians pictured were White men. I quickly checked the remainder of the posters and began taking them back down, concerned that the students in my classes would not see themselves represented as performers. Ultimately, however, I chose a different approach. I put the posters up and challenged the students to critique them—to identify who was missing and why that was a problem. When popular media and the majority of music representations do not include people of color or women, this lack of representation provides educators with an opportunity to challenge the images explicitly. As a young teacher, I encouraged students to notice whom this instrument manufacturer chose to portray as musicians. Now I might extend that conversation to ask larger ideological questions. The students clearly identified the racism and sexism operating in the representation of musicians on these posters; however, I missed the opportunity to have a broader conversation about racism and sexism in both music and society. Even so, my efforts at the time offered an opportunity for youth to practice critique—to notice inequity in representations.

Magali also suggested that explicit instruction may help foster the process of critiquing representations. At the Toronto Girls Rock Camp that Magali directed, youth at the camp participated in workshops that challenged them to think critically about messages the media propagated about body image. These workshops challenged campers to critique the gendered socialization process targeting them through the media and to resist it. When Casey taught there, she also pushed campers to think about issues of justice as they intersected with the arts, drawing on campers' strong sense of justice and fairness. Magali and Casey deliberately facilitated a process through which youth challenged expectations placed on women, both by society and by the media, to envision their own musical practices with full awareness of the manner in which the media often portrays women artists.

Second, in considering the artist alongside representations, educators navigate terrain fraught with stereotypes and underlying systems of patriarchy, heteropatriarchy, White supremacy, and classism. Artists who capitulate to the capitalist insistences on reproducing these systems may themselves perform a stereotype. tvu, for example, shared her experience with the music industry:

> I got an offer to write a theme song for a movie. They wanted a female rapper, and they wanted a song to be like a version of Beastie Boys "Girls, Girls, Girls," but it'd be called "Boys, Boys, Boys." It was just so gimmicky, you know? They just wanted a female voice, rap voice, to take on a very sexualized persona, and I couldn't really do it. And it left such a bad taste in my mouth for the industry in general, that I was kind of like, "Forget it. This really isn't for me." The people that I work with let me backtrack a bit. That made me realize that mainstream success wasn't going to be worth it to play that persona. I can't lie that well. So, I wouldn't have made it very far anyways.

In this instance, the music industry demanded that tvu play a particular role to achieve success by their standards. She refused and continued to perform on her terms. Calling on youth to enact a practice of noticing whose voices society privileges in musical practices demands that they examine underlying ideologies influencing artists. In doing so, youth develop a habit of considering the limits placed on certain people and further notice whose voices typically receive platforms and whose voices either do not or must perform in particular ways in order for society to recognize their contributions.[2]

In fostering a culture of questioning, music educators can also facilitate developing a practice of noticing which bodies typically play the role of the artist in music. What are the demographics of the artists whom music education and popular media continually highlight?[3] Noticing whom society characteristically celebrates as the artist and the roles or scripts that they perform publicly helps youth develop a habit of critiquing absences, presences, stereotypes, and industry demands in representation. In considering representations, recognizing the ideologies shaping any and all representations involves examining both what the representation itself communicates and what has informed this particular portrayal or performance.

Challenging Messages Communicated through Music

Alongside encouraging youth to challenge and critique the ideologies informing authority figures and representations, educators can also call upon students to explicitly engage messages communicated through music. In Chapter 2, El urged her son to be aware of the messages music communicates lest the vibrations enter his consciousness unchecked. Oppressive discourses permeate in society and manifest at times in music through patriarchal, White supremacist, and heterosexist ideologies (hooks, 2008/1994). Rather than shying away from music that propagates oppressive discourses, activist-musicians advocated for addressing it directly. Music presents an opportunity to initiate critique. Hollindale (1988) explains that literacy education typically focuses on *what* children read rather than *how* they read and suggests that a critical literacy program might help children read critically by posing questions to uncover ideologies present in children's literature. Music provides similar opportunities.

Patrick described a multifaceted approach to engaging misogynist music in the hip-hop program he directed in California:

> You can look at a misogynistic hip-hop song. There are teachers all day telling kids that that's a bad song—it's degrading. It's not as common for them to really break down and [provide] the tools for the youth to come up with that opinion on their own. Music is a perfect tool for critical thinking because we can break something down and have youth think about something in a more three-dimensional way. In that process, they become more critical thinkers. Now, they'll never hear a song the same way.

Like Pete, Patrick opposed an education that encouraged youth to uncritically reflect their teacher's perspectives. Instead, he wished to set the conditions for youth to arrive at their own conclusions by equipping them with tools for analysis—an important facet of Patrick's approach to community music education. He discussed ways in which youth can consider musical practices alongside lyrical analysis in order to break down the content in songs. In modeling a practice of critique, educators facilitate opportunities for youth to challenge misogynistic, racist, or otherwise oppressive lyrics. When music educators productively model challenging and critiquing oppressive lyrics, they demonstrate how young artists can address and critique oppressive structures in society and represent identity in ways that create spaces for all bodies.

Patrick offered a crucial strategy for educators to materially challenge the messages youth might receive in music:

> In our programs, I encourage all instructors to acknowledge the music that the kids listen to. It would not be fair for us to say, "Oh, turn that off. That's crap." There has to be some value that draws the youth to it and you need to address that: "Whoa! That beat is an amazing beat. But do you really like what the guy's saying? What do you think your mom thinks about what that guy is saying about women? If you had a daughter, what would you . . ." So it's not about telling them that it's right or wrong. It's about [asking]: "How would you feel if you were in this other person's shoes? Who's in power?" We talk about power a lot: "Who has the power in this song? Who's a possible victim of this song? Who might not enjoy this song and why?" So [I begin with]: "Yes, I also like this song because I think the beat is amazing. I think the way he's rapping is really creative. However, I challenge you, the student, to remake this song with other lyrics that might not be as damaging or disrespectful or oppressive to certain populations."

Patrick acknowledged the value of the song and did not dismiss reasons why youth might be drawn to it. After this acknowledgment, however, he challenged them to critique it, drawing on strategies of empathy and critiquing representations and oppressive discourses (also see Vaugeois, 2009, as cited in Chapter 3). In doing so, he seized the opportunity to educate, often referred to as seizing the "teachable moment" (Hyun, 2006). Horton asserts that in the process of enacting critical pedagogy, "what you know is the body of the material that you're trying to get people to consider, but instead of giving a lecture on it, you ask a question enlightened by that" (Horton & Freire, 1990, p. 146). Patrick's pedagogy in this community hip-hop program enacted Horton's words. Patrick encouraged instructors in the program to respect youth's music, while challenging them to critique it—and perhaps ultimately remake it. He drew upon empathy as a strategy in this process and asked youth to "put themselves in others' shoes." While Razack (2007) cautions us about the slipperiness of empathy, which I explicate in Chapter 6, Patrick challenged youth to consider the perspectives of those closest to them. Drawing upon empathy as a pedagogical strategy in this instance encouraged youth to identify populations marginalized by the song's message. Patrick intertwined empathy and power to help youth critically analyze oppressive lyrics. His questions about identifying a possible victim of the song or a mother's feelings about the lyrics required youth to consider the perspectives of others alongside the possible effects of misogynist lyrics. Patrick's practice of coupling empathy and power in discussions provided a powerful tool to uncover oppressive ideologies in lyrics.

Summary: Noticing Ideologies in Authorities, Representations, and Music

Noticing the ideologies that shape the discourses and actions in our various societal encounters comprises an important first facet of fostering a culture of questioning. When youth develop a habit of recognizing the ideologies that inform the actions of authorities, the privileging of particular kinds of representations, and the messages communicated in music, they begin to actively practice critique and refuse to accept the material they encounter without first considering and questioning it. Committing to both noticing and questioning may further help youth trust and value their own perspectives.

Identifying Lived Conditions

A second important facet of fostering a culture of questioning involves recognizing the conditions that shape one's own life and the lives of others. Teaching for *conscientization* (Freire, 2000/1970), or an active practice of critique, ultimately involves facilitating a process through which youth can identify the conditions and ideologies that affect their lives. Recognizing and naming the conditions that influence one's world requires developing a practice of noticing and a habit of critique. In Chapter 2, Patrick identified a process of self-reflection that he called "internal social justice" and noted that when analyzing a song like "The Message" by Grandmaster Flash and Furious Five, youth may see their own experiences in the music and realize truths about their neighborhoods and police behavior in their communities. I recall Patrick's words here from Chapter 2:

> [As an educator,] you break down a song like "The Message" by Grandmaster Flash and Furious Five, which talks about growing up in the projects—broken glass, everywhere. You take these themes and analyze why these themes are so prevalent in hip-hop music. Then you start talking about class. You start talking about racism. You start talking about history. Because the population of youth I predominantly work with are from the same background as the folks who are making the music in terms of class, neighborhoods, and what they're experiencing, that's the self-reflection aspect. 'Cause social justice is also about internal social justice. You're figuring out why you are the way you are, why the neighborhoods you live in are the way they are, why the police act the way they do in your neighborhoods.

Patrick thus encouraged youth to connect the experiences shared in lyrics of the songs they enjoyed to their own life experiences to come to realizations about race and class and injustices enacted on racialized, classed populations. In teaching them to draw connections and see themselves in the music they deeply valued, Patrick created space to challenge, critique, and possibly transform the conditions that affected their lives (Freire, 2000/1970). Exploring the commonalities between youth and groups represented in music offered opportunities for students to critique their experiences (Freire, 2000/1970; Greene, 1978).

Patrick's approach in this instance drew upon hip-hop to prompt youth to consider the conditions that affect their own lives. With its racialized and classed content, hip-hop may provide a medium to help youth "name their world," as Freire (2000/1970) describes. Dale and Hyslop-Margison (2010) assert that "understanding individual context and how these conditions influence perceptions of self and society is the fundamental starting point for transforming individual consciousness and enhancing social awareness" (p. 159). Patrick's teaching practice aligns with Freire's problem-posing education, wherein youth identify issues in their lives, in this case through music, in order to examine, critique, and ultimately challenge them.

Patrick facilitated an important conversation that called upon youth to examine the conditions that shape their lives by analyzing hip-hop lyrics. Such discussions call upon educators to directly and frankly discuss difficult issues that often create discomfort. Many of the critical thinking strategies activist-musicians suggested require music educators to ably facilitate what Singleton and Linton (2006) call "courageous conversations."[4] To address uncomfortable issues, Boler (1999) calls upon educators to foster a "pedagogy of discomfort" that encourages participants to

> engage in critical inquiry regarding values and cherished beliefs, and to examine constructed self-images in relation to how one has learned to perceive others. Within this culture of inquiry and flexibility, a central focus is to recognize how emotions define how and what one chooses to see, and conversely, not to see.
>
> (pp. 176–177)

Critical conversations and self-inquiry require teachers and students to look unflinchingly at difficult issues and engage in both self-critique and critique of the world around them. In the community hip-hop program he directed, Patrick facilitated youth's questioning of the conditions that shaped their lives. Lise also made courageous conversations a crucial part of her pedagogy and prioritized Indigenous issues in her work with youth in school music. Teachers with whom she collaborated made a concerted effort to tell stories of residential schools in Canada (Amagaolik, 2012), drawing on resources including children's books to make these hardships and traumas understandable and accessible to youth. In explicitly teaching about the violence of colonization and physical and cultural genocide, Lise fostered a keen sense of justice in the youth with whom she worked. She facilitated critical and courageous conversations (Singleton & Linton, 2006) with students and worked to make explicit the marginalization and violence around them. Some students had first-hand or familial experience with these traumas, while other students became aware of the effects of residential schools through their education. In this context, discussing the trauma and oppression experienced by Indigenous people may validate the knowledge of Indigenous students in the class while also making non-Indigenous students cognizant of the lived conditions Indigenous groups often face as a result of generations of oppression and genocide. While often challenging, these discussions comprise a key facet of any pedagogy intended to encourage a practice of critique.

Recognizing lived conditions as an aspect of a culture of questioning involves examining both one's own circumstances and the circumstances of others. Patrick and Lise both engaged youth in difficult conversations about identity and oppression. Understanding how identity corresponds with privilege and oppression may help youth name both their own world and the worlds of others and subsequently work to change them. These two activist-musicians further drew upon music as a means of recognizing oppressive conditions as they affect one's own life and the lives of others.

These first two phases of a culture of questioning—identifying the ideologies informing all encounters and recognizing the lived conditions of self and others—encourage youth to practice critique. When educators work alongside youth to help them identify ideologies and notice the forces that shape the world around them, they assist youth in developing a habit of noticing. Greene (1978) argues that the arts and humanities provide important opportunities for heightened consciousness and self-reflection. When we integrate the arts and humanities into education, "we need to do so consciously," she asserts, "with a clear perception of what it means to enable people to pay, from their own distinctive vantage points, 'full attention to life'" (p. 163). Fostering a habit of noticing requires youth to develop a practice of paying full attention to life.

Facilitating Coming to Voice: Dissent, Imagining, and Exemplars

After working alongside youth to develop a habit of noticing oppression and unjust conditions, educators may encourage youth to move to action. Activist-musicians suggested that teachers could facilitate youth's opposition to oppressive ideologies and conditions that students themselves identify by drawing on a number of strategies. Educators, they urged, can encourage dissent in the classroom, demonstrably imagine musical practices beyond the constraints of oppressive ideologies, and offer exemplars of anti-oppressive possibilities. When educators enact these strategies, they set the conditions for youth both to move to action and come to voice.

Dissent in the Classroom

In the discussion on ideology, Pete advocated for a culture of questioning through which youth could openly challenge authority. He envisioned a classroom in which teachers encourage youth to think for themselves and dissent accordingly. When educators create an environment in which dissent is valued, youth may learn that dissent is crucial to democratic society and that teachers will support them when they assert themselves. Pete subsequently argued that if educators encourage youth to question those in authority, students may gain the confidence to challenge both educators and politicians who propagate ideologies that differ from their own. When educating involves teaching youth to question authority, students may learn to critically challenge the world around them and assert themselves effectively.

Pete pointed to the tendency of teachers to forward their own ideologies in the classroom. In considering ways to help youth challenge authority, educators may encourage practicing dissent as vital to democratic music education (Gould, 2013; Schmidt, 2008). Moreover, in facilitating spaces in which youth may dissent, educators potentially foster genuine dialogue in the classroom (Freire, 2000/1970), as Pete suggested, and create spaces in which youth learn to strongly assert their perspectives. Such assertion requires practice, and classrooms can provide these opportunities. When we welcome dissent and explicitly teach youth to identify influential ideologies, they may develop the skills to challenge the discourses and actions they encounter in a manner that considers the perspectives of all. A practice of dissent aligns with the "culture of questioning" that Giroux and Giroux (2004, p. 123) position as crucial to education. In fostering such a culture, educators create space for recognition of, dissent from, and contestation of dominant ideologies. Enabling dissent in the classroom sets the conditions for youth to move to action when they notice injustice and to strongly assert their voices in the world.

Imagining Possible Musical Practices

Casey recognized the sexism that shaped representations of women engaged in musical practices and took a unique approach to the limitations and stereotypes communicated by the media. She presented a workshop called "The History of Women in Music" for the Girls Rock Camp in Toronto, Ontario, Canada. Her presentation encouraged students to think about

> the different ways in which we can imagine what a woman is and the histories of race and gender that circulate with women who play rock music. And thinking about who paves the way for us in Toronto specifically to pick up an instrument and play—or expand the idea of what music can be. Not just rock music . . . It's about imagining—being able to dream up a music practice that doesn't necessarily mean a guitar and

a bass, and a drum kit. That you can be punk rock and be a slam poet or an R&B artist.[5]

In this participatory workshop, Casey encouraged campers to clap and cheer when they recognized an artist, and she included pictures of famous artists, camp facilitators, and the campers themselves in the presentation. The presentation created possibilities for these young women to see themselves as artists while unsettling stereotypes of gendered and racialized performance roles. When music educators provide role models who are engaged in various musicking activities and who look like the students (Gould, 1996; Grant, 2000; Koza, 1992b, 1994b; Lind & McKoy, 2016; MacKay, 2009), that type of musical engagement becomes a genuine possibility in young people's imaginations. Casey deliberately showed representations of women enacting a multiplicity of musical practices. In offering different representations, Casey created space for youth to pursue roles, perhaps previously unimaginable or unavailable, and enact a musical practice that may not yet exist. In doing so, she directly addressed limitations placed on young women's musicking practices. Explicitly challenging stereotypical representations opens possibilities for who can participate in various musical practices. Casey's strategy to address inequity in musical participation and representation involved broadening the range of what was possible and creating a space for young women to invent themselves as artists. She herself recognized the lack of representation of women in music and refused to restrict the young women she taught by perpetuating societal limitations. In adopting this strategy, Casey challenged stereotypical representations of women in music. When women see themselves in leadership roles in music without the requirement to capitulate to dominant discourses, shifts in participation become possible. Casey imagined a different future for women musicians and taught directly to that vision—a process Freire (1998b) describes as *dreaming*. In music education, Juntunen et al. (2014) argue that "music teachers working in a fast-changing society could focus on envisioning their students' imaginary spaces for engaging with music and equipping them for leaping into what for the students would be the musically hitherto unexplored" (p. 251). Like Casey, they called upon music educators to imagine what might be possible for students without being restricted by current practices. Providing different representations in this way creates possible openings in formerly restricted musical practices.

Griffin similarly suggested that school music programs should focus on creating a space in which all youth participants can see themselves playing music:

> I think that there would also be simultaneously something in a pie-in-the-sky music program that worked really strongly against gendered associations of who does and who does not play music.

Griffin focused on gendered associations, as have many scholars (Abeles, 2009; Conway, 2000; Koza, 1994c; Lamb, 1987; Sinsabaugh, 2005). Casey's workshop modeled a diverse range of people engaged in music. Both of them purposefully de-centered gendered discourses in education. Griffin recognized the effects of patriarchy on young musicians and sought an approach to music education that refused to restrict youth's musical practices based on gender. In Chapter 3, Griffin strongly opposed the shaming that girls face in music, and their words here extend the importance of fostering mutually supportive spaces that actively counter patriarchy. We can extend these ideas to other forms of oppression including racism, heterosexism, and ableism. Griffin suggests that we make this challenge a vital part of our programs. When we communicate that all bodies can do music and do not limit the musical genres we engage, we create a space where youth can select their own musical practices and develop their unique voices, less inhibited by limited representations in their education. Importantly, Casey and Griffin both advocate for enacting these challenges and re-imaginings with young children. They seem to perceive that when the call to re-envision who participates in music, and how that participation looks and sounds, starts young, a different future may become possible. These imaginings and reimaginings similarly resonate with Freire's (1998b) notions of dreaming.

Providing Exemplars

Educators can also purposefully share anti-oppressive exemplars in order to encourage youth to assert themselves. In his efforts to address misogynist messages in hip-hop, Patrick intentionally provided socially conscious exemplars to contradict the oppressive discourses that youth encounter in music:

> There are a lot of [hip-hop] songs out there that very directly, mostly in a negative way, address sexuality issues. We take that, and we can break down songs that are not the most positive representation of gender issues or sexuality issues, but then we also take another song that addresses the issues in a more positive way. There are a lot of artists out there—the conscious hip-hop artists—that have amazing music that might not have the access to radio or be as known. And we take it, and we show the youth what it looks like to have somebody talk about those issues in a positive way, and still make great music.

Youth in Patrick's program ultimately created their own music, and Patrick wanted them to have positive examples of artists addressing complex issues through an anti-oppressive lens. hooks (2008/1994) describes the patriarchal assertions of misogyny and rape culture that the capitalist music industry demands of Black male rappers but notes, "Significantly, there are powerful alternative voices. Mass media pays little attention to those Black men who are opposing phallocentrism, misogyny, and sexism" (Kindle Locations 1731–1732). Patrick calls upon educators to highlight these "alternative voices"—socially conscious hip-hop artists resisting capitalist pressures to capitulate to patriarchy, racism, classism, and heterosexism. Ableism, while ubiquitous, is conspicuously absent in all of these discussions.

Taiyo took a different approach to providing exemplars. He integrated youth's own critical musical interests into his curriculum. He shared,

> A lot of the music I was really into as a teenager was really critical music—artists and musicians that were really critiquing the status quo in their music . . . [I'm] bridging that to how I'm trying to understand academic content. That is what I'm striving for always as an educator. What are the kids naturally into that is already critiquing the system, and what is it that I'm doing within class spaces that does that at the same time? Bridge that knowledge.

Taiyo's commentary directs attention to the importance of drawing on music to which youth already relate—a practice that resonates with ideas in culturally relevant pedagogy (Ladson-Billings, 1995, 2009), culturally responsive teaching (Gay, 2018; Lind & McKoy, 2016), and culturally sustaining pedagogy (Paris & Alim, 2014, 2017). In prioritizing a practice of critique, Taiyo suggested that educators align students' music that critiques the status quo to classroom content that enacts similar values. Centering youth's self-selected critical music can help educators foster students' critical thinking skills. Educators can work alongside youth to facilitate a critique of systems that affect them in ways that may prove productive for their lives. Taiyo drew upon musics that both interested the youth he taught and actively critiqued the system and he subsequently worked to broaden their critique to include other media and texts they encountered in the world. He elaborated upon critical work that already shaped students' worldviews in order to foster critical consciousness (Freire, 2000/1970) and analysis as daily practice. Considering Taiyo's ideas alongside Patrick's earlier work with misogynist music, we can see ways in which educators engage both oppressive and critical music to which youth relate in order to foster a practice of critique.

Liz and James also supported finding examples of critical music. They focused explicitly on connecting music to social movements and current issues. Liz strongly advocated for exposure to and analysis of current events through music. She wanted youth to critically investigate issues in the world around them and noted that music could support that work. Her organization, Music2Life, worked to create what Liz called a "soundtrack" for social justice concerns—a process that involved connecting critical music to varied social and environmental justice issues in order to facilitate Music2Life's goal of "moving hearts and minds." In his classroom, James connected social movements to musics that emerged from these resistance movements, as explored in Chapter 3. Like Taiyo, Liz and James looked for critical music to offer artistic exemplars of active critique. When educators provide exemplars of socially conscious music, youth can then apply their practice of noticing ideologies and lived conditions to creating their own music.

Summary: Facilitating Coming to Voice through Dissent, Imagining, and Exemplars

As educators facilitate youth's moving to action in this third phase of fostering a culture of questioning, activist-musicians suggested that creating an environment that both encourages and supports dissent would help youth learn to assert their own voices after analyzing discourse and situations for both ideologies and oppressive conditions. Casey and Griffin also encouraged educators to use their imaginations to dream past restrictive representations and ideologies—to help youth develop musical practices uninhibited by socialized expectations of which instruments or musical practices they may explore. Ultimately, Patrick, Taiyo, Liz, and James argued that providing exemplars of socially conscious music and musicians may help youth develop their own voices and may model ways for them to create accordingly. When educators create a space in which youth can dissent, demonstrably imagine uninhibited musical practices, and provide socially conscious exemplars, they set the conditions for youth to move to action through developing their own unique musical practice and strongly assert their voices in the world.

Musicking Anti-Oppression

While facilitating youth to move to action can involve encouraging dissent, imagining uninhibited musical practices, and offering positive exemplars, in music education, moving to action also entails musicking anti-oppression. Musicking anti-oppression engages the creating and songwriting practices explored in Chapter 4 and combines them with a rich practice of noticing and critiquing ideologies and lived conditions. When educators encourage youth to think critically about their encounters—musical or otherwise— teachers can subsequently facilitate opportunities to respond. While much of what activist-musicians suggested requires critical conversations, educators can also create possibilities for youth to address oppression musically by asserting their voices and their experiences through songwriting. Activist-musicians spoke passionately about directly engaging music in anti-oppression work. Casey, for example, challenged youth to think about what they would do, as artists, in oppressive conditions:

> When I did that presentation [for youth at the Girls Rock Camp], Pussy Riot was happening, which is a complicated thing.[6] What

happened to them is unfortunate, but using that contemporary example of having women's voices be oppressed in some way, and asking the question, "If this were to happen to you—if you felt like you were being treated unjustly—how do you communicate that in song? Or what sort of things do you want to talk about?"

In asking these questions, Casey addressed oppressive conditions directly and encouraged young women to make connections to their own artistic practices and lived experiences. She put forward music as a medium to speak back to oppression—a powerful *testimonio* (Cruz, 2012) opposing the dominant narrative. Her approach encouraged youth to think about how they might musically oppose oppressive conditions. In asking adolescents to consider how they might communicate feelings of injustice in a song, Casey draws on the rich tradition of music for justice issues, connecting youth to a long history of speaking back (see for example Gilbert, 2007; Hirsch, 2002; Kanaaneh et al., 2013; Turino, 2008). As they add their voices to this longstanding practice, these young women can assert their own experiences through music and name their worlds or identify the conditions that affect them through music (Freire, 2000/1970) in a dialogical music education. As noted in Chapter 4, young women who participated in the Girls Rock Camp used their music to communicate strong messages that were true to their experiences, such as, "We should all have the chance to play," and "We don't want to go to school because it doesn't feel fair to sit." Kirylo (2011) notes, "Embedded in the element of dialogue is criticality in problematizing the existential reality of the subject. . . . For the oppressed . . . to democratically participate, the chains of silence must be broken" (p. 147). Kirylo's note on breaking the silence about oppression underscores the importance of speaking about injustice. By drawing upon music to engage in dialogue, youth can speak back powerfully to oppressive discourses.

Like Casey, James and Patrick regularly encouraged youth to music about their experiences, following rigorous analysis. In fact, facilitating youth's creation of their own music served as the ultimate goal of both James' high school music program and Patrick's community hip-hop program. In placing anti-oppressive, socially-conscious hip-hop in dialogue with hip-hop that draws on oppressive discourses, for example, Patrick challenged youth to think deeply about music and move to action after analysis by creating their own music in opposition to dominant discourses. Creating opportunities for youth to music about their experiences through a critical lens provides openings for them to assert themselves and their experiences publicly and to actively resist oppressive conditions and ideologies.

James' work connecting social movements and music, similarly, created the possibility for youth to use music as a tool to speak to their social conditions. Through sharing the musics of social movements, he offered models of resistance music and music that critiques systemic injustice. Moreover, he created a space in which youth came to understand the ways that groups use music to resist the conditions that shape their lives. Youth in his program then created musical works that spoke to issues about which they cared deeply. In musicking about oppressive conditions, youth enacted a culture of questioning musically through critically examining and expressing their own experiences. Ultimately, in following Casey's, James', and Patrick's work, educators fostering activist music education combine a practice of critique and a habit of noticing with the songwriting process identified in Chapter 4, through which youth share their stories.

Summary

Enacting music education as political involves creating a culture of questioning (Giroux & Giroux, 2004) in which youth first notice and identify the ideologies shaping all of their encounters, subsequently recognize the lived conditions of self and others, and ultimately move to action. Moving through these three phases encourages youth to develop and value their own critical perspectives. Activist-musicians offered important ideas about actualizing a culture of questioning in music education. They suggested ways in which educators could facilitate youth's noticing ideologies circulating in the discourses and actions of authority figures, in representations in media and educational resources, and in musical lyrics. They further drew upon music to help youth recognize the conditions shaping their lives through exploring music and by engaging in courageous conversations (Singleton & Linton, 2006). Subsequently, facilitating youth's moving to action involves educators purposefully shaping an environment in which students can dissent following analysis, engaging the imagination in dreaming musical practices uninhibited by societal oppression, and providing socially conscious exemplars on which youth may model their own creative work. Ultimately, moving to action through coming to voice includes creating music that enacts a culture of questioning by exploring youth's own experiences.

Notes

1 Lise Vaugeois' (2009) "musical life histories" shared in Chapter 3 encourage music students to ask these very questions.
2 The National Football League (NFL) protests against racial injustice initiated by Colin Kaepernick clearly illustrate this idea. Football players have been "taking a knee" during the national anthem to protest police brutality and the state of racism in the United States since fall 2016. Trump and much of the White U.S. population have expressed outrage at these protests, calling players unpatriotic and urging them to stop their protest and play the game for the edification of the U.S. public (Gilmore, 2017; Washington, 2017).
3 I note here that the artists highlighted by popular media and by music education are often not the same groups.
4 While Singleton and Linton (2006) focus on conversations about race, I widen the subject matter to include difficult discussions across all identity categories, as well as conversations that specifically address oppression.

5 In Hess (2019), I present a discussion of identity politics that draws upon Casey's words and other participants' contributions in this chapter.
6 Pussy Riot, a feminist punk rock protest band, performed a song called "Punk Prayer," which protested Putin and attacked the Russian Orthodox Church (Tayler, 2012). Band members Maria Alyokhina and Nadezhda Tolokonnikova were imprisoned for the critique of Putin. The official charge was hooliganism. They served 22 months in prison and were released in late 2013 (Mullen, Magnay, & Hanna, 2013).

6 The Dangers of Activist Music Education

In Chapter 2, activist-musicians asserted that music could, in fact, be dangerous. Dangers also arise in music education contexts. Foucault (1983) contends that

> My point is not that everything is bad, but that everything is dangerous, which is not exactly the same as bad. If everything is dangerous, then we always have something to do. So my position leads not to apathy but to a hyper- and pessimistic activism. I think that the ethics-political choice we have to make every day is to determine which is the main danger.
>
> (pp. 231–232)

Chapters 3, 4, and 5 suggested possibilities for activist music education that centers connecting, honors lived experiences, and encourages critical thinking. In this chapter, I explore potential dangers of centering these ideas in music education. Like Foucault, in identifying the dangers, I do not advocate for apathy or inaction. Rather, I argue that recognizing the dangers inherent in activist music education will better equip teachers to navigate this potential in their classes as they implement practices that connect youth to each other and to their communities, honor their lived experiences, and develop their abilities to critique conditions that affect their lives. In Chapter 1, I challenged the potential for the tenets of critical pedagogy to reinscribe oppressive, problematic discourses and urged educators toward uncertainty (Lather, 1998). Having put forward activist-musicians' perspectives on a connective, expressive, and critical music education, I again mobilize a critical lens to consider possible dangers and reinscriptions and encourage educators to refuse to "figure it out," lest we reinscribe relations we hope to avoid. When we refuse to be the "One with the 'Right' Story" (Ellsworth, 1997, p. 137), this humility may allow us to better navigate the potential for reinscribing oppression. In seeking to implement activist pedagogy, we will undoubtedly, at times, reproduce relations and discourses that we wanted to avoid. Those moments when we "slip" provide important opportunities for conversations. I explore potential negative outcomes not in order to create fear about enacting such pedagogy, but rather to acknowledge what is possible. When we recognize these issues in our praxis, engaging them creates significant opportunities for growth, both personally and in our school communities. Addressing "mis-steps" provides a powerful model for youth to challenge similar issues and structures in their own lives. This chapter addresses potential for pedagogical slippages, rather than societal dangers teachers may face upon implementing this pedagogy. The afterword explores dangers that may emerge when implementing activist music education.

Connecting to Others as Fraught Territory

In Chapter 3, activist-musicians advocated for a connective music education that involved building community locally among education participants, linking musics to their histories, and using musical study to connect youth to unfamiliar groups of people. Connecting to Others through music, however, traverses fraught territory. This section explores possible dangers of attempting to connect to unfamiliar Others through introducing multiple musics. It examines the risks of hierarchization, cultural appropriation, stereotyping, exoticization, as well as the possibility of trauma that may emerge through rich contextualization. While activist-musicians perceived that fostering connection matters greatly in music education, without careful and thoughtful application, negative possibilities may result. Recognizing these possibilities allows us to treat them as instructive and engage any instances that occur with students.

Risks of Hierarchization: Centering Western Classical Music, Additive Curricular Practices, and Investments in Superiority

Activist-musicians suggested including a range of musics to foster openmindedness among youth in music classrooms. Introducing multiple musics, however, creates potential for hierarchization—a pseudo-Darwinian ordering of musics and the people who practice them (Gustafson, 2009). Encountering difference often inherently involves a process of ordering. The existence of this tendency requires educators to attend to any unintentional communication of hierarchy to students. Examining music education practices for teaching classical music and for broadening curricula to include many musics, as well as challenging the ways that engaging in multiple musics allows us to understand ourselves, provides a means to resist hierarchization.

    U.S. and Canadian music classrooms have long centered Western classical music. Teachers often teach Western classical music without contextualization, which allows it to assume a dominant place in the hierarchy of musics, unquestioned as "important music" (Bradley, 2007; Hess, 2015a; Schippers, 2010). Educators sometimes (quite politically) assert that classical music is apolitical or disinterested. Presenting classical music as disinterested or neutral enables educators to normalize it, creating the conditions for it to play a dominant role in curricula while positioning other musics as situated and political (Bradley, 2007, 2012a, 2017; Hess, 2015a; Schippers, 2010). Including multiple musics thus involves altering the approach to classical music to better contextualize it and reveal its historical location in the hierarchy of school musics.

In our eagerness to include a range of musics, moving beyond an additive curriculum helps address issues of hierarchization. Banks (2013) notes that content integration, while a typical first step in broadening curricula, is the most superficial dimension of multicultural education. Content integration involves adding "multicultural" content to the already-present curriculum—an additive model (Abril, 2003; Morton, 1994). In music education, that might entail maintaining the orchestral ensemble model while adding several fiddle tunes and arranged mariachi music, reinscribing the Western classical orchestra at the center of the program. When we add content to an already-existing program, rather than integrating it throughout the curriculum, we reinscribe these additions as "less than" their Western classical counterparts, creating a hierarchy of civilizations.

We might also consider how these musical endeavors allow us to understand ourselves. In literature, Morrison (1990) explains how a White reader may encounter an Africanist presence:

> Africanism is the vehicle by which the American self knows itself as not enslaved, but free; not repulsive, but desirable; not helpless, but licensed and powerful; not history-less, but historical; not damned, but innocent; not a blind accident of evolution, but a progressive fulfillment of destiny.
>
> (p. 52)

When introduced to different musics in music education, youth might easily understand themselves in relation to musics they encounter, and, perhaps, feel superior. Upon realizing the potential for students to hierarchize the musics introduced in music class, music educators may consider ways to foster respect for different musics and the people who practice them. Enacting rich contextualization, as activist-musicians suggested in Chapter 3, helps students understand musics as distinct human practices and creates opportunities to consider community contexts and recognize people behind these musics. Bryan cautioned,

> The whole system doesn't have to be overhauled necessarily. It's just about looking at different people and different traditions. Finding little tidbits about other musical cultures sometimes just perpetuates that kind of exoticization where it's like, "We only have mysterious bits of information about this tradition." But that's not true. It's just as fully formed as anything else.

In looking for alternatives to hierarchization, multicentricity (Dei, 2003)—a pedagogy that positions perspectives as equal centers—offers possibilities for music education. Within multicentricity, Europe becomes one among many, albeit a materially significant perspective due to legacies of the colonialism and racial oppression that advantaged Western European perspectives in curricula. Giving equal weight to multiple perspectives and identifying the historical and present privileging of Eurocentricity provides a means to challenge hierarchization. In implementing curricula with multiple musics, remaining aware of potential hierarchization and refusing to believe there is only one possible way to address it may help educators respond to issues of privileging musics and perspectives that emerge in the classroom. Music, including classical music, serves to explore, affirm, and ultimately celebrate our values (Small, 1998). We want to ensure, however, that including multiple musics to celebrate values does not involve ranking musics and feelings of superiority. If such ranking occurs, we can engage it.

The Danger of Cultural Appropriation

As music educators broaden curricula to include many musics, issues of appropriation and power arise. Young (2008) asserts that cultural appropriation occurs when "members of one culture (I will call them *outsiders*) take for their own, or for their own use, items produced by a member or members of another culture (call them *insiders*)" (p. 5, emphasis in original). Introducing musics from multiple cultures involves extracting musics from their contexts for classroom use. Activist-musicians raised concerns about cultural appropriation when discussing both curricula that include many musics and the practice of contextualization. Feld (2000a) describes a phenomenon called *schizophonia* [1]—the splitting of sound from its source typically through technology—in the context of appropriating Pygmy music into Western genres. Clothed in the façade of respect, Feld discusses artists' use of Pygmy musics without credit or recognition—an erasure of the music's originators. Casey stated,

> You wipe out the history of so many people by cutting it up and sampling it. It gets to a point where the person, or people, or the community of people who were behind that music aren't even there anymore.

The erasure of a group of people through the sampling Casey described enacts schizophonia (Feld, 2000a).[2]

Rather than erasing contexts and engaging in schizophonia, educators can consider power relations thoughtfully in musical engagements. As Bradley (2006b) reminds us, "the choice to include or not particular musical genres in curricular materials makes the question 'what music' always and unavoidably 'whose music'?" (p. 335). Musics emerge from people. Honoring sources instead of erasing them allows for meaningful engagement with different musics. Feld (2005b) asserts that "[a]ppropriation means that the question 'Whose music?' is submerged, supplanted, and subverted by the assertion, 'Our/my music'" (p. 238). Ethical engagement with multiple musics requires refusing such submersion (or appropriation). In music education, considering the power relations at work when a dominant group performs music of a minoritized group compels us to think through ways to mitigate the dynamics that may reinscribe those same hierarchies and structures that enabled oppression. Performing musics respectfully involves rich contextualization and explicit class discussions about power. As Casey noted in Chapter 3, discussing cultural appropriation with children, while purposeful, can also be playful.

In working to contextualize and mitigate power relations, additional complexities emerge. Music educators often lack knowledge across multiple musics. While many music educators comfortably engage with two musical traditions—perhaps Western classical music and Western vernacular music, or, in my case, Western classical music and Ghanaian (Ewe) music—extensive knowledge of many musical traditions is rare, unrealistic, and not a particularly fair expectation of music educators. Music publishers frequently step in to address this knowledge gap, capitalizing on teachers' desire to include musics beyond their areas of expertise. Various publications result, such as classical ensemble arrangements of folk songs that often draw on stereotypical ideas about the musical tradition engaged by arrangers who are frequently White. Such arrangements, while perhaps well-meaning, further remove musics from their contexts, appropriating them into foreign instrumentation and often straightening, simplifying, and Whitening rhythms and melodies (Gustafson, 2009; Hess, 2018c; Trinka, 1987). Engaging these types of arrangements creates opportunities to discuss cultural appropriation and consider the changes made to the music for classroom use. As Casey noted in Chapter 3, educators and students can question any music's origins and consider

> who were the people that were playing that music before 15 teenagers started playing it in some type of ensemble. Giving it a context might change the way that people engage in the music and ultimately create a better performance, and a better understanding, or a better communication of that music to an audience.

These arrangements offered by publishers provide a means to engage different musical practices. Rather than dismiss them outright, we can discuss them, and, in doing so, as Casey elucidates, perhaps offer a better communication to an audience of the intentions of the music.

Broadening school music curricula might further allow us to interrogate ways to engage different musics without separating sound from source in an appropriative manner. How can we maintain a music's integrity when including it in music education? A band arrangement of an Indigenous piece can replicate colonization—the removal of Indigenous music from its context, followed by its brutal reshaping into a version unrecognizable by the communities from which it emerged. Extending music curricula can easily become a violent exercise of cultural appropriation. Educators can instead mindfully recognize the potential violence, choosing not to erase it, but to engage it with students. Such conversations potentially encourage broader discussions about cultural appropriation that may lead youth to call out such violence when they encounter it—for example, in Halloween costumes.

Musics change when they enter schools; separation from community practices automatically occurs. As we recontextualize musics by bringing them into music classrooms (Schippers, 2010), we can purposefully center ethical processes and recognition when we perform and engage with these musics in new ways in the classroom. Acknowledging contexts and peoples who practice different musics when engaging in mash-up or remix culture, for example, is distinct from erasing origin. Centering principles such as respect and reciprocity may help educators formulate ethical practices when engaging with multiple musics.

As Lise noted in Chapter 4, when we practice "curriculum as mirror" (Style, 1996) with a classroom population of predominantly middle-class White students, a responsibility lies with educators to broaden their perspectives beyond mere reflection of their (often) privileged realities. Despite inherent dangers of cultural appropriation, limiting students' experiences to what they already know misses important opportunities to expose students to diverse perspectives. Broadening youth's experiences requires mindful pedagogy. When engaging different musical traditions, educators may frankly discuss appropriation in a way that encourages open critique of problematic practices and representations, thus facilitating education participants to critically center questions of power. Casey, Bryan, and Griffin all strongly supported including such discussion. Engaging Lise Vaugeois' (2009) questions to map the "musical life histories" of musics shared in Chapter 3 provides a possible entry point to consider musics critically.

The Dangers of Stereotyping

Introducing many musics also potentially encourages stereotyping. When youth learn what Bradley (2006b) calls "global song," here extended to include instrumental musics, stereotyping becomes both possible and likely if this learning occurs in at least two ways. First, when music educators fail to contextualize music, youth may draw upon images of the *always already Other* (Meiners, 2001)—what they believe about the group of people behind a particular music based on media representations and other public images and discourses. Second, music education uses the problematic term *culture bearers* to describe individuals who work with youth in schools or communities on a musical practice for which they are cultural insiders. Engaging culture bearers is common approach in music education. I examine the potential for stereotyping in both practices.

Meiners (2001) argues that we carry "ready-made" images of the Other—ever-present and waiting for us to engage. Bradley (2003, 2006b) worries that when music educators fail to provide contextual information for songs learned in global choral music, students will imagine the context for songs encountered, drawing upon these "ready-made" images. Students then potentially "invent Otherness"—a term Bradley extends from Morrison's (1990) "inventing Africanness." Relying upon media-influenced stereotypical images of the always already Other, students apply already-present knowledge in order to understand musical encounters. When students lack context for a song, they may "borrow" a context rooted in stereotypes and racist ideology.

When singing a song from Ghana, for example, if not provided with context, students may draw upon the always already Other amalgamated from multiple sources, including the media, to create their own context for the music they perform. Doing so becomes problematic when NGO infomercials solely encompass the images of Africa available to the students. The ease of accessing these ready-made images of the Other reminds us to provide detailed context about all musics studied in order to offer an experience that encourages youth to situate current learning in the context of other musics and other histories.

The second issue involves the question of "culture bearers." Music educators often draw upon culture bearers—cultural insiders brought into the classroom or community group to represent the culture under study—to provide an experience for students and alleviate the stress of not being able to personally enact a musical tradition. The term *culture bearer* problematically implies that only certain individuals have "culture" and further suggests a duty to share said culture for others' consumption, a move bell hooks (1992) calls "eating the Other." The terminology more covertly implies that White individuals lack culture, as music education culture bearers typically consist of people of color.

The practice itself may create additional issues. Many music educators advocate for employing culture bearers when teaching "world music." While the term (coined over 20 years ago) and practice remain prevalent, multiple scholars critique this practice. Solís (2004) describes the notion of culture bearers as discriminatory, as do Racy, Marcus, and Solís (2004) in the same volume. Moreover, Trimillos (2004) describes *culture bearers* as Indigenous artists expected to possess unlimited cultural knowledge and represent an entire group of people. Music education scholars similarly problematize employing culture bearers (Hess, 2013a; Klinger, 1996; Vaugeois, 2009). Vaugeois (2009), for example, explicates the way society understands Indigenous Canadian artist Eddy Robinson:

> Eddy Robinson cannot escape the designation *First Nations musician*, either in how he understands himself or in how he is taken up by others, precisely because his life, his identity, and his social location are profoundly shaped by the material and discursive structures of racism. Correspondingly, the same systemic effects that shape the identities available to Robinson also produce White musicians as not-raced and recognized as autonomous individuals. That is, the privileged social locations of not-racialized people derive from the same structures and discourses that produce marginalized locations. . . . In other situations, gender, class, and able-bodied status might also leap out as identity markers, suddenly making people embodying these designations visible against a background of assumed homogeneous normalcy.
>
> (p. 17, emphasis added)

In considering an orchestral violinist as a "culture bearer," Vaugeois further notes:

> [W]e would likely not notice the whiteness of the violinist as a marker of identity and would be interested, instead, in knowing about her ideas and how she understands her work. Is a White artist then a normal guest in which social locations are incidental and therefore not noticed or scrutinized while racialized guests are assumed to have an identifiable raced, classed, and gendered location? We would no doubt be interested in hearing from other violinists.
>
> (pp. 16–17)

Asking individuals to represent entire cultures easily leads to stereotyping. Klinger (1996) challenges the possibility that so-called culture bearers will represent stereotypes in classrooms, conceiving instead a potential for "multiple authenticities"—multiple legitimate versions of the same piece of music from different individuals within an ethnic group. While music education gradually abandons notions of authenticity for "recontextualization" (Schippers, 2010)—situating musics into new contexts—Klinger's notion acknowledges musics' multiplicity and variety. "We would," Vaugeois (2009) notes, "no doubt be interested in hearing from other violinists" (p. 17). When music educators invite experienced musicians from various cultural practices to share their music, rather than asking one person to stand in for an entire culture, we may consider inviting multiple artists and providing detailed contextual information in order to offer youth a contemporary, realistic perspective of different communities.

A further complication emerges when we consider how colonialism and slavery constituted Others (and continues to constitute Others) as subhuman in order to subjugate or dispose of them (Giroux, 2006; Goldberg, 1993; Mills, 1997). When people understand other people as "less than," atrocities become possible. Stereotyping participates in dehumanization. When one lacks a complex and realistic understanding of different groups of people, it perhaps becomes easier to negate them. Stereotyping already undermines the humanity of Others. When individuals and groups then act on such negation, however, perhaps through violence, this practice becomes dehumanizing, with material and sometimes fatal consequences. Purposefully contextualizing or employing multiple musicians may allow us to avoid participating in any practice that dehumanizes Others.

The Risks of Exoticization

Additional risks of exoticization—unrealistic and imagined perceptions of the Other as exotic— emerge from the same practices that produce stereotyping. hooks (1992) asserts that

> The commodification of Otherness has been so successful because it is offered as a new delight, more intense, more satisfying than normal ways of doing and feeling. Within commodity culture, ethnicity becomes spice, seasoning that can liven up the dull dish that is mainstream White culture.
>
> (p. 21)

Engaging many musics in music class amounts in some ways to commodifying Otherness—offering an experience of the so-called *Other* through a mediated form: music. Music distinct from Western classical and Western vernacular music thus becomes the "spice"—a taste of the "exotic" for youth studying unfamiliar musics. I consider the potential for exoticization across three music education practices: studying and performing unfamiliar music through music education resources, engaging with music featuring unfamiliar instruments or sounds, and working with "culture bearers" in music education contexts.

Encountering unfamiliar musics through printed resources in music education presents many of the same issues that emerge in examining the potentials for stereotyping and exoticization. Bradley (2009a) notes, for example, that the type of engagement with global song that world music publications encourage may "produce and reiterate romanticized notions of people and cultures, reiterate stereotypes, and leave prejudices unchallenged" (p. 106). We want to avoid such romanticization in music education. While failing to provide context in musical study creates potentials for stereotyping and imagining the Other, that same practice may also facilitate romanticizing various groups. Many music education resources, as previously discussed, offer limited contextual information and alter the music significantly. Educators' awareness of these issues helps us work against exoticization through rich contextualization.

Complexities also emerge when aurally encountering unfamiliar musics. Jason integrated Chinese traditional instruments into some of his music, and we discussed these ideas extensively:

JASON: For any minority composer, it's always interesting [to consider] one's ethnic identity and then the perceptions of music. I always wondered if I were not an American-born Chinese, but my music came from Shanghai and I emerged with this compositional voice and these works and my way of playing the violin—with that backstory— the trajectory of my life in the market would be different. If I were of any other ethnicity doing exactly what I'm doing, that backstory would affect perception. And I'm aware of that and that's why I do give some thought [to] where I'm coming from and who I am.

JULIET: Do you think your music would be perceived more positively if you were from Shanghai originally?

JASON: In certain circles, yes. Because it would be. There's the fascination with the Other. Even though I think most people realize that there's not this cultural essentialism. It's not like there's something in my chromosomes that made me create this Asian music or inflection. It's something learned. Culture is learned. That being said, my ethnicity has shaped my childhood, my life; it has affected what I'm interested in and what I believe. Music is an arena to construct identity, not abstractly, but out of one's life. That's why when I use Chinese instruments, I feel biographical resonance. Could someone else blend those instruments? Sure. And it would have a different meaning for them. Our construction of identity is a continual act of imagination.

Jason considered the complexities of identity in audience reception to his work. He also identified the "fascination with the Other" that leads individuals to embrace particular musics and "eat the Other" (hooks, 1992). Youth exposed to Jason's music could easily romanticize the figure behind the sounds they hear. Jason's intentions, however, refused this romanticization. He spoke of purposefully combining Chinese and Western instruments:

> Using Chinese [instruments]—it's like I hear the overtones of my family's voice. Usually with traditional instruments and Western instruments, to the listener at first, there's the novelty. "Wow, I never heard an erhu played with a tuba. Or the pipa with the string bass." So the ear will go to that novelty, but I don't write for that novelty. It's not like hitting a gong signifies the entrance of something Chinese sounding. It's not a signifier of ethnic identity. But it's a part of a democracy of sounds where all sounds are equal. Over the course of the piece, the novelty wears off for the listener and they're hearing music. Pretty soon, they're used to the sound of this experience.

Jason's music offers a non-colonial fusion that allows listeners to value all sounds (and cultures). In creating a democracy of sounds without hierarchy, Jason normalized what he had previously defined as *novelty*, rather than allowing romanticization. His music provides an approach to engaging unfamiliar sounds while refusing exoticization.

Engaging so-called "culture bearers" also creates possibilities for exoticization. Individuals who enter music class to share musical experiences from their home culture play particular roles. Critiquing the engagement of culture bearers, Klinger (1996) notes, "I don't think Johnny Moses presented enough information about himself to bring him out of the stereotypical view of Native Americans. He looked the part, with his braids and beads. In some ways he presented a stereotype" (pp.108–109). Music educators implicitly call upon culture bearers to embody particular roles in classroom interactions. The individual in Klinger's research may or may not have represented himself in a manner inconsistent with his daily life. Students in his class, however, may exoticize other Indigenous community members based on their experiences with Moses. Sharing one's musical culture requires performing oneself as a subject of some kind. Consistent with the contextualization practices suggested in Chapter 3, educators might seek multiple perspectives alongside facilitating frank discussions of the potential for stereotypes and exoticization.

When music educators invite musicians of varied musical practices into our classrooms, what, precisely, do we expect? An Ewe master drummer, for example, may present a stereotype that leads students to exoticize both him and Ghana, his country of origin. His success as a teacher of Ewe music in North America, however, perhaps hinges on his ethnicity and further requires him to minimize his identity as a now-U.S. citizen. How can music educators move beyond a practice that creates potential for exoticization while also providing a living to many musicians? The complexity of this issue requires discussion in the classroom, as well as in the profession.

Possible Trauma through Music Education

In Chapter 3, activist-musicians advocated for deep contextualization of all musics studied in order to connect musics to their histories. Rich contextualization practices, however, introduce the possibility of trauma. Activist-musicians pointed to the potential of trauma or re-experiencing trauma stemming from the study of musics that emerged from trauma, oppression, and violence. Caruth (1993) notes that "traumatic disorders reflect the direct imposition on the mind of the unavoidable reality of horrific events, the taking over—psychically and neurobiologically—of the mind by an event that it cannot control" (p. 24). We live in a time characterized by "a cultural politics of trauma" (Ranck, 2000, p. 199). Legacies of historical traumas such as slavery, lynchings in the United States, and genocides that have occurred around the world—as well as present-day traumas that include but are not limited to the ongoing genocide of Indigenous peoples, the #MeToo Movement, police violence against people of color, mass shootings, and the forced separation of children from their parents at the U.S./

Mexico border—have effects that ripple throughout every student population. At the individual level, an alarming number of youth personally experience trauma through abuse and/or oppression (see for example U.S. Department of Health & Human Services, 2017). Given the ubiquity of trauma, grappling with its complexities and unknowability becomes essential for music educators.

Simon, Rosenberg, and Eppert's (2000) edited collection suggests that traumatic history and even trauma itself are sources of knowledge from which one might develop pedagogy. Rather than avoiding traumatic material, music educators might lean into these encounters and see what learning becomes possible. Britzman (2000) suggests that educators might "approach history as an incomplete project of becoming an ethical subject in relation to other ethical subjects" (p. 37). Engaging with traumatic histories through musicking and musical encounters may allow us to do the work of becoming ethical subjects. Grappling with what Britzman (1998) calls "difficult knowledge" may require a "working through of our own relationships with loss" (Salverson, 2000, p. 72). Resistance, defensiveness, and anxiety may occur as natural responses among students and should be read as "signs of potential rather than evidence of pathology" (Salverson, 2000, p. 72) and an indication that youth are caring for themselves.

Engaging material that emerges from trauma may produce difficult emotions; doing so may also allow us to wrestle with experiences of loss and trauma in a structured environment. Eppert (2000) engages Joy Kogawa's novel *Obasan*, about Japanese internment in Canada, to explore how literature calls us to respond to trauma and difficult knowledge. Eppert notes, "The 'claim' of address both staked and exerted by this literature calls upon readers not to read indifferently or purely for pleasure but to themselves become answerable—both to this literature and to its historical referents" (Newton, 1995, p. 11, as cited in Eppert, 2000, p. 214). Kogawa's novel, Eppert asserts, calls upon readers to become answerable—to respond to these traumatic circumstances. Music, like literature, also calls us to respond. Rather than considering music as an aesthetic object (Reimer, 2003), engaging music as a human practice involves answerability—an imperative to deeply consider the humanity inherent in every musical practice.

This imperative to engage, however, does not necessarily account for the effects that engaging musics that emerged from trauma may produce. Traumatic material (or any material) may trigger and potentially provoke a flashback or re-experiencing of trauma. Experiences that may trigger are difficult to predict and specific to individuals. Any classroom engagement has the potential to trigger a trauma response. Because potential triggers are challenging to predict, educators can simply teach with knowledge of what might occur. Educators also may re-experience their own unhealed traumas when engaging traumatic material or perhaps in response to encountering a student's trauma that resonates with their own past experience. If such responses occur, educators should ensure that they, too, have the support they require. Given the ubiquity of trauma, teachers should keep in mind the likelihood that many students may have trauma histories and become aware of the types of responses that youth with Post-Traumatic Stress Disorder (PTSD) may exhibit.[3] After cultivating such awareness, educators can turn to music and shape their pedagogy with the full knowledge that some material may trigger, using music as a means for "working through" (Salverson, 2000), rather than avoiding, difficult or sensitive material.

Lise developed a possible approach for engaging traumatic material in her work exploring Indigenous musics that balanced discussions between community strengths and the oppressions experienced. She noted the traumatic potential of exploring Indigenous musics and histories in the context of ongoing projects of colonialism and genocide in Canada (see Chapter 3). Teaching Indigenous music in a class of both Indigenous and non-Indigenous students (White students and students of color) requires educators to recognize the range of experiences of students in the class. In considering the history of residential schools (MacDonald & Hudson, 2012) and the number of missing and murdered Indigenous women in Canada (Brant, 2017; Razack, 2002), we realize that Indigenous youth have likely either experienced trauma directly, witnessed it, or know of it indirectly through the experiences of family and community members. Between 1980 and 2012, the Royal Canadian Mounted Police's (RCMP) 2014 report acknowledged 1200 missing or murdered Indigenous women (Brant, 2017). Moreover, in 2009, 67000 Indigenous women over the age of 15 reported having survived violence in the preceding 12 months—a rate of violence three times that of non-Indigenous women (Brennan, 2011). The challenge becomes supporting and working through these traumas when teaching Indigenous musics.

Lise routinely prioritized Indigenous issues in her teacher education classes. She noted that Indigenous students in her class in 2014 objected to examining the violence enacted on the Indigenous community and the ongoing colonial project;[4] instead, they asked her to focus on community strengths. Lise felt hesitant, however, to only focus on strengths given the traumas enacted on the Indigenous community in Canada across centuries. The suggestion of focusing on strengths from the students Lise taught, however, provides a possible way to teach musics entangled in traumatic histories. Teachers might find ways to provide a balance between traumatic histories and a community's cultural wealth (Yosso, 2005).

As music educators, we can be clear about short-term and long-term class content when beginning a class, allowing youth to ready themselves for difficult topics. "Trigger warnings" also offer advance notice to "allow those who are sensitive to these subjects to prepare themselves for reading about [encountering] them, and better manage their reactions," (Manne, 2015); trigger warnings do not provide an excuse not to engage but do allow students to prepare to take care of themselves as needed.[5]

Activist-musicians identified the potential for traumatizing or re-experiencing trauma through engagement with musics that emerged from trauma, oppression, and violence. Rather than avoiding potentially traumatic material, educators can engage it carefully with full awareness of the inherent dangers of such critical discussions. No class participant need offer up their experiences for class discussion; youth may, if they wish, but teachers should be explicit that cultural "insiders" need not feel compelled to represent their community. Broaching these difficult conversations with youth in schools and monitoring carefully for adverse responses requires purposeful attention. Awareness of potential for re-experiencing trauma prompts educators to balance curricula between community strengths and oppressions. As educators navigate teaching musics rooted in oppression and trauma, we can limit both the prolonged nature of conversations and repetition of details. Instead, educators can integrate discussion and musical work, moving back and forth between music and conversation.

In considering the moral imperative to engage traumatic material as a source of knowledge, educators might ultimately consider students' right to refuse. Commissioned by the Red Cross to write a play about land mines, Salverson (2000) notes:

> When I accepted the Red Cross commission to meet and in some way pass on the story of land mines, I decided that this matter of the right to refuse story was critical. Deborah Britzman reminds us that when education engages with the right of refusal, what gets opened up is the territory of psychic trauma and the internal conflicts the listener brings to testimony.
>
> (p. 62 citing Britzman, 1998, p. 117)

While teachers will likely view students' non-engagement in any educational encounter as less than ideal, perhaps when engaging traumatic material we can trust, having built a classroom community based on respect, that youth who disengage may actually be choosing to take care of themselves. We can affirm this choice by honoring it and purposefully varying classroom activities so that musicking and discussion integrate in ways that engagement becomes possible for different people at different times. While music educators do not seek to traumatize or trigger youth through sharing musics, doing so may provoke a trauma response and offer potential for a "working through" (Salverson, 2000). Engaging these musics and difficult issues carefully may create conditions for a future in which youth can themselves challenge situations that are potentially traumatizing and also prioritize taking care of themselves when they recognize their own triggers in different circumstances.

Summary: The Difficulties of Connecting to Others

The inherent risks of hierarchization, cultural appropriation, stereotyping, and exoticization when connecting to unfamiliar Others through music education reaffirm the importance of connecting to histories, as noted in Chapter 3. Rich contextualization potentially resists practices of cultural appropriation, stereotyping, and exoticism, in particular. Deep contextualization, however, may open the possibility for trauma to be (re)-experienced. Educators can view trauma as a source of knowledge as they work to situate musics realistically while honoring any possible trauma responses. Multiple possible negative outcomes may result from engaging multiple musics in the classroom. Awareness of this potential and refusing to "figure out" the "right" pedagogy may allow us to better navigate these possibilities and to engage students in conversation about them if they occur. Reinscribing unhelpful relations will likely occur at times when teaching a wide range of musics and working toward connection. Rather than avoiding this practice because of the negative possibilities, we can instead use the ways that we "slip" as opportunities for conversation and growth.

The Risks of Expressing Lived Experiences

Freire's (2000/1970) pedagogy centers the lived experiences of the classroom community. His approach to literacy with Macedo, for example, draws texts and vocabulary directly from participants' struggles (Freire & Macedo, 1987). Honoring lived experiences through music education and subsequently encouraging youth to share their stories musically may not actually address or transform oppressive relations. Having youth express experiences may, in fact, reinscribe dominant power structures. In order to limit possible reinscriptions, this section explores ways that expressing lived experiences may fail to unsettle unproductive power dynamics. I identify risks associated with music's empathetic potential and the way it can allow audiences to understand themselves as "tolerant" or as saviors. I further reengage possibilities of cultural appropriation in the context of creative work. While I do not take up issues of mandatory reporting that may follow any revelation of abuse or harm, having explored these concerns in Chapter 4, I note here that this issue is perhaps the most serious possible result of asking youth to share their stories.

The Limitations of Empathy

Scholars increasingly point to music education's potential to foster empathy (Laird, 2015; Winter, 2013; Zhang, 2017). While empathy often creates connection, fosters understanding, and remains a valuable goal for music education, centering lived experiences of the Self and Others can, on occasion, foster empathy unproductively. In connecting to musics and experiences of unfamiliar Others, as explored in the previous sections and in Chapter 3, feeling empathy becomes both possible and likely, but such feelings sometimes fail to alter oppressive discourses. Moreover, when we share lived experiences through songwriting, as suggested in Chapter 4, these stories may provoke empathy that similarly fails to unsettle oppression. Empathy often provides a hopeful starting point for understanding others. As educators, we want to ensure that empathy is productive.

We might easily identify empathy as a lofty aim for connecting to Others through engagement with a range of musical practices. Empathy, however, may prove counterproductive, requiring caution and humility. Razack (2007) interrogates what she calls "stealing the pain of Others," and describes a letter written by philosopher John Rankin to his slave-holding brother, which graphically recounted the horrors of slavery (p. 376, citing Hartman, 1997). Razack (2007) asserts that Rankin identifies "so readily with the slave's pain that he exists in place of the other and his own complicity and privilege is thereby obscured" (p. 377). Razack (2007) argues that "passive empathy produces no action towards justice but situates the powerful Western eye/I as the judging subject, never called upon to cast her gaze at her own reflection" (p. 387). She challenges readers to consider two questions: "Who benefits from the production of empathy? Who should feel empathy for whom, and what has been gained other than a 'good brotherly feeling'" (p. 390)? Empathy's potential to erase complicity leads to a failure to recognize one's own implication in current and historical oppressions. Identifying so deeply with the Other and the pain of the Other may make movement forward impossible. This type of empathy can re-center Whiteness and other dominant identities, encouraging pity and "good brotherly feeling" (Razack, 2007, p. 390) rather than action. Moreover, Caruth and Keenan (1995) write,

> Empathy is what the public is supposed to learn to feel, but it solidifies the structure of discrimination. In this case, empathy as a kind of understanding or of relation seems to reinforce the gesture of exclusion rather than the recognition.
>
> (p. 264)

Feeling empathy for the Other as distinct from the Self may further relegate the Other to a space apart, re-centering the Self in the process.

In music education, including varied musics in the curriculum and encouraging connections with Others through musics that emerge from oppression may generate the type of empathy that facilitates further exclusion, erases complicity, reinscribes dominant subjectivity, and fails to produce justice or change. Recognizing this potential allows music educators to re-center complicity and the importance of action while still encouraging empathy. As educators, we want to ensure that empathy creates productive actions. "Good brotherly feeling" (Razack, 2007, p. 390) does not necessarily move us forward by itself. It can easily result in self-congratulation (Hess, 2013a) for extending kindness and tolerance[6] toward Others and the reinscription of distance between Self and Other, enabling us to do nothing more than merely feel. Feeling, while important, remains only part of creating change. Instead, as educators, we can focus on action and consider how to engage our new knowledge toward justice, recognizing the role that acknowledging complicity plays in enacting work for justice.

When we move away from encountering the experiences of unfamiliar Others to encouraging youth to put forward their own experiences through songwriting, we create the potential for empathy of the type Razack (2007) and Caruth and Keenan (1995) describe. If students engage in songwriting in a way that fosters empathy, we might consider ways to make that feeling productive rather than re-centering listeners' feelings. The stasis empathy can bolster will not help address issues youth identify in their music. Instead, class communities may thoughtfully consider ways to create opportunities for the greater school community to move to action to transform the problems to which youth point.

A Question of Audience Desires

As we encourage youth to tell their stories, we must also examine audience desires related to storytelling. Razack (1998) argues that people of color are often encouraged to share their experiences for the edification of White people. She further contends that these stories contribute to the way that White people understand themselves. Such stories, for example, may allow dominant groups to know themselves as empathetic, open-minded or "tolerant," and benevolent—emotions that may fail to lead to action or systemic change. In Chapter 5, I drew upon hooks (2008/1994) to note that middle-class White people consume "gangsta rap" because they "want to be down" with what occurs in communities to which they have limited access (Kindle Locations 2376–2380). Navigating a need for stories to capitulate to dominant desires may prove difficult. As educators, in expressing systemic inequities through story, we might again underscore the importance of action. Controlling how dominant groups engage with stories from the margin remains impossible. Awareness that audiences may draw upon stories to understand themselves as empathetic and "tolerant," however, may help music educators frame stories carefully from a position of strength, rather than need or deficit. Moreover, we can help youth understand that dominant society sometimes consumes stories from the margin in order to produce themselves in particular ways. Considering the potential for such consumption—the "eating the Other" that hooks (1992) describes—may influence how youth choose to shape their music. Importantly, the desire for stories from the margin may extend across identities and proves troubling when dominant groups play the role of consumer.

Encouraging youth to share stories that are difficult also potentially positions them in the world in terms of their struggles rather than their strengths. Moreover, seeing youth struggle may foster salvationist tendencies in audiences. Freire (2000/1970) reminds us of the role that the oppressed

144 *The Dangers of Activist Music Education*

must play in their own liberation (p. 66). Underscoring youth agency may help educators navigate the salvationist tendencies that may emerge in listeners upon hearing difficult stories. Such tendencies reinscribe the hierarchical relationship between teacher and students, audiences and young artists. Recognizing the potential for salvationist responses from audiences allows us to focus on action and transforming difficult situations that may be rooted in systemic issues.

The songwriting practices put forward by activist-musicians as a means to share lived experiences perhaps provide an opportunity for youth to speak back powerfully to conditions that affect them. Detroit youth participants in a songwriting project at a community music school, for example, use songwriting to reframe deficit discourses about their lives (Hess, 2018a).[7] While music provides a potential medium for audiences to understand themselves as tolerant or "good," music educators can underscore youth agency and actively center action and transformation (Freire, 2000/1970).

Schizophonia and Cultural Appropriation in Storytelling

While I explored the potential for cultural appropriation at length earlier in this chapter when considering connecting to Others through music, I reengage these ideas briefly here to acknowledge the immense potential for cultural appropriation in songwriting. Casey noted previously that artists often borrow from different cultural traditions without recognition, splitting sounds from sources or participating in schizophonia (Feld, 2000a, 2005a). In encouraging youth to share their stories, including through remix culture, as explored in Chapter 4, teachers can extend conversations about cultural appropriation to include discussions about assigning credit when warranted and navigating decisions about the appropriateness of incorporating different musical traditions into music one creates. Music educators can initiate conversations with youth about "borrowing" and consider embedded power dynamics in such actions. Many of the concerns already raised about cultural appropriation in relation to connecting to Others' musical practices also apply to the creative process, reminding music educators to stay mindful of the appropriative potential in encouraging youth to tell their stories musically.

Summary: Issues of Empathy, Audience, Cultural Appropriation, and Risk in Sharing Lived Experiences

Sharing lived experiences in ways that produce empathy or allow audiences to perform themselves as tolerant and benevolent or engage in salvationism may easily reinscribe oppressive discourses unless educators purposefully position music to move toward action. Expressing experiences through songwriting can shift this undesired potential if we focus this practice on effecting change, while remaining mindful of the potential for cultural appropriation. Storytelling through songwriting, however, may pose risks to student artists. As noted in Chapter 4, educators, as mandatory reporters of abuse, assault, and neglect, must report any disclosure received from students. In encouraging youth to express their lived realities through music, educators may learn of circumstances that necessitate reporting—a practice that may fail to improve the conditions they experience (Campbell et al., 2010). Recognizing the potential to reinforce both oppression and dominant discourses helps educators to thoughtfully consider Freire's (2000/ 1970) imperative to name the world in order to transform it. In acknowledging that some of the results of encouraging youth to share their experiences may be unproductive, we can attend to those issues as they arise and re-center action.

Dangers of Enacting Music Education as Political

Freire (2000/1970) calls upon students to name the world. Activist-musicians offered a number of possibilities to explicitly enact music education politically in alignment with Giroux and Giroux's (2004) "culture of questioning." In particular, they emphasized learning to think critically and underscored ways that youth could engage in music to identify structures and systems of oppression that shape the experiences of many youth in schools. In proffering politicized music education, however, potential for microfascism[8] emerges when enacting an activist agenda. In this section, I explore this possibility and consider ways in which a Freirian discourse of empowerment may reinscribe oppression and/or colonialism.

Microfascism

In Chapter 2, activist-musicians identified the fascistic potential of music; music can unify a group of people around a particular idea, or what Bradley (2009b) calls "that magic feeling," that manifests through a performance in which the community feeling of unity becomes overwhelming. Keil (2005) describes this phenomenon as the "urge to merge" (p. 98). Similarly, enacting activist music education in schools reveals potential for fascism or microfascism. The *Oxford Dictionary* defines *fascism* as "extreme authoritarian, oppressive, or intolerant views or practices" (English Oxford Living Dictionaries, 2019). *Microfascism*, following Deleuze and Guattari (2005/ 1987), differentiates fascist and totalitarian regimes from microfascist impulses—smaller-scale authoritarian moves that thread through capitalist society. In this case, the common feeling or idea involves embracing activism or revolution without room for dissent. Proscribed action diverging from dominant practices may become authoritarian upon implementation:

> Obliging students to speak to current issues that shape their lives, while perhaps seemingly innocuous, may enact just as stringent and

authoritarian an agenda as a music curriculum that centers Western classical music and Western standard notation. Dissent from a revolutionary musical agenda may not be any more possible than dissent from ensemble-based instruction.

(Hess, 2018d, p. 43)

Revolution and activism in music education, then, potentially become dogma, failing to create space for creative engagement. When revolution becomes curriculum, educators may enact the same authoritarian, oppressive, or intolerant practices of fascism. Revolution-as-dogma lacks flexibility. Many music educators carefully consider curriculum as they implement it in their classrooms. To dogmatically implement an agenda of revolution lacks the attention to context and student populations that activist-musicians identified as crucial in Chapter 3.

Social justice education now comprises a significant body of literature in music education scholarship (see for example Benedict et al., 2015; Bowman, 2007a; Gould et al., 2009). The proliferation of social justice discourse indicates both a timeliness and an openness to implementing activist music education.[9] Activism in schools, however, must avoid becoming a dogmatic antidote to the oppressive discourses and power structures that shape students' lives. Instead, educators can engage activism thoughtfully and with humility—adapting to community issues and engaging youth's explicit needs and challenges.

> A curriculum cannot simply be revolutionary; it must be revolutionary in relation (and always in relation) to the larger oppressive power structures at play. . . . As productive as the conversations about social justice work in music education are (see, for example, Benedict et al., 2015; Gould et al., 2009), there is an ever-present danger that social justice agendas in music education may, in fact, become a strict ideology that fails to allow for opposition or dissent, thus aligning with the definition of fascism. Any revolutionary work in schools must thus avoid dogma and allow room for multiple narratives.
>
> (Hess, 2018d, p. 43)

Awareness of activist music education's potential to replicate fascistic relations helps educators to thoughtfully consider ways to engage activist and/or revolutionary ideas in their classrooms. Activist-musicians in Chapter 2 noted music's propensity toward fascism—what Bryan identified as "galvaniz[ing] people around an idea, almost irrelevant of the content of the song in some cases, but just the feeling." Music's inherent ability to unite people around a feeling or an idea, coupled with its historical role in doing so to foster violence in Nazi Germany (Turino, 2008), for example, requires caution (Bradley, 2009b). Creating room for dissent and expressing different ideas will help music educators implement any activist curricular agenda.

Empowerment and Classroom Hierarchies

Education enacted to foster conscientization (Freire, 2000/1970) and empowerment may further reinscribe hierarchical power relations. Kirylo (2011) notes that for Freire,

> Conscientização (conscientization) is an unfolding process that awakens critical awareness (Freire, 1994). It is not a process that is static, nor formulaic; rather conscientization assumes an understanding of our unfinishedness, implying it is a "requirement" in becoming more authentically human "if we are to deepen our awareness of our world, of facts, of events, of the demands of human consciousness to develop our capacity for epistemological curiosity" (Freire, 1998a, p. 55). Stated another way, "Conscientization refers to the process in which men [and women], not as recipients, but as knowing subjects achieve a deepening awareness both of the sociocultural reality that shapes their lives and of their capacity to transform that reality" (Freire, 1985, p. 93).
>
> (Kirylo, 2011, p. 149)

"Awakening" critical consciousness may exacerbate classroom power dynamics between students and teacher. Rather than the reciprocal students-teachers/teacher-student relations that Freire (1971, p. 67) desires, education for critical consciousness implies students' lack of consciousness—an assumption that tips the balance of power toward the teacher. The inherent hierarchization in assuming that educators know more about students' "sociocultural realit[ies]" than do youth themselves limits potential for empowerment—a term that itself implies the presence of an "empowerer" rather than youth agency. The notion that conscientization helps youth become more "authentically human" also fails to recognize their already-present humanity, viewing youth from a deficit perspective.

Activist-musicians' emphasis on critical thinking in Chapter 5 potentially privileges educators' perspectives of youth's realities, which may fail to account for the specificities and nuances of their circumstances. Keeping in mind the Freirian ideal of reciprocity in teacher-student and students-teachers' relations, despite the difficulties inherent in its practical implementation (Dei & Sheth, 1997; Ellsworth, 1989; Ladson-Billings, 1997), calls for attention to the dynamics of educators aiming for conscientization among student populations. Music, as Patrick noted in Chapter 5, provides a valuable medium for analyzing realities presented through lyrics. While maintaining a critical orientation in discussion remains important in order to avoid reinscribing oppressive discourses and practices (Hess, 2014), educators may allow themselves to be open to multiple interpretations of musical encounters, positioning themselves as facilitators who ask thoughtful questions to provoke courageous conversations (Singleton & Linton, 2006). "Empowerment," conceptually, may exacerbate the power dynamics between teachers and students. Given this dynamic, educators might instead find ways for students to seize their own agency and assert it, perhaps through songwriting practices that allow them to speak to their lived realities.

Summary: Microfascism and "Empowerment"

Complex power relations weave through attempts to enact activist music education. Activist-musicians identified critical thinking as fundamental to political engagement in music education. Thinking critically involves asking hard questions about presences and absences in music education, as modeled by Vaugeois' (2009) questions on musical life histories (Chapter 3). Classroom practices that allow room for thinking, challenging, and inquiry will help educators interested in activism and social justice avoid dogmatic implementation of this curriculum. Moreover, challenging discourses of empowerment unsettles the power dynamics in the classroom and encourages youth agency. While empowerment seems hopeful, as Ellsworth (1989) notes, the notion can in fact exacerbate the power of the teacher in the classroom. Noticing these dogmatic and hierarchical possibilities encourages educators to reflect upon their activist pedagogy and look for any emergent oppressive tendencies.

Summary

Facilitating activist music education as suggested by activist-musicians in Chapters 3, 4, and 5 involves connecting to Others, sharing lived experiences, and fostering critical thinking. These same pedagogical moves, however, pose multiple risks. As such, following Lather (1998), I urge educators to remain uncertain and avoid "figuring out" activist pedagogy. Attempting to connect musically to unfamiliar Others may create possibilities of hierarchization, cultural appropriation, stereotyping, and exoticization. Situating musics historically may also recall encounters with trauma when the music studied emerges from oppression. Centering lived experiences may create further difficulties—perhaps fostering empathy for the realities of Others in a way that prevents action or change or enabling audiences to perform themselves as tolerant by consuming stories. Sharing stories may also generate potential for the cultural appropriation described in the section on connecting.

As noted in Chapter 4, encouraging youth to express their experiences through music may further pose risks to students who resist both personal and systemic injustices when the stories shared reveal situations that require reporting. Avoiding the dogmatic or microfascistic implementation of a politicized activist curriculum further requires educators to thoughtfully account for context and foster dissent in classroom practice. The discourse of empowerment, moreover, may not serve youth well, as it centers the teacher rather than encouraging youth agency. As Foucault (1983) argues,

"If everything is dangerous, then we always have something to do" (pp. 231–232). Remaining uncertain will help us navigate these potential risks or dangers. While activist music education across notions of connection, expression, and critique offers great potential, keeping these possible dangers in mind will help educators implement a thoughtful, connective, and deeply political music education that honors youth's lived experiences. In teaching, reinscribing relations we do not want to support is inevitable. Awareness of this possibility allows us to decide purposefully how we will address these "slips." Transparently repairing accidental reinscriptions of oppression with youth models a mechanism for them to address such occurrences in their own lives.

Notes

1 Feld (2005a) credits Canadian composer R. Murray Schafer for coining the term *schizophonia*.
2 Feld (2000b) describes a specific sampling process through which a sample of Afunakwa's voice makes her context unnecessary. He argues: "Through this progression one hears how what was once distinctly Afunakwa's world is now up for a new sharing, becoming, ultimately, a world where her voice is no longer necessary to her imagined presence" (p. 155). Feld concludes, "Afunakwa is not a person but a sound" (p. 165).
3 Students with PTSD may experience the following symptoms: "a re-experiencing of the event, the avoidance of situations that may trigger the event, the numbing of responses, and forms of arousal upon exposure to triggering phenomena" (Ranck, 2000, p. 197, drawing on the *Diagnostic and Statistical Manual of Mental Disorders*).
4 See Walcott (2000) for a distinct but related discussion considering the resistance Black students exhibited when he addressed the Middle Passage, slavery, and trauma in his teaching.
5 Leaving the classroom may create further issues, as it may reveal a student's personal experiences without their consent. Creating a classroom environment in which youth regularly do what they need to in order to take care of themselves may alleviate some of these issues.
6 The notion of *tolerance* is problematic. *Tolerance* literally involves enduring someone or something one does not entirely support. Embedded in multicultural movements in Western nations, tolerance rarely extends beyond superficial engagement with the Other or what Alibhai-Brown (2000) calls the "3S" model of multiculturalism: "saris, samosas, and steel drums" (p. 33). Deeper interaction typically lies beyond the scope of tolerance.
7 In Chapter 4, Casey called this type of songwriting a practice for youth to address issues in a way that is "honest and true [to] their experience."
8 See Hess (2018d) for an extended version of this argument.
9 *Activism* and *social justice* are not synonymous. *Social justice* is a slippery term, rarely defined in the literature. Scholars take it up regularly through both critical and liberal frameworks. As a term, *activism* is also slippery. For the purposes of this book, I define *activism* following Kuntz (2015) in the introduction. While I employ the term activism *because* of its openness, I simultaneously recognize that both *activism* and *social justice* are vague terms that are rarely defined with specificity.

Conclusion
A Tri-Faceted Pedagogy for Future Activism

The 20 activist-musicians provided important considerations of ways in which music education may embolden youth to challenge oppressive ideologies and to connect to one another and to others more removed from their realities, as well as to honor and share their own lived experiences. Activist-musicians put forward music education as connective, communicative, and critical. Listening to their voices—given their work supporting identity politics, speaking out against oppression, and using music to share important stories—provides a way forward for music education in a manner that supports those with the least amount of privilege while heightening awareness among more privileged students of the oppressions faced by others. Drawing on the work in Chapters 3, 4, and 5, in particular, in this chapter, I outline pedagogies that emerge from activist-musicians' assertions about music education. I therefore put forward a pedagogy of community based on activist-musicians' emphasis on connectivity, a pedagogy of expression rooted in both honoring lived experiences and sharing them through music, and a pedagogy of noticing that emerges from activist-musicians' work on critical thinking. Combining these pedagogies sets the conditions for future activism among youth and offers a possible practical enactment of critical pedagogy for music education.

A Pedagogy of Community

Considering activist-musicians' emphasis on both music and music education as connection, I offer a pedagogy of community as the first facet of activist education. In Chapter 3, activist-musicians outlined a tri-faceted education of connection, underscoring the importance of building community, linking musics to their histories and sociopolitical contexts, and connecting youth to unfamiliar others through engagement with a broad range of musics. A multifaceted pedagogy of community, then, involves connecting with others, with histories, and with larger societal narratives. Such an education also encourages understanding one's location both in relation to others and in relation to history. Music is a human practice—an idea that activist-musicians asserted and reiterated.

A pedagogy of community begins with a practice of building community in the classroom, as outlined in Chapter 3. Educators looking to build community among students in their class work to foster a mutually-supportive space, as Griffin noted, to encourage youth's musicking. When music educators facilitate a practice of community through music, students learn about both the importance of listening to the voices of others and the appropriate time to step forward and offer leadership—moving back and forth between what Taiyo called "solo" or "lecturing space" and a supportive role. When teachers give youth important responsibilities, that sense of trust further serves to build the classroom community. This first facet of a pedagogy of community focuses on fostering connections between individuals in the immediate classroom community, encouraging youth to both develop and trust their own unique voices and to value the contributions of others.

The second facet of a pedagogy of community involves connecting the musics studied to their histories, linking musics to their sociopolitical and sociohistorical contexts, and refusing any artificial dichotomy between music and other "subjects." Activist-musicians argued for the rich contextualization of all musics. This type of contextualization includes thinking deeply about the lived musical contexts that predate any incarnation of music in the classroom, considering (and utilizing if available) the instruments typically used in any musical practice studied, and translating all text in languages other than the official school language in order for youth to understand the meaning of the texts they perform and hear. Educators can, moreover, encourage youth to consider how publishers and educators may alter musics for classroom use and further challenge and discuss any possibility of cultural appropriation while navigating potential for traumatization or re-experiencing trauma. In striving to link musics to their histories, music educators can draw connections between disciplines, as well as to social movements. A rich contextualization process in the classroom may thus help youth understand the context of their own struggles and the challenges faced by their communities and the communities of Others. In Chapter 3, Griffin suggested studying individual artists to help youth understand the life of an individual "as a node connected to others in a matrix of social relations." Griffin felt that examining artists in this way would help youth understand their own lives in relation to others. This pedagogy of community advocates rich contextualization to help youth understand themselves in a wider matrix of social relations, through engagement with a broad range of musics.

The third facet of a pedagogy of community involves engaging a wide variety of musics in a way that encourages youth to connect to Others by exploring musical practices beyond the familiar. Chapters 3 and 4 both draw upon Style's (1996) conceptualization of curriculum as window and mirror. In prioritizing connecting to Others, this pedagogy focuses on providing a window for youth to look out into the world. Educators may first present musics familiar to youth in the class, grounding them in their own musicking practices and providing a window into musicking occurring in the local community before looking beyond the immediate school context. Introducing a wide range of musics provides youth with glimpses into the lives of Others through engagement with their musical practices and with a variety of instruments. In drawing upon musical traditions other than those familiar to educators and students, a number of activist-musicians noted the potential for cultural appropriation. Remaining aware of the possibility for appropriation, however, may help educators to navigate introducing different musics with respectful and ethical recontextualization. Centering a wide range of musics for classroom study allows educators to foster a connection between youth and the larger global community.

A pedagogy of community, then, emphasizes connecting on three levels. First, youth engage with each other in the local classroom community, fostering a mutually-supportive environment in which they learn to value their own contributions and those of other community members. Second, youth connect music to its sociopolitical and sociohistorical context in a way that allows them to understand their own lives and the lives of Others in a wider matrix of social relations. Finally, youth encounter unfamiliar Others through examining different musical traditions that provide a window into both the local community and the wider global community. Educators looking to enact a pedagogy of community strive to facilitate what Taiyo called a "practice of community" among youth in the classroom, alongside continual development of contextual knowledge and experiences with multiple musical traditions.

A Pedagogy of Expression

A pedagogy of expression emerges from activist-musicians' emphasis on musicking as a way to tell stories. Their desire to share lived experiences through music initially requires a practice of honoring lived experiences, grounding youth firmly in their own realities. A pedagogy of expression thus involves both valuing youth's experiences and encouraging them to share those experiences through music. Such a practice also potentially encourages them to value others' lived realities as they begin to share their stories and listen to the narratives of others.

Implementing a place-based curriculum can honor youth's lived experiences in schools. Magali noted, for example, the importance of considering what youth in Ferguson, Missouri, needed after the murder of 18-year-old Michael Brown in 2014, and advocated for connecting curriculum directly to context, with full consideration of the school population. Emphasizing Style's (1996) mirror, a place-based education focuses on reflecting youth's experiences back to them in a way that validates and affirms their lives. Enacting place-based education allows educators both to recognize the complexities in youth's lives and to honor their contributions. This type of education draws upon the literatures of culturally relevant pedagogy

(Gurgel, 2016; Koza, 2006; Ladson-Billings, 1995, 2009), culturally responsive teaching (Gay, 2018; Lind & McKoy, 2016), and culturally sustaining pedagogy (Paris & Alim, 2014, 2017) and looks first to students' experiences before crafting a curriculum. Honoring and centering youth's lived realities in the curriculum validates their contributions and perspectives.

In honoring youth's experiences, educators can encourage sharing stories through music. Activist-musicians, as active artists, suggested a rich songwriting process as a means to share stories and experiences. A pedagogy of expression encourages the articulation of experiences through music—an active practice of naming the world (Freire, 2000/1970). Eighteen of the 20 activist-musicians advocated for songwriting as a key element of the curriculum. They looked for ways to provide accessible tools to facilitate creation and wanted to see youth write lyrics and music true to their own realities.

Sharing their stories through music perhaps provides students with an outlet for processing their experiences and connecting their own lives to larger narratives in order to heighten the possible impact of their musics. Educators looking to foster this pedagogy of expression in the classroom may take up the role of what Allsup (2016) calls "fellow adventurers"—educators working alongside students to explore what may become possible. In creating a space in which youth may choose to share their experiences, educators must remain mindful to make the expression of lived experiences a choice, as some issues and realities may be rooted in trauma or in experiences that youth may not want known, such as addiction and poverty, for example. Encouraging youth to share only as they see fit allows them to maintain control of the information known about them.

A Pedagogy of Noticing

A pedagogy of noticing comprises the important third facet of activist music education. In recognizing both music and music education as political (Freire, 1993), activist-musicians encouraged a practice of critical thinking through which youth learn to critique the world around them, to name the conditions and ideologies that shape their lives and the lives of others, and to challenge those conditions toward transformation (Freire, 2000/1970). This pedagogy of noticing encourages youth to notice oppression and the ideologies that influence it, even when (perhaps especially when) it does not affect them, and to question what they encounter in daily interactions. In doing so, youth learn to recognize not only oppressions that affect their group directly, but also oppressions across multiple identities, learning to notice not only racism, for example, but also ableism. Through a practice of critical thinking and a culture of questioning (Giroux & Giroux, 2004), youth learn to challenge and critique the oppressive representations, texts, and discourses that surround them. Patrick suggested multiple ways to draw upon hip-hop and hip-hop lyrics to foster critical thinking. Upon regularly engaging in a practice of noticing, as fellow-adventurers (Allsup, 2016), teachers and students may consider how to directly address oppression through their musical work.

Enacting a pedagogy of noticing involves an astute practice of critique on the part of the teacher; educators themselves notice, critique, and challenge the injustices that surround them. In doing so, teachers work to facilitate that same habit of questioning and noticing among youth in the classroom, engaging them in courageous conversations (Singleton & Linton, 2006) about social justice and oppression, while remaining mindful of the hierarchizing potential inherent in Freirian (2000/1970) notions of conscientization and empowerment (Ellsworth, 1989; Ladson-Billings, 1997; Siddhartha, 2005). Teachers may set the conditions for noticing, while leaving room for youth to seize that power and assert their voices.

Remaining Aware of Potential Dangers

Enacting this tri-faceted pedagogy for activist music education requires vigilance against potential dangers. As educators, we will likely "slip" and reinscribe relations we wish to avoid. Noticing these reinscriptions as they occur allows us to address these possibilities with students. The issues identified in Chapter 6 linger in every move toward initiating the pedagogies of community, expression, and noticing. Any pedagogy of community through which youth connect to Others through music poses risks of hierarchization, cultural appropriation, exoticization, stereotyping, and trauma. A pedagogy of expression may similarly emphasize empathy in a manner that ultimately reinscribes oppression and facilitates cultural appropriation. Encouraging youth to share their experiences may also place them at risk of capitulating to audience desires. In further facilitating a pedagogy of noticing, educators must resist any dogmatic implementation of an activist agenda, remaining both thoughtful and attentive to context. Freirian notions of empowerment and conscientization (Freire, 2000/1970) may also reinforce the hierarchy between teachers and students in a manner that privileges the teacher and limits youth agency. Remaining aware of these negative possibilities and centering them in discussion when they emerge helps educators to mindfully implement this tri-faceted pedagogy for activist music education in collaboration with youth. In seeking to construct activist music education, I encourage music educators not to "figure it out" (Lather, 1998)—to decide any right or appropriate implementation of this pedagogy. Rather, I urge educators to remain uncertain and know that reinscribing oppression is a possibility. "Slipping" is inherently human. How we address those "slips" with students matters greatly.

Redefining Activist Music Education

In order to now redefine what constitutes activist music education, I recall Kuntz's (2015) definition of activism, shared in the Introduction, as a working definition of *activism* for this volume. Kuntz asserts that

> In a general sense, to engage in activism is to in some way work for social change. As such, activism requires an imaginative or creative element—the ability to understand ourselves as other than we are. More specifically, activism involves the determined intervention into the normative processes and practices that govern the world in which we live. As a practice of intervention, activism necessarily remains grounded in the realm of the material; activist practices are material practices. Through activism one might seek to generate new meanings, new ways of considering and engaging within the world.
>
> (p. 28)

Activism thus works toward transformation, a key element of Freirian pedagogy (Freire, 2000/1970). Enacting activism involves creative imagining—dreaming of what Walcott (2009) calls the "something more possible," the something that emerges from its "location between brutality and something different," where cultures fuse and mix when forced to cohabit together (p. 170, citing Hall, 2003, p. 193). Activism also involves material action that drives change. Activism is a creative praxis, one that looks to circumnavigate systems and structures of oppression to find a better way forward.

Kuntz' definition of *activism* resonates with critical pedagogy. Freirian dialogue in education involves reflection, a process of naming the world, subsequent action, and transformation as a result of naming the world, and a return to reflection (Darder, 2017; Freire, 2000/1970). Material action—action leading to material changes—is crucial to critical pedagogy and also essential to transformation. Imagining also plays a vital role in critical pedagogy. Freire (1998a) perceives the unfinishedness inherent in humanity and the imperative in education to transform and ameliorate current conditions. Giroux (2017a) notes that

> [Critical thinking in critical pedagogy] was about offering a way of thinking beyond the seeming naturalness or inevitability of the current state of things, challenging assumptions validated by "common sense," soaring beyond the immediate confines of one's experiences, entering into a dialogue with history, and *imagining a future that would not merely reproduce the present.*
>
> (p. xii, emphasis added)

Dreaming, Freire (1998b) reminds us, "is not only a necessary political act, it is an integral part of the historico-social manner of being a person. . . . There is no change without dream, as there is no dream without hope." (p. 81). Critical pedagogy thus involves that same imperative of material action and imagination that Kuntz (2015) identifies when engaging in a classroom practice of thinking critically about the world.

Activist-musicians asserted that music as an artistic practice provides the opportunity to foster connections between peoples, to communicate important stories and lived experiences, and to offer a political perspective. Music education likewise offers an opening to connect people, to honor and share experiences through music and music pedagogy, and to engage in thinking critically about the world—naming it in order to transform it (Freire, 2000/1970). This tri-faceted pedagogy for activist music education emphasizes the importance of building community both locally and in the wider community, honoring and sharing lived experiences for the purposes of expression and resistance, and noticing injustice—not merely the injustice enacted on one's own group, but across identities, in a manner that is intersectional (Collins, 2000; Crenshaw, 1995).

Both activism, following Kuntz' (2015) definition, and critical pedagogy, however, involve material action. While educators, together with students, may engage in the pedagogy of community, expression, and noticing, these practices unto themselves do not guarantee action. I argue that, instead, they set the conditions for activism. When youth learn at a young age to build connections within and beyond their communities, music education creates the possibilities for youth to prioritize their communities—to actively strive to support one another and look to connect to their immediate communities and further foster connections to people who they might not otherwise encounter beyond their local context. In fostering community, providing rich contextualization for all musics, and actively engaging in musical practices that span the musicking traditions from a wide number of groups, music education communicates the value of human beings—all human beings. This pedagogy of community emphasizes the rich histories that accompany all musics, highlighting the strength that can emerge from intense oppression. Moreover, once the "novelty" of engaging with unfamiliar people and sounds dissipates, as Jason indicated in Chapter 6, such pedagogy enables a democracy of sounds that places traditions in conversation with one another. A pedagogy of community emphasizes connections and further underscores the inherent value of listening to all contributions, rather than undermining perspectives that differ from one's own. In and of itself, a pedagogy of community may not result in action. I assert, however, that it sets the conditions for youth to seek connections in their lives and value the perspectives of others.

Encouraging a pedagogy of expression may not ultimately initiate action. Valuable learning, however, occurs when educators actively seek to honor youth's own lived experiences and encourage them to share those experiences through music. A pedagogy of expression provides the creative element of activism that Kuntz (2015) identifies. When educators honor youth's lived realities, they communicate strongly that youth are of value and their experiences matter. Youth, consequently, may begin to value and trust their own voices (Hess, 2013b), recognizing their perspectives as important and vital to the community in which they live and learn. Encouraging youth to share their perspectives through songwriting offers an important opportunity for them to nurture their artistic voices—to explore different ways of expressing ideas, stories, and emotions through music, and to develop a musical practice that allows their words and their experiences to ring out into the world. Finding one's voice musically and fostering a practice that captures the integrity of one's experiences involve an innately musical process of coming to voice (Freire, 2000/1970). Through a pedagogy of expression, youth learn to assert their presence in their communities (Hess, Watson, & Deroo, 2019)—to speak for themselves and recognize their contributions as valuable and important while simultaneously recognizing when to listen and put forward the contributions of others. In expressing their ideas and their experiences, their music may encourage changes in their local communities, particularly when they name the world as they see it and clearly identify the challenges they face. If material changes do not occur, at the very least, a pedagogy of expression sets the conditions for youth to continue the practice of asserting their voices in the world, sometimes through artistic practice and sometimes through other mechanisms. Such a pedagogy teaches youth that their experiences matter; it further communicates that some adults will listen and respond when they speak. Moreover, if imagination is crucial in activism, as Kuntz (2015) underscores, the pedagogy of expression and the opportunity to find one's own artistic voice provide a significant means by which to practice imagining a different possible future and perhaps engage in the kind of collective envisioning identified in Chapter 4.

A pedagogy of noticing, similarly, does not necessarily lead to action. Noticing injustice, however, signals youth's astute analysis of the conditions and discourses that shape their lives and the lives of others with whom they may be less familiar. To notice and to name are actions unto themselves. Noticing and naming lie in opposition to acceptance and complacency. The complex process of noticing the injustices that shape one's own existence involves recognizing systems and structures that oppress. In Chapter 5, Patrick pointed to a potential way to analyze hip-hop texts that aligns with youth's own experiences, to foster recognition of systemic conditions rather than isolated or individualized circumstances.

Activist-musicians strongly advocated for connecting individual experiences to larger social movements, refusing an individualization of the systemic (Castagno, 2014; Giroux, 2006; Goldberg, 2009). Noticing the injustices enacted upon groups of which one is not a member, however, perhaps requires more specific prompts. Recognizing systems and structures as they affect and marginalize different groups across all identities requires an intersectional understanding of oppression (Collins, 2000; Crenshaw, 1995) and a willingness to notice and name the unjust conditions that affect others in a manner that does not foster complacency or settle for empathy but pushes toward transformation. Noticing encompasses a hopeful first step toward action. When youth learn to notice intersectional injustices, this pedagogy sets the conditions for resistance.

Initiating Freirian dialogue in the classroom, as noted previously, involves processes of reflection, naming the world, engaging in action as a result of this naming, and returning subsequently to reflection (Darder, 2017; Freire, 2000/1970). Reflection brings together all three facets of this tri-faceted pedagogy for music education. A pedagogy of community facilitates the consideration of histories and the manner in which they weave throughout the present, allowing all participants in education to contemplate the ways we are connected to one another. In validating and honoring our lived experiences, a pedagogy of expression encourages youth to engage with their experiences as valid and important. Moreover, a pedagogy of noticing emboldens youth to consider the conditions and ideologies that shape their experiences. The second aspect of the process—naming the world—again draws on a pedagogy of expression to engage in a process of identifying these experiences and asserting them to the world. This expression emerges from noticing oppressive conditions and identifying them through reflection. A pedagogy of community further allows us to situate the expression of experiences in relation to both historical and present contexts and the lived realities of others.

The next stage—action—as indicated, may remain more elusive in school music education. Indeed, Sloboda (2015) observes that music education is far from the ideal vehicle for social justice; he argues that music educators who value social justice may benefit from reevaluating their professional field of activity to choose a field where they can effect more direct action (p. 545). While music education may not be the most impactful means to effect social justice, it can contribute to creating the conditions for change-making in profound ways. The processes of reflection and naming the world create great potential for action. Whether or not educators can work alongside youth to realize action depends at least somewhat on the definition of *action*. If we define *action* only as transformative change, this activist music education may perhaps set the conditions without actualization. If, however, we define *action* as the changes created when youth attach value to their experiences and risk asserting them in their communities, this tri-faceted pedagogy may in fact encourage small transformations. These microtransformations may be internal changes but may become significant as youth call out oppression when they see it and refuse, as Giroux (2017a) notes, the reinscription of the status quo or the reproduction of the present (p. xii). The return to reflection then allows for contemplation of any changes that occurred through the initial process and further indicates a constant process of forward movement.

Taken together, a pedagogy of community, expression, and noticing push toward the recognition of the humanity in Self and Others. While it may not produce action directly toward change and transformation, this learning of the inherent value of human experiences across all identity categories sets the conditions for action. Hate, oppression, and White supremacy continually manifest in both new and familiar ways, and the so-called "alt-right" is taking hold in multiple contexts globally (Giroux, 2017b; MacKinnon, 2017; Marsh, 2017; Nowak & Branford, 2017; Taylor, 2016). Against this backdrop, an education that encourages youth to recognize the humanity in all diminishes the power of oppressive regimes by fostering attentive and critical youth who value the experiences of others and believe in the importance of their own voices and the voices of others, alternating, as Taiyo noted, between solo and lecturing space and the space to support others. This deep valuing of others' perspectives, coupled with the tools to recognize and name injustice and express their ideas powerfully in the world, sets the conditions for transformation and encourages an unwillingness to settle when global, national, and local systems and structures oppress others. Freire (2000/1970) argues that reflection without action is *verbalism*, while action without reflection is *activism* (pp. 87–88). This pedagogy of community, expression, and noticing brings together action and reflection—a rich Freirian praxis for music education.

The activist-musicians offered crucial perspectives on the manners in which music can connect individuals with their local and global communities, provide a vehicle for expressing lived experiences and sharing stories, and offer an opportunity to think more critically about the world. Their artistic praxes embody these ideals, and who they are as artists, educators, and individuals shape their thoughts for music education. In beginning this project, I sought to shape some kind of activist music education rooted in the activism and music of these 20 individuals. I asked, given their creative endeavors and their experiences with both activism and music, what they would have wanted as a child in music class. Their ideas emerged directly from their artistic practices. Music enacted as connection and an opportunity to engage in a practice of community gave way to asserting a music education profoundly about connection and community. Their recognition of music as an important vehicle to share stories led to a pedagogy in which music educators both valued youth's experiences and facilitated the expression of these experiences musically. Finally, the recognition of music as deeply political fostered a music education in which youth learn to critically assess and name the world, noticing injustices and challenging them. This activist music education thus emerges directly from lived musical practices of activist-musicians—individuals who recognize injustices across multiple identities and concentrate their musical efforts toward heightening awareness and moving to action. At a time when suppression and oppression submerge minoritized voices, this music education pedagogy seeks to facilitate the expression of lived experiences, to develop an artistic practice that is deeply political, rooted in valuing Self and Others, and to bring people together. Such music education sets the conditions for future activism and intensive work for social justice. Moreover, rooted in artistic practices, this tri-faceted music education centers musicking. Pedagogies of community, expression, and noticing simultaneously help youth develop their own musicking practices while encouraging them to foster connections, express their ideas, and think deeply about their experiences and encounters through musicking. Activist music pedagogy thus not only fosters musicianship among youth, but also encourages them to music thoughtfully.

This tri-faceted pedagogy centers love, hope, care, and ethics. The music education these activist-musicians suggest privileges connection, expression, and critique over opposition. Instead of encouraging youth to individually refuse particular oppressive conditions, the activist-musicians set the conditions for youth to value themselves and their communities, drawing on what Yosso (2005) calls "community cultural wealth" in their opposition, rooting their assertions in deep connections with others. Youth's musical assertions draw upon lived experiences that link to larger narratives in a manner that may encourage audiences to truly listen to the message and potentially act on it. Activist-musicians modeled a way to musically engage in the community, resist apathy, and speak to issues of import to their lives. Activist music education fosters critical civic engagement while communicating to youth the value of their voices and their experiences, and the community of strength upon which they can draw.

Conclusion: A Critical Praxis for Music Education

This critical praxis—a combination of theory and practice, of reflection and action—offers a possible way forward for music education rooted in connection, expression, and criticality. When critical educators looked to Freire for a critical pedagogy method to apply across contexts, Freire refused (Dale & Hyslop-Margison, 2010; Freire & Macedo, 1998). Instead, he called for educators to reinvent critical pedagogy for their specific situations. Darder's (2017) study, for example, provides illustrations of the ways in which different educators enact critical pedagogy. Similarly, I do not offer this tri-faceted pedagogy rooted in activist-musicians' praxes as a method. Rather, in putting forward these pedagogical ideas, I note that as music educators, we must first consider our specific contexts and apply these notions in a manner that works for the individuals we teach. Many of the pedagogical perspectives offered by activist-musicians apply across multiple contexts, but there also may be circumstances in which, for example, youth may not wish to music about their experiences. In honoring their experiences then, as educators, we may recognize cultivating a songwriting practice as perhaps less crucial for our community than drawing on remix culture with youth.

In this volume, I put forward a possible praxis for music educators—a pedagogy that draws upon theory combining the rich tradition of critical pedagogy with the lived experiences and perspectives of activist-musicians to underpin practice. Darder (2017) observes,

> It is significant to note that Paulo Freire moved from speaking of the relationship between theory and practice as a "union" in *Pedagogy of the Oppressed* (1970) to an "alliance" in *The Politics of Education* (1985). The

shift marked more than simply a semantic distinction. His concern was the manner in which the concept of "union" could cause teachers to artificially collapse or dissolve two distinct, although connected, moments of knowing into one another and to lose the significance of each dialectical contribution to the ongoing construction and remaking of knowledge in our lives.

(p. 74)

This activist music education presents an opportunity for us to combine theory and practice, action and reflection, honoring their alliance without eliding them. In further encouraging a practice of Freirian (2000/1970) dialogue in our classrooms—a process that involves reflection, naming, action, and return to reflection—we facilitate a process of identifying oppressive conditions through music, fostering connections, and expressing perspectives. Action, however, as noted, remains somewhat uncertain. The ambiguity of what may result when enacting such pedagogy does not reveal a flaw. Instead, I view this uncertainty as a space of openness (Allsup, 2016), of intense possibility. Many possibilities emerge when youth learn that we, as educators, value their experiences and encourage their participation in shaping the very conditions that affect their lives. Music, as activist-musicians asserted throughout these chapters, provides a unique opportunity for expression that listeners perhaps receive more easily, as tvu noted, than more didactic messages through speech. If the call to action always already involves a critical imagining of what may be possible when we refuse to further reproduce the present (Giroux, 2017a), musicking, as an intensely creative activity, can play a key role in this collective envisioning.

At this juncture in time, music education must matter; it must honor the humanity in all and resist injustice loudly and musically. The life's work of these activist-musicians provides a powerful model for music education—a model that celebrates community, honors lived experiences, provides musical means to share them, and encourages a praxis of noticing and resisting injustices across multiple identities. Listening to their voices helps our discipline imagine a different possible future—a collective envisioning of all that music education can do and be.

Afterword—Taking Courage
Implementing Activist Music Education

Implementing activist music education requires courage. Teachers choosing activist music pedagogy face significant challenges as they facilitate and navigate the different effects of this pedagogy. External forces drastically shape teachers' actions. This afterword addresses these external forces, as well as societal constraints placed on teachers not previously taken up in the book. The overwhelming emphasis on standardized testing, scores, and ranking deeply influences what becomes possible in schools. Exploring ways to address this pressure remains important to implementing a pedagogy that prioritizes critical thinking. Stark societal divides may also emerge in the classroom and the school when students grapple with the issues raised through this pedagogy. Preparing to navigate discord thus becomes an important aspect of implementation. Teachers may themselves face resistance from their communities as they implement what some may see as a "leftist, liberal agenda." This afterword offers suggestions for responses to such criticisms. Taking courage and initiating (or continuing) activist music education ultimately helps youth build community and connect with others, express their stories and their ideas, notice injustice(s), and critique the world around them. Considering possible difficulties teachers may face allows us to better address these issues as they emerge.

Competing Roles for Teachers: Navigating the Global Education Reform Movement

Teachers face significant challenges in the wake of the Global Education Reform Movement, which has proliferated since the 1980s, resulting in major changes to arts education. Sahlberg (2011) identifies a number of features of this education movement: the standardization of teaching and learning, a focus on literacy and numeracy, the teaching of a prescribed curriculum with seemingly predictable and uniform outcomes, the borrowing of market-oriented reform ideas from the corporate world to apply to education, and the use of high-stakes accountability measures through standardized testing (p. 103). These elements form the current backdrop for music education. In a climate that prioritizes standardized testing, music educators must balance their own educational philosophies against accountability-era literacy and numeracy priorities. Music teachers may be evaluated based on students' standardized test scores (Robinson, 2017) and face pressure to contribute to student success on standardized tests. While standardized tests purportedly focus on higher-order thinking skills (Smith & Szymanski, 2013), the way that education discourse describes these skills fails to capture the focus on ideology that is central to the type of critical thinking discussed in this book. Smith and Szymanski (2013) note,

> Critical thinking is probably the most current label for what many call analytical reasoning, synthesis, problem-solving, or higher mental processes (Scriven & Paul, 1992). Lewis and Smith (1993) indicate that much of the confusion surrounding the definition of higher order thinking comes from the inconsistent use of the term critical thinking. They noted that "critical thinking has been assigned at least three distinct meanings: (a) critical thinking as problem solving, (b) critical thinking as evaluation or judgment, and (c) critical thinking as a combination of evaluation and problem solving."
>
> (p. 18, citing Lewis & Smith, 1993, p. 134)

These definitions of critical thinking focus on problem-solving, rather than problem-posing (Goulet, 1996). Evaluation or judgment and a problem-solving approach do not necessarily encourage youth to examine the root of the problem. After gaining experience with critiquing discourses and experiences for underlying ideologies, standardized tests perhaps present an opportunity for all education participants to consider why tests value only particular kinds of critical thinking (problem solving), and in so doing, privilege certain raced and classed identities. Thinking about the ideologies that shape the Global Education Reform Movement and standardized tests themselves may illuminate the need for a different path forward in education—a result perhaps both undesirable and unsettling to corporate accountability reformers but nonetheless imperative. Recognizing cognitive dissonance can become part of what we do as music teachers. Contributing to students' development of alternate forms of critical thinking then becomes a contribution relevant to both activist music education and broader goals within the present-day educational context.

Upon encouraging youth to develop a habit of critique, we might also work to ensure through collective analysis that they understand what types of thinking produce "right answers" on standardized tests. Contrary to Lorde's (2007/1984) assertion that the "master's tools will never dismantle the master's house," Delpit (2006/1995) argues that giving minoritized students tools to navigate a system incongruous with their own experiences is essential for student success until dismantling the system becomes possible.[1] Delpit (2006/1995) describes a bidialectical dictionary activity for a language class that allows students to explore the ways they speak at home versus the ways they speak at school in order to support students in "code switching" to achieve success in school. In music class, we may focus on fostering critical analytical skills that allow students to recognize the ideologies that require particular codes in different situations, noticing, for example, reasons why standardized tests do not typically reward a culture of questioning (Giroux & Giroux, 2004). In this accountability era, however, encouraging youth to employ the demanded codes to succeed until teachers, students, parents, and communities initiate systemic change ensures that the effects of centering problem-posing education rather than problem-solving education do not make the current situation even more deleterious.

Pedagogical Concerns: Navigating a Divided Community

When inviting youth to name their experiences, speak to issues that affect them, and consider their identities in relation to their realities, we might expect some level of contention or disagreement in the classroom and school community. Having already established structures for addressing any oppressive speech or action, we might consider ways to encourage listening in our school communities. In the public sphere, opposition and disagreement are common. The organization of most governments by political party fosters division, as choosing one of the available sets of governing tenets becomes part of what we do as citizens. We will likely experience these same types of ideological differences as we delve into challenging issues in music classrooms. As educators, we may be hesitant to encourage any politicized music education because of the divisions that it may produce. Rather than shying away from such possibilities, however, we can lean into the discomfort and see what we might learn from each other.

As Stauffer (2017) asserts, failing to listen to each other has greatly contributed to a climate of division in the United States. She proposes that we learn to listen radically—"mindfully, patiently, imaginatively, repeatedly, and intentionally" (p. 8)—to understand the perspectives of those with whom we disagree. Rather than listening to persuade others of our own viewpoints, we can listen with the aim of understanding. In the classroom, we can practice and encourage students to employ reflective listening strategies (Ferrara & LaMeau, 2015) that repeat what listeners think they have understood from others to ensure that the message communicated reflects the speaker's perspective. In this way, students learn to recognize the humanity present across different views.

In a climate of discord, division becomes a teaching opportunity. How might we listen across disparate viewpoints and still function as a community? How do we distinguish between oppressive perspectives and perspectives that simply encompass different ideals than our own? When listening across disparate perspectives becomes curriculum, and reflective and radical listening become routine practices, youth may develop the skills not only to assert their perspectives but to recognize different views as valid and important. Embracing contention in schools equips youth to better address discord in their communities. Through music education, they learn to consider views that differ from their own and differentiate between perspectives that are different and perspectives that are oppressive. Creating space for contention in the classroom can feel uncomfortable; leaning into the discomfort, however, may create space for students to develop the skills that are critical to civic engagement in the wider community. Rather than shying away from discord, we can encourage respectful conversation across disparate views, with clear parameters about oppressive discourse.

Facing Resistance from the Community

Teachers implementing activist music education may also face resistance from their local communities and, in some cases, from large segments of the population because of a perceived lack of congruence between beliefs or actions deemed appropriate at home versus at school.[2] Administrators and community stakeholders may accuse educators of propagating a "liberal leftist agenda" or criticize or discipline teachers for engaging music they deem profane or inappropriate (see for example Fearnow, 2014; Stephenson, 2018; Willis, 2017). Historically, teachers have often faced opposition for teaching what Zimmerman and Robertson (2017) identify as controversial issues, often because of concerns that students will adopt teachers' perspectives at the expense of familial values. Despite resistance, after surveying various school district policy documents, Zimmerman and Robertson determine that "[f]or the first time in our history, indeed, teaching controversial issues has become the official 'best practice' in American schools" (p. 94). They argue that engaging with contentious issues in schools teaches youth how to "do" democracy (p. 62). Such work further encourages youth to engage respectfully with each other in discussion (p. 98).

While some of the issues youth may choose to pursue in activist music education may meet Zimmerman and Robertson's definition of a *maximally controversial issue*, this tri-faceted approach to music education does not encourage a particular ideology. Rather, it builds community relations, situates musics in their contexts, and encourages youth to acknowledge the humanity embedded in all musical practices and express their responses to their lived experiences. It further urges youth to consider the ideologies and discourses that shape their encounters. While the public sometimes fears that students will take their teachers' perspectives (Zimmerman & Robertson, 2017, pp. 19–20), activist music education does not propagate a particular perspective but rather aims to give youth the tools to make informed decisions about the circumstances and issues they encounter. Noticing and identifying the ideologies that shape one's conditions are not solely leftist or liberal practices; they instead are practices of truly "naming the world"—identifying the influences that inform one's encounters. Activist music education encourages students to learn to think deeply about issues and to practice engaging respectfully with each other across disparate perspectives. It is therefore explicitly non-partisan.

As argued in Chapter 5, education is inherently political. Ideologies and numerous discourses shape every pedagogical move. Striving for connection, expression, and noticing are, of course, political and situated. These same ideals, however, form the cornerstone of an education that positions youth as thoughtful and committed members of their communities. A pedagogy of community urges youth to consider both each other and those groups that may be less familiar, as well as exploring the situatedness of music in human practices. A pedagogy of expression encourages students to value their own experiences and those of others and to assert their voices through processes of coming to voice and naming the world. Ultimately, a pedagogy of noticing asks youth to deeply consider the forces that shape their experiences. Implementing an education that teaches youth to value community, express their ideas and experiences musically, and notice ideologies simply creates the conditions for youth to engage their world on their own terms.

By encouraging educators to lean into the discomfort of doing this work when facing resistance, I do not intend to minimize possible risks to teachers. Educators, for example, have been disciplined for use of music deemed profane (Fearnow, 2014; Stephenson, 2018; Willis, 2017). As such, mindfully selecting elements of this tri-faceted pedagogy for the needs and climate of each individual community becomes important. As noted, activist music education is not an instructional method, and as Freire insisted (as cited in Freire & Macedo, 1998), each implementation must be a reinvention. Specific forms of possible resistance and risk vary greatly across contexts, which require educators to shape local plans for implementation, rather than more generalized pedagogical plans. Music educators can then carefully consider their communities and decide what will be possible, perhaps emphasizing a pedagogy of community through cultivating togetherness through ensemble, for example, while selecting small ways to address and identify ideologies. All three facets of the pedagogy create productive possibilities. Emphasizing the respect and recognition that a pedagogy of community engenders while finding more subtle ways of encouraging youth to name their world and identify dominant ideologies still positions music education as fundamental to recognizing the humanity present in all. Considering the local climate, both within the classroom and in the larger community, remains crucial in all aspects of implementation.

Not Just "One More Thing"

With all of the external pressures teachers face, implementing activist music education may seem like just one more task to add to the long list of expectations placed on educators. Cultivating community, expression, and a practice of noticing, however, easily falls within the realm of what music teachers already do as socially engaged community members. As previously noted, *ensemble* means "together" in French. Encouraging youth to find ways to be in the world together while honoring each other's contributions already comprises an important aspect of music teacher practice. Similarly, expression easily becomes an extension of performing and listening to music—three deeply interrelated actions. The third facet—noticing and critique—then becomes a habit for youth to develop and through which to look for the ideologies and discourses circulating in all the material they encounter. While this habit may take time to develop initially, once it becomes ingrained and firmly rooted in students' thought processes, it happens relatively quickly. The emphasis on musicking in all senses of the word, coupled with a habit of noticing, is already common practice for many music educators. Centering community, expression, and noticing occurs not at the expense of the music, but with it and through it. Magali and James, for example, both noted the importance of technical instrumental instruction integrated with youth songwriting practices. Engaging this tri-faceted pedagogy, then, involves recognizing when to integrate technical instruction to help learners take their musicking to the next level. What this tri-faceted pedagogy offers is a particular focus and not an additional responsibility—a way to make our work meaningful through the centering of musicking as a human practice, a means of expressing deeply important ideas and experiences, and a medium to consider discourses and ideologies.

Conclusion: Taking up the Challenge

As educators, we may face challenges on a number of fronts upon implementing activist music education. In this era of high-stakes accountability, we navigate external pressures to "teach-to-the-test" in ways that work in opposition to a critical approach to education. We may further worry about difficult issues or discord that may emerge from the curriculum. Moreover, we might face resistance from our immediate communities, and perhaps regional or national opposition to our efforts. Implementing activist music education may indeed seem like simply another responsibility placed on educators rather than an already-routine part of music teacher praxis. Realizing this pedagogy, however, becomes a way to make music education even more deeply meaningful and further allows educators to shape our social engagement in society in ways that center humanity. Pedagogically, we understand the value of the practices of community, expression, and noticing put forward by activist-musicians and recognize these ideals as defensible to any concerned stakeholders. I thus urge music educators to take courage. This political moment (and arguably every political moment) requires youth who will deeply consider the discourses they encounter, recognize the humanity in all, and lift up their voices when they deem it important. Encouraging these priorities allows youth to play a thoughtful and engaged role in society. In this moment, we must take heart and bravely step onto the path forward.

Notes

1 Ravitch (2010) describes a bleak picture of the effects of standardized testing and school choice in the United States. As long as these measures remain evaluative of students, teachers, and schools, however, success on the tests is important to continued federal support.
2 Band directors from Spring Lake Park High School outside of St. Paul, Minnesota, for example, intentionally centered instrumental compositions by women and composers of color in their band programs (Wastvedt, 2017) and faced significant national backlash (personal correspondence).

Appendix
The Activist-Musicians

Karl Buechner (born December 23, 1970) is an American musician from Syracuse, New York, best known as the front man for the metalcore band Earth Crisis. He is also the singer for Freya, Path of Resistance, Vehement Serenade, Apocalypse Tribe, and 1000 Drops of Venom. In the mid- to late 90s, Buechner attained great popularity within the hardcore music scene as the front man of Earth Crisis, due to their outspoken advocacy for the straight-edge and vegan lifestyles. He has been featured on and interviewed by CNN, CBS, *The New York Times*, and Fox News, and has addressed the U.S. Congress about teens and substance abuse. (from https://en.wikipedia.org/wiki/Karl_Buechner)

DANakaDAN is an alternative rap artist from Los Angeles, California. His eclectic style draws on inspiration from artists such as Macklemore, Mike Shinoda (Linkin Park), and Kanye West. On top of music, DAN is best known for his work as a lead producer and personality with pioneer digital artists Wong Fu Productions and musicians Far East Movement. Through his work with these artists, he has produced over 150 digital films, features, and music videos, including his personal documentary series, *AKA DAN*, in which he documents his life as a Korean adoptee meeting his biological family for the first time, including an identical twin brother he had not previously known about. His digital work has been seen by millions online. He recently worked with NBC to put out the sequel to the documentary *AKA SEOUL*, which is currently making its rounds in the film festival circuit. He has been featured on MSNBC, BBC, NPR and has even been invited to the White House, where he took part in activities to help amplify the work of the Asian Pacific American community to the Washington, D.C., community. As an artist, he has been able to travel the world, performing in South Korea, Singapore, and Malaysia. He has collaborated with other digital artists like David Choi, The Kinjaz, Ki Hong

Lee, Clara C, and more. DAN's second full-length album, *Escape from L.A.*, was released in 2017. For more information, please visit him on social media: @DANakaDAN.

Bryan DePuy is an artist, game developer, and audio engineer based in Toronto, Canada. Since coming of age in the DIY/punk scene of Washington, D.C., he has aspired to balance creative practice with ongoing accountability to the communities that support him, as well as a commitment to anti-racist, anti-colonial, and feminist ideals. Originally interested in very loud music and very bad drawing as his primary means of expression, he has subsequently dabbled in many artistic disciplines, slowly transitioning toward a focus on digital and interactive media. Most recently, he has developed or co-developed a small handful of video games, some of which may eventually be available to the wider public. Despite spending far too much time trying to wring deeper meaning from ugly strings of code, he continues to play and record music in the post-punk band SPOILS and works with his partner on a number of artistic and political projects in and around the city. Most of all, he remains grateful for and inspired by the opportunity to collaborate with steadfast friends, loving family, and brilliant creative allies.

James Dumlao is a first-generation Filipino American multi-instrumentalist, educator, activist, and performer. From the classroom to the stage, his influences stem from critical ethnic studies pedagogy to formal and informal music training from San Francisco State University. As a people's artist, James has supported many community-based events and social-justice actions as a drummer, vocalist, and trumpet player for the band Dirty Boots, connecting his artistry to social justice and serving the people. James is a member of Salupongan International, a solidarity network which advocates for the Lumad (Indigenous peoples of Mindanao, Southern Philippines) and their right to self-determination and ancestral domain. James also is currently an ethnic studies and music teacher at Downtown High School in San Francisco, a project-based continuation school highly rooted in social justice, which provides alternative education to inner-city youth who have not been successful in traditional high schools. He is co-teacher of the MMARSS Project (Music and Math Alive in Resistance to Social Systems), and his students engage in music praxis, field experiences, and service learning around a social justice theme, culminating with composing, recording, and performing original songs that reflect what they have explored throughout the semester. James stands in solidarity with the people's struggle for self-determination and liberation.

Griffin Epstein self-identifies as a White settler and anti-Zionist Ashkenazi Jew who has been working in education, community organizing, and formal frontline social service provision since 2005. Griffin holds an M.A. and a Ph.D. from OISE/University of Toronto and currently teaches in the School of Social and Community Services at George Brown College. Griffin has musical roots in the New York City anti-folk scene and currently plays in the post-punk band SPOILS (http://torontospoils.bandcamp.com).

Patrick Huang, a.k.a. DJ Phatrick, is a second-generation Chinese American who started deejaying as a teenager at house parties in Sugar Land, Texas, before starting college in the Bay Area at UC Berkeley, where he became involved in grassroots activism, using hip-hop as a tool for organizing and education. After graduating, he co-founded the Oakland-based Bay Unity Music Project (BUMP), a music program for youth and young adults. Moving to Los Angeles in 2008, he combined his loves for music and education by running digital music programs that teach production, recording, and performance to youth in low-income neighborhoods through the Sessions L.A. program. As a musician, producer, and audio engineer, DJ Phatrick is a member, along with MCs Kiwi and Bambu, of the Native Guns, a political hip-hop group. He went on to produce much of Bambu's music, including the *Party Worker* and *Prey For The Devil* albums.

Jason Kao Hwang (composer/violin/viola) explores the vibrations and language of his history in his music. The 2018 El Intruso International Critics Poll voted him Violinist of the Year. Burning Bridge, his octet of Chinese and Western instruments, recently released *Blood*. *Jazziz Magazine* named their first album, *Burning Bridge*, one of the top albums of 2012. *Downbeat Magazine* named his quintet *Sing House* one of the best albums of 2017. His 2015 album, *Voice*, received critical acclaim. The 2012 Downbeat Critics' Poll voted him Rising Star for Violin. In 2011, his albums *Symphony of Souls*, for improvising orchestra, and *Crossroads Unseen*, by his quartet EDGE, received international acclaim. *Opera News* named his *The Floating Box: A Story in Chinatown*, one of the top ten opera recordings of 2005. As a violinist, he has worked with William Parker, Pauline Oliveros, Will Connell, Jr., Zen Matsuura, Butch Morris, Reggie Workman, Patrick Brennan, and Tomeka Reid. He has received support from Chamber Music America, U.S. Artists International, the National Endowment for the Arts (NEA), and the Rockefeller Foundation. For Young Audiences NY, he created cross-curricular methods to teach music and self-empowerment. He also taught Asian American music, a course he originated for New York University (NYU). Mr. Hwang currently teaches sound design at NYU.

Laura Kaminsky is a composer of opera, orchestra, chamber, vocal, and choral music with "an ear for the new and interesting" (*New York Times*). Recently cited in the *Washington Post* as "one of the top 35 female composers in classical music," her scores often address current social and political issues such as sustainability, war, and human rights. Her music is "full of fire as well as ice, written in an idiom that contrasts dissonance and violence with tonal beauty and meditative reflection" (*American Record Guide*). She recently made waves with her opera *As One* (co-librettists Mark Campbell and Kimberly Reed), which premiered at the Brooklyn Academy of Music (BAM) in 2014 and is now the most frequently performed contemporary opera in North America. In the 2017–2018 season, *As One* was the only opera by a living composer among the top 25 operas produced. Two more collaborations with Campbell and Reed include *Some Light Emerges*, for Houston Grand Opera and *Today It Rains*, for Opera Parallèle and American Opera Projects. With Reed, she has been commissioned by a consortium led by the Santa Fe Opera and San Francisco Opera to create a new opera, *Hometown to the World*, inspired by the Postville immigration raid. Other commissions include a piano quintet for Ursula Oppens and the Cassatt String Quartet, and her seventh string quartet for the Fry Street Quartet. Head of composition at Purchase College Conservatory of Music/SUNY, she is a composer-mentor at Washington National Opera's American Opera Initiative at the Kennedy Center. www.laurakaminsky.com

Chucky Kim is a Los Angeles-based music producer, mixing engineer, and bassist. Spanning genres, his unique production process incorporates unique generative environments to aid artists in exploring out-of-the-box creative experiences. He is currently artistic director of CultureHub Studios (Los Angeles), a creative center that explores the convergence of art and technology. He is also currently serving as an advisor/producer to BiotaBeats, an initiative of the MIT Media Lab and the East Meets West bookstore (EMW) in Boston. As a graduate of Harvard Divinity School, he has written extensively on community studies, the nature of creativity, and ethical formation. His most recent productions, *Great Sinners EP* (HC Smith) and *Ukulele Days* (Cynthia Lin), gained first-round Grammy nominations (Best Rock Song, Best Rock Album, Best Rock Performance) and *Billboard* #8 (World Albums) and #15 (Jazz Albums) respectively.

DJ L'Oqenz is a powerful, creative, and influential force. A deejay, producer, music director, sound designer, and cultural curator, L'Oqenz's passion for music and multi-layered creativity has garnered the attention of local and international audiences. From her home in Toronto to scenes in Los Angeles, New York, Singapore, the Caribbean and the U.K., her undeniable skills on the turntables, innovative musical vision, and respected artistic leadership have transcended the worlds of music, theatre, visual arts, and multi-media. Spinning and producing everything from hip-hop to progressive soul, world music to funk and Jazz, L'Oqenz's musical trajectory is travelling at the speed of hard-driven, beat-laden sound. (from www.thedrake.ca/happenings/2017/7/1/dj-lo qenz/)

Magali Meagher is founder and co-director of Girls Rock Camp Toronto, an organization that creates the conditions for girls and trans-identified youth to learn about themselves and others through music making. A musician with 20 years' experience, Meagher has performed and toured with The Phonemes, The Hidden Cameras, Hank, and Metal Kites, as well as touring extensively in North America and Europe as a solo artist. As a board member of Blocks Recording Club, she was active in bringing to life a vision to create alternative economies for music creation, promotion, and dissemination that has left a lasting impression on Toronto's independent music community. Meagher completed a master's degree in environmental studies at York University, where she researched arts-based learning environments and music and girlhood. She is currently a Toronto Arts Council Leaders Lab Fellow.

Casey Mecija is a multi-disciplinary artist and Ph.D. student (University of Toronto) whose work explores Filipinx futurity and aesthetics, the political potentials of popular culture, and psychoanalytic theories of aesthetics. Her essays and performances draw from queer theory, cultural studies, and diaspora studies. In particular, she theorizes the aesthetic experience of making and encountering sound that bears the trace of diasporic longing. Mecija's films have screened internationally and nationally, showcased in Canada at The Reel Asian Film Festival and Inside Out, Toronto's LGBTQ film festival. Mecija is also an award-winning multi-instrumentalist. She played in an orchestral pop band (Ohbijou) and, in 2016, released her first solo album, entitled *Psychic Materials*.

Nobuko Miyamoto is a song/dance/theater maker who began a career in films and Broadway but found her own voice in 1970 as an activist and troubadour in the Asian American movement, co-creating the album *A Grain of Sand*. Founding Great Leap (GL) in 1978 to create stage works reflecting the Asian American experience, she later transformed GL to respond to the 1992 L.A. Uprising, producing *A Slice of Rice, Frijoles and Greens* to collaborate with artists of color; after 9/11, she used the arts as a process to deepen understanding between faith communities. Climate change now has Nobuko and Dan Kwong creating environmental music videos—*BYO Chopstix, Mottainai*, and *Cycles of Change*— that can be seen on YouTube. Nobuko has created song and dances in the Japanese Obon tradition, danced by thousands at Obon Festivals. Partnering with Quetzal, she co-produces FandangObon, a pluri-ethnic festival celebrating art, culture, and environment. For more information, www.greatleap.org

Taiyo Na (Taiyo Ebato) is a musician, writer, and educator. His work spans two decades of cultural and pedagogical contributions to urban communities. He was honored in 2010 by Governor David A. Paterson and the State of New York for his "legacy of leadership to the Asian American community and the Empire State." The short film/music video to his 2008 song "Lovely To Me (Immigrant Mother)" was heralded by MTV Iggy as "the realest thing seen in a while." The 2010/2011 collaboration albums *Home:Word* and *Home:Word* [Deluxe Edition], with hip-hop duo Magnetic North, included a number of chart-topping songs in Asia, and his "Artist Takeovers" playlist was featured on Spotify in 2017. His writing has appeared in *Aperture, Hyphen*, and *Lantern*. As an educator, his areas of practice include transformative justice, culturally responsive pedagogy, inclusion, and coaching basketball.

Lee Phenner is an award-winning writer and holds an M.F.A. in creative writing from Emerson College, where she received Duprey awards for screenwriting and poetry and was selected for the Ploughshares International Fiction Seminar at Kasteel Well, Netherlands. Her creative works include the screenplay *Celia Now and Then*, which placed in the MORE Women in Film Screenplay Contest, and *Circle of the First*, a choral work co-written with Robert D. Terrio that premiered in 2010. She is a member of the Martin Luther King, Jr. Committee in Arlington, Massachusetts, StageSource, and the Small Theatre Alliance of Boston, and is an associate member of the Dramatists Guild of America. Her current work, the musical *A Pint of Understanding*, explores race and racism in the U.S. context. (www.apintofunderstandingthemusical.com/about).

SKIM weaves together stories of love and resilience through their sultry singing mixed with their fiery rap lyrics. They flow through elements of hip-hop and indigenous Korean cultures seemingly seamlessly, dedicated to cultivating their music further and playing their part in local and global struggles for social change. Their reach is continuously expanding as their soulful sounds break through emotional barriers and political borders—whether on HBO's *Def Poetry* or on Pacifica Radio, at college campuses or juvenile halls, at LGBT or senior care centers, harmonizing with the Chicago Children's Choir or chanting with the October 22nd Coalition to Stop Police Brutality, Repression and the Criminalization of a Generation. SKIM engages audiences everywhere and defies simple categorization. Along with working on collaborative multimedia and community-based projects, SKIM is currently a member of Koreatown Immigrant Workers' Alliance, Alternative Intervention Models, Tuesday Night Project, and ICU Love2Live. (from www.reverbnation.com/skimmusic)

Pete Shungu (stage name Afro D) is a trumpet and piano player, hip-hop emcee, and spoken-word artist who uses music as a tool to build community, protest injustice, and strive for positive social change. He has released two jazzy, soulful hip-hop albums, *Elevation* and *Strength in Numbers*, and has been featured on countless more albums with artists of all styles. He was born and raised in New Jersey and attended college at Tufts University. He then lived primarily in and around Boston before moving to the Midwest in January 2017, and settling in Champaign, Illinois, where he currently works at the University of Illinois and plays trumpet in a local R&B band called Nuclei. His roots extend way beyond these places, as his father is from the Democratic Republic of Congo and his mother is from Kansas. At times, he weaves his own multicultural and multiracial identity into his music. His father, Daniel Shungu, is a particular inspiration to him, having started his own nonprofit organization, United Front Against Riverblindness (www.riverblindness.org), which works to combat the debilitating disease of riverblindness in the DR Congo. Pete is a lifelong educator who has worked with youth in a variety of capacities: as a classroom teacher, college counselor, mentor, and workshop facilitator on topics ranging from challenging -isms to writing rhymes. He is also a family man, proud partner to Melissa and father to young daughters Malia and Naima.

Liz Stookey Sunde is the daughter of legendary folksinger and activist Noel Paul Stookey (Peter, Paul & Mary). She saw much of the world by the time she was 5. Growing up among artists dedicated to causes, she witnessed the profound capacity of music to enlighten audiences and drive action. Today, this perspective fuels her work as a change agent. For more than 25 years, Liz has helped nonprofit organizations develop creative solutions to their communication, organizational, and fundraising challenges. In addition, she has served for more than 15 years as founder and creative director of the nonprofit Music2Life (music2life.org), showing advocacy groups new ways to use music as a strategic communications tool. In this role, Liz has organized national social-justice songwriting contests, designed educational and entertainment events and tours, facilitated collaborations among artists, nonprofits, and community stakeholders, and developed online music-based resources to support the work of social movements. Liz lives in Wilder, Vermont, with her husband and two teenage sons.

Lise Vaugeois, Ph.D., lives in Thunder Bay, Ontario, where she is a conductor, composer, scholar and activist. Her research on music education and social justice is concerned with the role of "civilizing projects," as expressed in music education practices, in producing and rationalizing hierarchies of who counts as fully human. Her teaching is concerned with the development of pedagogical spaces in which educators and students can explore social, political, and philosophical issues, together with questions of signification (through musical experiences), with respect to public performance, community development, and social and material change. She teaches professional year and graduate courses at the Faculty of Education, Lakehead University. In addition to her university teaching, she has worked as an artist-educator in schools, community centers, and with incarcerated youth. She spends her free time kayaking on Lake Superior whenever she can.

Theresa "tvu" Vu is a senior vice president of engineering at AppNexus. tvu was the first developer hired at AppNexus and, with a tiny but dedicated team of engineers, built the real-time ad-serving system that is now the largest independent ad tech platform in the world (more than 150 billion impressions daily, globally). In 2015, she was named on LinkedIn's Next Wave list of the top ten professionals under 35 in marketing/advertising. When she is not coding, tvu is part of the hip-hop group Magnetic North and Taiyo Na, whose album *Home:Word* hit #3 on the Japanese hip-hop charts. *Home:Word [Deluxe Edition]* is a culmination of three years of creative partnership between artists Magnetic North and Taiyo Na. Without devaluing the concert tours, music videos, or newfound international success, Magnetic North and Taiyo Na are proudest of their Holla Benefit Concert Series (2009's Home for the Holla'Days, 2010's Home for the Holla'Days II and 2011's Holla for Japan), which have collectively raised over $30,000 for charity. Collaborating with other like-minded musicians to put on concerts to aid urgent causes has brought their passions for music and social responsibility together in the most fulfilling of ways.

References

Abeles, H. (2009). Are musical instrument gender associations changing? *Journal of Research in Music Education, 57*(2), 127–139.
Abrahams, F. (2005a). The application of critical pedagogy to music teaching and learning. *Visions of Research in Music Education, 6*, 1–16.
Abrahams, F. (2005b). Critical pedagogy for music education editorial. *Visions of Research in Music Education, 6*, 1–2.
Abrahams, F. (2006). Critical pedagogy for music education: A best practice to prepare future music educators. *Visions of Research in Music Education, 7*(1), 1–8.
Abrahams, F. (2007). Musicing Paulo Freire: A critical pedagogy for music education. In P. McLaren & J. L. Kincheloe (Eds.), *Critical pedagogy: Where are we now?* (pp. 223–237). New York: Peter Lang.
Abrahams, F. (2009). Hosanna, Hanukah, and hegemony: Anti-Semitism in the music classroom. In E. Gould, J. Countryman, C. Morton, & L. Stewart Rose (Eds.), *Exploring social justice: How music education might matter* (pp. 325–342). Toronto, ON: Canadian Music Educators' Association.
Abril, C. R. (2003). *Beyond content integration: Multicultural dimensions in the application of music teaching and learning* (Ph.D. dissertation), The Ohio State University, Columbus, Ohio.
Abril, C. R. (2010). Opening spaces in the instrumental music classroom. In A. C. Clements (Ed.), *Alternative approaches in music education: Case studies from the field* (pp. 3–14). Toronto, ON: Rowman & Littlefield Publishers.
Abril, C. R. (2012). A national anthem: Patriotic symbol or democratic action? In D. G. Hebert & A. Kertz-Welzel (Eds.), *Patriotism and nationalism in music education* (pp. 77–94). Burlington, VT: Ashgate.
Adamek, M. S., & Darrow, A.-A. (2010). *Music in special education* (2nd ed.). Silver Spring, MD: The American Music Therapy Association.
Adderley, C., Kennedy, M., & Berz, W. (2003). "A home away from home": The world of the high school music classroom. *Journal of Research in Music Education, 51*(3), 190–205.
Ahmed, S. (2000). *Strange encounters: Embodied others in post-coloniality*. New York: Routledge.
Aidi, H. D. (2014). *Rebel music: Race, empire, and the new Muslim youth culture*. New York: Vintage Books.
Akom, A. A. (2009). Critical hip hop pedagogy as a form of liberatory praxis. *Equity & Excellence in Education, 42*(1), 52–66. doi:10.1080/10665680802612519

References

Alibhai-Brown, Y. (2000). *After multiculturalism*. London: Foreign Policy Centre.

Alim, H. S. (2007). Critical hip-hop language pedagogies: Combat, consciousness, and the cultural politics of communication. *Journal of Language, Identity, and Education, 6*(2), 161–176. doi:10.1080/15348450701341378

Allsup, R. E. (2002). *Crossing over: Mutual learning and democratic action in instrumental music education* (Ed.D. doctoral dissertation). Columbia University, Teachers College, New York.

Allsup, R. E. (2003a). Mutual learning and democratic action in instrumental music education. *Journal of Research in Music Education, 51*(1), 24–37.

Allsup, R. E. (2003b). Praxis and the possible: Thoughts on the writings of Maxine Greene and Paulo Freire. *Philosophy of Music Education Review, 11*(2), 157–169.

Allsup, R. E. (2016). *Remixing the classroom: Toward an open philosophy of music education*. Bloomington: Indiana University Press.

Amagaolik, J. (2012). Reconciliation or conciliation? An Inuit perspective. In S. Rogers, M. DeGagné, J. Dewar, & G. Lowry (Eds.), *Speaking my truth: Reflections on reconciliation and residential schools* (Vol. 1, pp. 37–47). Ottawa, ON: Aboriginal Healing Foundation.

American Academy of Pediatrics (2009). Policy statement—Impact of music, music lyrics, and music videos on children and youth. *Pediatrics, 124*(5), 1488–1494. doi:10.1542/peds.2009-2145

Anderson, C. A., Carnagey, N. L., & Eubanks, J. (2003). Exposure to violent media: The effects of songs with violent lyrics on aggressive thoughts and feelings. *Journal of Personality and Social Psychology, 84*(5), 960–971. doi: 10.1037/0022-3514.84.5.960

Anyon, J. (1981). Social class and school knowledge. *Curriculum Inquiry, 11*(1), 3–42.

Apple, M. (2003). Freire and the politics of race in education. *International Journal of Leadership in Education, 6*(2), 107–118. doi:10.1080/13603120304821

Apple, M. (2004). *Ideology and curriculum*. New York: RoutledgeFalmer.

Applebaum, B. (2010). *Being White, being good: White complicity, White moral responsibility, and social justice pedagogy*. New York: Lexington Books.

Au, W. (2005). Fresh out of school: Rap music's discursive battle with education. *The Journal of Negro Education, 74*(3), 210–220.

Baker, F. (2013). Music therapists' perceptions of the impact of group factors on the therapeutic songwriting process. *Music Therapy Perspectives, 31*, 138–143.

Baker, F. (2015). What about the music? Music therapists' perspectives on the role of music in the therapeutic songwriting process. *Psychology Of Music, 43*(1), 122–139. doi:10.1177/0305735613498919

Baker, F., & Krout, R. E. (2012). Turning experience into learning: Educational contributions of collaborative peer songwriting during music therapy training. *International Journal of Music Education, 30*(2), 133–147. doi:10.1177/0255761411427103

Baker, F., Wigram, T., Stott, D., & McFerran, K. (2008). Therapeutic songwriting in music therapy. *Nordic Journal of Music Therapy, 17*(2), 105–123. doi:10.1080/08098130809478203

Banks, J. A. (2013). Multicultural education: Characteristics and goals. In J. A. Banks & C. A. McGee Banks (Eds.), *Multicultural education: Issues and perspectives* (8th ed., pp. 3–23). Hoboken, NJ: Wiley.

Bartel, L. (2004). Introduction: What is the music education paradigm? In L. Bartel (Ed.), *Questioning the music education paradigm* (pp. xii–xvi). Toronto, ON: Canadian Music Educators' Association.

Bates, V. (2012). Social class and school music. *Music Educators Journal*, *98*(4), 33–37.
Bejarano, B. L. S. (2005). Who are the oppressed? In C. A. Bowers & F. Apffel-Marglin (Eds.), *Rethinking Freire: Globalization and the environmental crisis* (pp. 48–67). Mahway, NJ: Lawrence Erlbaum Associates, Publishers.
Benedict, C. (2007). Naming our reality: Negotiating and creating meaning in the margin. *Philosophy of Music Education Review*, *15*(1), 23–35.
Benedict, C., Schmidt, P. K., Spruce, G., & Woodford, P. G. (Eds.) (2015). *The Oxford handbook of social justice in music education*. New York: Oxford University Press.
Berger, L. M. (2000). The emotional and intellectual aspects of protest music. *Journal of Teaching in Social Work*, *20*(1), 57–76. doi:10.1300/J067v20n01_05
Beverley, J. (1993). *Against literature*. Minneapolis: University of Minnesota Press.
Birkenshaw-Fleming, L. (Ed.) (1996). *An Orff mosaic from Canada*. Toronto, ON: Schott.
Boler, M. (1999). *Feeling power: Emotions and education*. New York and London: Routledge.
Bourdieu, P. (1973). Cultural reproduction and social reproduction. In R. Brown (Ed.), *Knowledge, education, and social change: Papers in the sociology of education* (pp. 71–112). London: Tavistock Publications.
Bowman, W. D. (2002a). Discernment, respons/ability, and the goods of philosophical praxis. *Action, Criticism & Theory for Music Education*, *1*(1), 2–36.
Bowman, W. D. (2002b). Educating musically. In R. Colwell & C. Richardson (Eds.), *The new handbook of research on music teaching and learning* (pp. 63–84). New York: Oxford University Press.
Bowman, W. (Ed.) (2007a). Theorizing social justice in music education. [Special issue]. *Action, Criticism & Theory for Music Education*, *6*(4).
Bowman, W. D. (2007b). Who's asking? (Who's answering?): Theorizing social justice in music education. *Action, Criticism & Theory for Music Education*, *6*(4), 1–20.
Bradley, D. (2003). *Singing in the dark: Choral music education and the other*. Paper presented at the Fifth International Symposium for the Philosophy of Music, Lake Forest College, IL. Retrieved from www.researchgate.net/publication/267624308_Singing_in_the_Dark_Choral_Music_Education_and_The_Other on December 23, 2017.
Bradley, D. (2006a). Education, multiculturalism, and anti-racism—Can we talk? *Action, Criticism & Theory for Music Education*, *5*(2), 1–30.
Bradley, D. (2006b). *Global song, global citizens? Multicultural choral music education and the community youth choir: Constituting the multicultural human subject* (Ph.D. dissertation), Ontario Institute for Studies in Education, University of Toronto, Toronto, ON.
Bradley, D. (2007). The sounds of silence: Talking race in music education. *Action, Criticism & Theory for Music Education*, *6*(4), 132–162.
Bradley, D. (2009a). Global song, global citizens? The world constructed in world music choral publications. In E. Gould, J. Countryman, C. Morton, & L. Stewart Rose (Eds.), *Exploring social justice: How music education might matter* (pp. 105–119). Toronto, ON: Canadian Music Educators' Association.
Bradley, D. (2009b). Oh that magic feeling! Multicultural human subjectivity, community, and fascism's footprints. *Philosophy of Music Education Review*, *17*(1), 56–74.
Bradley, D. (2012a). Avoiding the "P" word: Political contexts and multicultural music education. *Theory into Practice*, *51*(3), 188–195. doi:10.1080/00405841.2012.690296
Bradley, D. (2012b). *Living with ghosts: Trauma theory and pedagogy*. 2nd Symposium on LGBT Studies and Music Education. Retrieved from www.researchgate.net/publication/326881478_Living_with_Ghosts_Trauma_Theory_and_Pedagogy

Bradley, D. (2015). Hidden in plain sight: Race and racism in music education. In C. Benedict, P. K. Schmidt, G. Spruce, & P. G. Woodford (Eds.), *The Oxford handbook of social justice in music education* (pp. 190–203). New York: Oxford University Press.

Bradley, D. (2017). Standing in the shadows of Mozart: Music education, world music, and curricular change. In R. D. Moore (Ed.), *College music curricular for a new century* (pp. 205–222). New York: Oxford University Press.

Brady, J. (1994). Critical literacy, feminism and a politics of liberation. In P. McLaren & C. Lankshear (Eds.), *Politics of liberation: Paths from Freire* (pp. 142–143). London: Routledge.

Brant, J. (2017). Missing and murdered indigenous women and girls in Canada. *The Canadian Encyclopedia*. Retrieved from www.thecanadianencyclopedia.ca/en/article/missing-and-murdered-indigenous-women-and-girls-in-canada/

Brennan, S. (2011). Violent victimization of Aboriginal women in the Canadian provinces, 2009. *Component of statistics Canada catalogue*, 85–002-X. Minister of Industry, Statistics Canada. Retrieved from www.statcan.gc.ca/pub/85-002-x/2011001/article/11439-eng.pdf

Britzman, D. (1998). *Lost subjects, contested objects: Toward a psychoanalytic inquiry of learning*. Albany: State University of New York Press.

Britzman, D. (2000). If the story cannot end: Deferred action, ambivalence, and difficult knowledge. In R. I. Simon, S. Rosenberg, & C. Eppert (Eds.), *Between hope and despair: Pedagogy and the remembrance of historical trauma* (pp. 27–57). New York: Rowman & Littlefield Publishers, Inc.

Brooks, D. A. (2011). Nina Simone's triple play. *Callaloo, 34*(1), 176–197.

Brooks, J. (2015). Mass-mediated protest music and mobilization: Synthesizing the civil sphere's EMM-framing theory. *Theory in Action, 8*(3), 1–26. doi:10.3798/tia.1937-0237.15014

Brown, J. (2016). *The road to Soweto: Resistance and the uprising of 16 June 1976*. Rochester, NY: James Currey.

Bruner, J. S. (2006). *In search of pedagogy: Volume I*. New York: Routledge.

Buck-Morss, S. (2003). *Thinking past terror: Islamism and critical theory on the left*. New York: Verso.

Burnard, P. (2000). How children ascribe meaning to improvisation and composition: Rethinking pedagogy in music education. *Music Education Research, 2*(1), 7–23.

Burton, J. F., Roosevelt, E., & Cohen, I. J. (2002). *Confinement and ethnicity: An overview of World War II Japanese American relocation sites*. Seattle: University of Washington Press.

Bylica, K. (2018). *Subversive rabble-rousing: Interrupting school silencing*. Paper presented at the MayDay Group Colloquium 30: Understanding the Role of Curriculum in Contemporary Learning Communities, University of Western Ontario, London, ON.

Caldas, S. J. (2006). *Raising bilingual–biliterate children in monolingual cultures*. Tonawanda, NY: Multilingual Matters Ltd.

Campbell, K. A., Cook, L. J., LaFleur, B. J., & Keenan, H. T. (2010). Household, family, and child risk factors after an investigation for suspected child maltreatment: A missed opportunity for prevention. *Archives of Pediatrics & Adolescent Medicine, 164*(10), 943–949. doi:10.1001/archpediatrics.2010.166

Campbell, N. I., & LaFave, K. (2005). *Shi-shi-etko*. Toronto, ON: Groundwood Books, House of Anansi Press.

Campbell, P. S., Connell, C., & Beegle, A. (2007). Adolescents' expressed meanings of music in and out of school. *Journal of Research in Music Education, 55*(3), 220–236.

Caruth, C. (1993). Violence and time: Traumatic survivals. *Assemblage, 20*(April), 24–25.
Caruth, C., & Keenan, T. (1995). "The AIDS crisis is not over": A conversation with Gregg Bordowitz, Douglas Crimp, and Laura Pinsky. In C. Caruth (Ed.), *Trauma: Explorations in memory* (pp. 256–272). New York: Johns Hopkins University Press.
Castagno, A. E. (2014). *Educated in whiteness: Good intentions and diversity in schools*. Minneapolis: University of Minnesota Press.
Collins, P. H. (2000). *Black feminist thought: Knowledge, consciousness, and the politics of empowerment* (2nd ed.). New York: Routledge.
Colwell, R. (2005). Taking the temperature of critical pedagogy. *Visions of Research in Music Education, 6*, 1–15.
Connery, M. C., John-Steiner, V. P., & Marjanovic-Shane, A. (Eds.) (2010). *Vygotsky and creativity: A cultural-historical approach to play, meaning making, and the arts*. New York: Peter Lang.
Conway, C. M. (2000). Gender and musical instrument choice: A phenomenological investigation. *Bulletin of the Council for Research in Music Education, 146*, 1–16.
Countryman, J. (2009). Stumbling towards clarity: Practical issues in teaching global musics. In E. Gould, J. Countryman, C. Morton, & L. Stewart Rose (Eds.), *Exploring social justice: How music education might matter* (pp. 23–37). Toronto, ON: Canadian Music Educators' Association.
Crenshaw, K. (1995). Mapping the margins: Intersectionality, identity politics, and violence against women of color. In K. Crenshaw, N. Gotanda, G. Peller, & K. Thomas (Eds.), *Critical Race Theory: The Key Writings that Formed the Movement* (pp. 357–383). New York: The New Press.
Cross, I. (2014). Music and communication in music psychology. *Psychology Of Music, 42*(6), 809–819. doi:10.1177/0305735614543968
Cruz, C. (2012). Making curriculum from scratch: Testimonio in an urban classroom. *Equity & Excellence in Education, 45*(3), 460–471. doi:10.1080/10665684.2012.698185
Dairianathan, E., & Lum, C.-H. (2012). Soundscapes of a nation(alism): Perspectives from Singapore. In D. G. Hebert & A. Kertz-Welzel (Eds.), *Patriotism and nationalism in music education* (pp. 111–130). Burlington, VT: Ashgate.
Dale, J., & Hyslop-Margison, E. J. (2010). *Paulo Freire: Teaching for freedom and transformation—The philosophical influences on the work of Paulo Freire (Vol. 12)*. New York: Springer.
Dalton, T. A., & Krout, R. E. (2006). The grief song-writing process with bereaved adolescents: An integrated grief model and music therapy protocol. *Music Therapy Perspectives, 24*(2), 94–107.
Darder, A. (2017). *Reinventing Paulo Freire: A pedagogy of love* (2nd ed.). New York: Routledge.
Darder, A., Baltodano, M. P., & Torres, R. (2009). Critical pedagogy: An introduction. In A. Darder, M. P. Baltodano, & R. Torres (Eds.), *The critical pedagogy reader* (2nd ed., pp. 1–26). New York: Routledge.
Davis, J. F. (2001). *Who Is Black? One nation's definition*. University Park: Pennsylvania State University Press.
Davis, J. H. (2007). *Why our schools need the arts*. New York: Teachers College Press.
Dei, G. J. S. (2003). *Anti-racism education: Theory and practice*. Halifax, NS: Fernwood.
Dei, G. J. S. (2006). Introduction: Mapping the terrain—Towards a new politics of resistance. In G. J. S. Dei & A. Kempf (Eds.), *Anti-colonialism and education: The politics of resistance* (pp. 1–23). Rotterdam, NY: Sense Publishers.

Dei, G. J. S., & Asgharzadeh, A. (2001). The power of social theory: The anti-colonial discursive framework. *Journal of Educational Thought, 35*(3), 297–323.

Dei, G. J. S., & Sheth, A. (1997). Limiting the academics of possibilities: A self-reflective exercise in Freirian politics. In P. Freire, J. W. Fraser, D. Macedo, T. McKinnon, & W. T. Stokes (Eds.), *Mentoring the mentor: A critical dialogue with Paulo Freire* (pp. 143–173). New York: Peter Lang.

Deleuze, G., & Guattari, F. (2005/1987). *A thousand plateaus: Capitalism and schizophrenia* (B. Massumi, Trans.). Minneapolis: University of Minnesota Press.

Delgado, R. (2000). Storytelling for oppositionists and others: A plea for narrative. In R. Delgado & J. Stefancic (Eds.), *Critical race theory: The cutting edge* (2nd ed., pp. 60–70). Philadelphia, PA: Temple University Press.

Delgado, R., & Stefancic, J. (2001). *Critical race theory: An introduction*. New York: New York University Press.

Delpit, L. D. (2006/1995). *Other people's children: Cultural conflict in the classroom*. New York: The New Press.

Delpit, L. D. (2012). *"Multiplication is for White people": Raising expectations for other people's children*. New York: The New Press.

DeNora, T. (2000). *Music in everyday life*. Cambridge, U.K.: Cambridge University Press.

DeNora, T. (2013). "Time after time": A Quali-T method for assessing music's impact on well-being. *International Journal of Qualitative Studies on Health and Well-Being, 8*(1), 1–13. doi:10.3402/qhw.v8i0.20611

Dewey, J. (1966). *Democracy and education*. New York: Free Press.

DiAngelo, R. (2011). White fragility. *International Journal of Critical Pedagogy, 3*(3), 54–70.

Draves, T. J. (2008). Music achievement, self-esteem, and aptitude in a college songwriting class. *Bulletin of the Council for Research in Music Education, 178*(Fall), 35–46.

Elliott, D. J. (1995). *Music matters: A new philosophy of music education*. Oxford, U.K.: Oxford University Press.

Elliott, D. J. (Ed.) (2005). *Praxial Music Education: Reflections and Dialogues*. New York: Oxford University Press.

Elliott, D. J., & Silverman, M. (2015). *Music matters: A philosophy of music education* (2nd ed.). New York: Oxford University Press.

Elliott, D. J., Silverman, M., & Bowman, W. D. (Eds.) (2016). *Artistic citizenship: Artistry, social responsibility, and ethical praxis*. New York: Oxford University Press.

Ellsworth, E. (1989). Why doesn't this feel empowering: Working through the repressive myths of critical pedagogy. *Harvard Educational Review, 59*(3), 297–324.

Ellsworth, E. (1997). *Teaching positions: Difference, pedagogy, and the power of address*. New York: Teachers College Press.

Elpus, K. (2015). National estimates of male and female enrolment in American high school choirs, bands and orchestras. *Music Education Research, 17*(1), 88–102. doi:10.1080/14613808.2014.972923

Elpus, K., & Abril, C. R. (2011). High school music ensemble students in the United States: A demographic profile. *Journal of Research in Music Education, 59*(2), 128–145. doi:10.1177/0022429411405207

Elpus, K., & Carter, B. (2016). Bullying victimization among music ensemble and theatre students in the United States. *Journal of Research in Music Education, 64*(3), 322–343. doi:10.1177/0022429416658642

English Oxford Living Dictionaries (2019). "Fascism." Retrieved from https://en.oxforddictionaries.com/definition/fascism on March 6, 2019.

Eppert, C. (2000). Relearning questions: Responding to the ethical address of past and present others. In R. I. Simon, S. Rosenberg, & C. Eppert (Eds.), *Between hope and despair: Pedagogy and the remembrance of historical trauma* (pp. 213–230). New York: Rowman & Littlefield Publishers, Inc.

Escobar, E. (1994). The heuristic power of art. In C. Becker (Ed.), *The subversive imagination: Artists, society, and responsibility*. New York: Routledge.

Eyerman, R., & Jamison, A. (1998). *Music and social movements: Mobilizing traditions in the twentieth century*. New York: Cambridge University Press.

Fanon, F. (1963). *The wretched of the earth* (R. Philcox, Trans.). New York: Grove Press.

Fearnow, B. (2014). Teacher suspended for assigning Lil Wayne lyrics as homework. *CBS Tampa Bay*, February 4. Retrieved from https://tampa.cbslocal.com/2014/02/04/teacher-suspended-for-assigning-lil-wayne-lyrics-as-homework/ on November 26, 2018.

Feld, S. (2000a). The poetics and politics of Pygmy pop. In G. Born & D. Hesmondhalgh (Eds.), *Western music and its Others: Difference, representation, and appropriation in music* (pp. 254–279). Los Angeles: University of California Press.

Feld, S. (2000b). A sweet lullaby for world music. *Public Culture*, *12*(1), 145–171.

Feld, S. (2005a). From schizophonia to schismogenesis: On the discourses and commodification practices of "world music" and "world beat." In C. Keil & S. Feld (Eds.), *Music Grooves* (2nd ed., pp. 257–289). Tuscon, AZ: Fenestra Books.

Feld, S. (2005b). Notes on "world beat." In C. Keil & S. Feld (Eds.), *Music Grooves* (2nd ed., pp. 238–246). Tuscon, AZ: Fenestra Books.

Ferrara, M. H., & LaMeau, M. P. (2015). Active or reflective listening. In M. H. Ferrara & M. P. LaMeau (Eds.), *Social skills* (pp. 54–59). Farmington Hills, MI: Gale.

Fiore, M. (2015). Pedagogy for liberation: Spoken word poetry in urban schools. *Education and Urban Society*, *47*(7), 813–829. doi:10.1177/0013124513511269

Fitzpatrick, K. R. (2013). Motherhood and the high school band director: A case study. *Bulletin of the Council for Research in Music Education*, *196*, 7–23. doi:10.5406/bulcouresmusedu.196.0007

Folkestad, G. (2002). National identity and music. In R. A. R. MacDonald, D. J. Hargreaves, & D. Miell (Eds.), *Musical identities* (pp. 151–162). New York: Oxford University Press.

Foucault, M. (1983). Afterword—On the genealogy of ethics: An overview of work in progress. In H. L. Dreyfus & P. Rabinow (Eds.), *Michel Foucault: Beyond structuralism and hermeneutics* (2nd ed., pp. 229–252). Chicago, IL: University of Massachusetts Press.

Foucault, M. (1994). Security, territory, and population. In P. Rabinow & N. Rose (Eds.), *The essential Foucault: Selections from the essential works of Foucault 1954–1984* (pp. 259–262). New York: The New Press.

Freire, P. (1970a). The adult literacy process as cultural action for freedom. *Harvard Educational Review*, *40*(2), 205–225.

Freire, P. (1970b). Cultural action and conscientization. *Harvard Educational Review*, *40*(3), 452–477.

Freire, P. (1971). *Pedagogy of the oppressed* (M. B. Ramos, Trans.). New York: Herder and Herder.

Freire, P. (1985). *The politics of education: Culture, power, and liberation*. New York: Bergin & Garvey.

Freire, P. (1993). *Pedagogy of the city*. New York: The Continuum Publishing Company.

Freire, P. (1994). *Education for critical consciousness*. New York: Continuum.

Freire, P. (1998a). *Pedagogy of freedom: Ethics, democracy, and civic courage*. New York: Rowman & Littlefield.

Freire, P. (1998b). *Pedagogy of hope: Reliving pedagogy of the oppressed*. New York: Bloomsbury.

Freire, P. (2000). *Pedagogy of the heart*. New York: Continuum.

Freire, P. (2000/1970). *Pedagogy of the oppressed: 30th anniversary edition* (M. Bergman Ramos, Trans.). New York: Continuum.

Freire, P., & Macedo, D. (1987). *Literacy: Reading the word and the world*. London: Routledge.

Freire, P., & Macedo, D. (1998). *The Paulo Freire reader*. New York: Continuum.

Frith, S. (1996). Music and identity. In S. Hall & P. Du Gay (Eds.), *Questions of cultural identity*. London: SAGE Publications.

Gadotti, M., & Torres, C. A. (2009). Paulo Freire: Education for development. *Development and Change, 40*(6), 1255–1267.

Garfield, L. (2017). Thousands of women will wear pink "pussy hats" the day after Trump's inauguration. *Business Insider*, January 18. Retrieved from www.businessinsider.com/pussy-hats-womens-march-washington-trump-inauguration-2017-1 on December 22, 2017.

Gay, G. (2018). *Culturally responsive teaching: Theory, research, and practice* (3rd ed.). New York: Teachers College Press.

Gaztambide-Fernández, R. (2008). The artist in society: Understandings, expectations, and curriculum implications. *Curriculum Inquiry, 38*(3), 233–265.

Gilbert, S. (2007). Singing against Apartheid: ANC cultural groups and the international anti-Apartheid struggle. *Journal of Southern African Studies, 33*(2), 421–441.

Gilmore, S. (2017). Trump, taking a knee in the NFL and the true meaning of patriotism. *Maclean's Canada*, September 24. Retrieved from www.macleans.ca/news/world/trump-taking-a-knee-in-the-nfl-and-the-true-meaning-of-patriotism/ on December 30, 2017.

Giroux, H. A. (2006). *Stormy weather: Katrina and the politics of disposability*. Boulder, CO: Paradigm Publishers.

Giroux, H. A. (2009). Critical theory and educational practice. In A. Darder, M. P. Baltodano, & R. Torres (Eds.), *The critical pedagogy reader* (2nd ed., pp. 27–51). New York: Routledge.

Giroux, H. A. (2017a). Forward: Paulo Freire and the courage to be political. In A. Darder (Ed.), *Reinventing Paulo Freire: A pedagogy of love* (2nd ed., pp. xi–xvii). New York: Routledge.

Giroux, H. A. (2017b). White nationalism, armed culture and state violence in the age of Donald Trump. *Philosophy and Social Criticism, 20*(10), 1–24. doi:10.1177/0191453717702800

Giroux, H. A., & Giroux, S. S. (2004). *Take back higher education: Race, youth, and the crisis of democracy in the post-Civil Rights era*. New York: Palgrave Macmillan.

Goldberg, D. T. (1993). *Racist culture: Philosophy and the politics of meaning*. Cambridge, U.K.: Blackwell.

Goldberg, D. T. (2009). *The threat of race: Reflections on racial neoliberalism*. Malden, MA: Wiley-Blackwell.

Goldwin, R. A., & Kaufman, A. (Eds.) (1988). *Slavery and its consequences: The constitution, equality, and race*. Washington, D.C.: American Enterprise Institute for Public Policy Research.

Gordon, M. (2009). Toward a pragmatic discourse of constructivism: Reflections on lessons from practice. *Educational Studies, 45*(1), 39–58. doi:10.1080/00131940802546894

Gould, E. (1992). Gender-specific occupational role models: Implications for music educators. *Update: Applications of Research in Music Education, 11*(1), 8–12.

Gould, E. (1994). Getting the whole picture: The view from here. *Philosophy of Music Education Review, 2*(2), 92–98.

Gould, E. (1996). *Initial involvements and continuity of women college band directors: The presence of gender-specific occupational role models* (Ph.D. dissertation), University of Oregon, Eugene.

Gould, E. (2007). Social justice in music education: The problematic of democracy. *Music Education Research, 9*(2), 229–240.

Gould, E. (2008). Devouring the other: Democracy in music education. *Action, Criticism, and Theory for Music Education, 7*(1), 29–44.

Gould, E. (2013). Companion-able species: A queer pedagogy for music education. *Bulletin of the Council for Research in Music Education, 197*, 63–76.

Gould, E., Countryman, J., Morton, C., & Stewart Rose, L. (Eds.) (2009). *Exploring social justice: How music education might matter.* Toronto, ON: Canadian Music Educators' Association.

Goulet, D. (Ed.) (1996). *Education for critical consciousness.* New York: Continuum Publishing.

Gowan, J. (2016). A polysemy of meanings: Music education for critical pedagogy. *Canadian Music Educator, 57*(3), 23–28.

Grande, S. (2010). Red pedagogy. *Counterpoints, TEACH BOLDLY! Letters to teachers about contemporary issues in education, 356*, 199–207.

Grant, D. E. (2000). *The impact of mentoring and gender-specific role models on women college band directors at four different career stages* (Ph.D. dissertation), University of Minnesota, Minneapolis.

Green, L. (2001). *How popular musicians learn: A way ahead for music education.* New York: Ashgate Press.

Green, L. (2002). Exposing the gendered discourse of music education. *Feminism & Psychology, 12*(2), 137–144.

Green, L. (2003). Music education, cultural capital, and social group identity. In M. Clayton, T. Herbert, & R. Middleton (Eds.), *The cultural study of music: A critical introduction* (pp. 263–273). New York: Routledge.

Green, L. (2008). *Music, informal learning and the school: A new classroom pedagogy.* London: Ashgate.

Greene, M. (1978). *Landscapes of Learning.* New York: Teachers College Press.

Greene, M. (1982). Education and disarmament. *Teachers College Record, 84*(1), 128–136.

Greene, M. (1995). *Releasing the imagination: Essay on education, the arts, and social change.* San Francisco, CA: Jossey-Bass.

Greene, M. (2000). Imagining futures: The public school and possibility. *Journal of Curriculum Studies, 32*(2), 267–280. doi:10.1080/002202700182754

Greene, M. (2001). *Variations on a blue guitar: The Lincoln Center Institute lectures on aesthetic education.* New York: Teachers College Press.

Greene, S., Burke, K. J., & McKenna, M. K. (2013). Forms of voice: Exploring the empowerment of youth at the intersection of art and action. *The Urban Review, 45*, 311–334.

Grigsby Bates, K. (2017). Race and feminism: Women's March recalls the touchy history. *NPR*, January 21. Retrieved from www.npr.org/sections/codeswitch/2017/01/21/510859909/race-and-feminism-womens-march-recalls-the-touchy-history on December 22, 2017.

Gurgel, R. (2016). *Taught by the students: Culturally relevant pedagogy and deep engagement in music education*. Lanham, MD: Rowman & Littlefield.

Gustafson, R. I. (2009). *Race and curriculum: Music in childhood education*. New York: Palgrave Macmillan.

Hall, S. (1997). The spectacle of the "Other." In S. Hall (Ed.), *Representation: Cultural representations and signifying practices* (pp. 223–290). London: SAGE Publications Ltd.

Hall, S. (2003). Creolization, diaspora, and hybridity in the context of globalization. In O. Enwezor, C. Basualdo, U. M. Bauer, S. Ghez, S. Maharaj, M. Nash, & O. Zaya (Eds.), *Créolité and creolization: Documenta 11 platform 3*. Ostfildern, Germany: Hatje Cantz.

Hallman, H. L. (2009). "Dear Tupac, you speak to me": Recruiting hip hop as curriculum at a school for pregnant and parenting teens. *Equity & Excellence in Education, 42*(1), 36–51. doi:10.1080/10665680802612642

Hanisch, C. (2006/1969). The personal is political. In S. Firestone & A. Koedt (Eds.), *Notes from the second year: Women's liberation: Major writings of the radical feminists*. New York: Radical Feminism.

Hartman, S. V. (1997). *Scenes of subjection: Terror, slavery, and self-making in 19th century America*. New York: Oxford University Press.

Hartocollis, A., & Alcindor, Y. (2017). Women's March highlights as huge crowds protest Trump: "We're not going away." *The New York Times*, January 21. Retrieved from www.nytimes.com/2017/01/21/us/womens-march.html on December 22, 2017.

Haynes, D. J. (1997). *The vocation of the artist*. New York: Cambridge University Press.

Hebert, D. G., & Kertz-Welzel, A. (2012). Introduction. In D. G. Hebert & A. Kertz-Welzel (Eds.), *Patriotism and nationalism in music education* (pp. 1–6). Burlington, VT: Ashgate.

Hess, J. (2008). *The Sankofa Drum & Dance Ensemble: An opportunity for growth and exploration* (M.Mus.Ed. major research paper), University of Toronto. Toronto, ON.

Hess, J. (2010). The Sankofa Drum and Dance Ensemble: Motivations for student participation in a school world music ensemble. *Research Studies in Music Education, 32*(1), 23–42.

Hess, J. (2013a). Performing tolerance and curriculum: The politics of self-congratulation, identity formation, and pedagogy in world music education. *Philosophy of Music Education Review, 21*(1), 66–91.

Hess, J. (2013b). *Radical musicking: Challenging dominant paradigms in elementary music education* (Ph.D. dissertation), University of Toronto, Toronto. Retrieved from https://tspace.library.utoronto.ca/handle/1807/43593

Hess, J. (2014). Radical musicking: Toward a pedagogy of social change. *Music Education Research, 16*(3), 229–250. doi:10.1080/14613808.2014.909397.

Hess, J. (2015a). Decolonizing music education: Moving beyond tokenism. *International Journal of Music Education, 33*(3), 336–347.

Hess, J. (2015b). Upping the "anti-": The value of an anti-racist theoretical framework in music education. *Action, Criticism & Theory for Music Education, 14*(1), 66–92.

Hess, J. (2016). Balancing the counterpoint: Exploring musical contexts and relations. *Action, Criticism & Theory for Music Education, 15*(2), 46–72.

Hess, J. (2017). "How does that apply to me?" The gross injustice of having to translate. *Bulletin of the Council for Research in Music Education, 207–208*, 81–100. doi: www.jstor.org/stable/10.5406/bulcouresmusedu.207-208.0081

Hess, J. (2018a). Detroit youth speak back: Rewriting deficit perspectives through songwriting. *Bulletin of the Council for Research in Music Education, 216*, 7–30.

Hess, J. (2018b). A "discomfortable" approach to "world music": Reenvisioning contextualized "world music education." *Philosophy of Music Education Review, 26*(1), 24–45. doi:10.2979/philmusieducrevi.26. 1. 03

Hess, J. (2018c). Musicking marginalization: Periphractic practices in music education. In A. M. Kraehe, R. Gaztambide-Fernández, & B. S. Carpenter II (Eds.), *The Palgrave handbook of race and the arts in education* (pp. 325–346): Cham, Switzerland: Palgrave Macmillan.

Hess, J. (2018d). Revolutionary activism in striated spaces? Considering an activist music education in K-12 schooling. *Action, Criticism & Theory for Music Education, 17*(2), 22–49. doi:10.22176/act17. 2. 21

Hess, J. (2018e). Troubling whiteness: Navigating white subjectivity in music education. *International Journal of Music Education, 36*(2), 128–144. doi:10.1177/ 0255761417703781

Hess, J. (2019). Singing our own song: Navigating identity politics through activism in music. *Research Studies in Music Education, 41*(1), 61–80. doi:10.1177/ 1321103X18773094

Hess, J., Watson, V. W. M., & Deroo, M. (2019). "Show some love": Enacting literacy presence and musical presence as civic engagement in the Verses Project. *Teachers College Record, 121*(5), Online first. Retrieved from: www.tcrecord.org/Content.asp?ContentId=22662

Hickey, M. (1997). The computer as a tool in creative music making. *Research Studies in Music Education, 8*(1), 56–70. doi:10.1177/1321103X9700800106

Hill, M. L. (2009). Wounded healing: Forming a storytelling community in Hip-Hop Lit. *Teachers College Record, 111*(1), 248–293.

Hill, M. L., & Petchauer, E. (2013). *Schooling hip-hop: Expanding hip-hop based education across the curriculum*. New York: Teachers College Press.

Hirsch, L. (Writer) (2002). *Amandla! A revolution in four-part harmony*. In S. Simpson & L. Hirsch (Producers). Canada: Alliance Atlantis.

Hoffman, A. R. (2012). Performing our world: Affirming cultural diversity through music education. *Music Educators Journal, 98*(4), 61–65. doi:10.1177/ 0027432112443262

Hollindale, P. (1988). *Ideology and the children's book*. Oxford, U.K.: The Thimble Press.

hooks, b. (1992). *Black looks: Race and representation*. Boston, MA: South End Press.

hooks, b. (1994). *Teaching to transgress: Education as the practice of freedom*. New York: Routledge.

hooks, b. (2008/1994). *Outlaw culture: Resisting representations*. New York: Routledge.

Horton, M. (1998). *The long haul: An autobiography*. New York: Teachers College Press.

Horton, M., & Freire, P. (1990). *We make the road by walking: Conversations on education and social change*. Philadelphia, PA: Temple University Press.

Howard, T. C. (2013). How does it feel to be a problem? Black male students, schools, and learning in enhancing the knowledge base to disrupt deficit frameworks. *Review of Research in Education, 37,* 54–86.

Hyun, E. (2006). *Teachable moments: Re-conceptualizing curricula understandings.* New York: Peter Lang.

Jorgensen, E. R. (1995). Justifying music instruction in American public schools: A historical perspective. *Arts Education Policy Review, 96*(6), 31–38.

Juntunen, M.-L., Karlsen, S., Kuoppamäki, A., Laes, T., & Muhonen, S. (2014). Envisioning imaginary spaces for musicking: Equipping students for leaping into the unexplored. *Music Education Research, 16*(3), 251–266. doi:10.1080/14613808.2014.899333

Kanaaneh, M., Thornsén, S.-M., Bursheh, H., & McDonald, D. A. (Eds.) (2013). *Palestinian music and song: Expression and resistance since 1900.* Bloomington: Indiana University Press.

Kaschub, M. (2009). Critical pedagogy for creative artists: Inviting young composers to engage in artistic social action. In E. Gould, J. Countryman, C. Morton, & L. Stewart Rose (Eds.), *Exploring social justice: How music education might matter* (pp. 274–291). Toronto, ON: Canadian Music Educators' Association.

Kaschub, M., & Smith, J. (Eds.) (2013). *Composing our future: Preparing music educators to teach composition.* New York: Oxford University Press.

Keil, C. (2005). Participatory discrepancies and the power of music. In C. Keil & S. Feld (Eds.), *Music Grooves* (2nd ed.). Tuscon, AZ: Fenestra Books.

Keil, C., & Feld, S. (2005). *Music Grooves* (2nd ed.). Tucson, AZ: Fenestra Books.

Kelly, D. M., & Brooks, M. (2009). How young is too young? Exploring beginning teachers' assumptions about young children and teaching for social justice. *Equity & Excellence in Education, 42*(2), 202–216. doi:10.1080/10665680902739683

Kennedy, M. (2004). Put the "play" back in music education. In L. Bartel (Ed.), *Questioning the music education paradigm* (pp. 62–73). Toronto, ON: Canadian Music Educators' Association.

Kennedy, M. A. (2002). "It's cool because we like to sing": Junior high school boys' experience of choral music as an elective. *Research Studies in Music Education, 18* (June), 24–34.

Kennedy-Moore, E., & Watson, J. C. (2001). How and when does emotional expression help? *Review of General Psychology, 5*(3), 187–212.

Kertz-Welzel, A. (2005). The pied piper of Hamelin: Adorno on music education. *Research Studies in Music Education, 25*(1), 1–12. doi:10.1177/1321103X050250010301

Kertz-Welzel, A. (2012). Lesson learned? In search of patriotism and nationalism in the German music education curriculum. In D. G. Hebert & A. Kertz-Welzel (Eds.), *Patriotism and nationalism in music education* (pp. 23–42). Burlington, VT: Ashgate.

Kincheloe, J. L. (2009). Critical complexity and participatory action research: Decolonizing "democratic" knowledge production. In D. Kapoor & S. Jordan (Eds.), *Education, participatory action research, and social change: International perspectives* (pp. 107–121). New York: Palgrave Macmillan.

Kinney, A. (2012). Loops, lyrics, and literacy: Songwriting as a site of resilience for an urban adolescent. *Journal of Adolescent & Adult Literacy, 55*(5), 395–404.

Kirylo, J. D. (2011). Freirian themes. *Counterpoints, 385,* 143–163.

Klarman, M. J. (2004). *From Jim Crow to Civil Rights: The Supreme Court and the struggle for racial equality.* New York: Oxford University Press.

Klinger, R. (1996). *Matters of compromise: An ethnographic study of culture-bearers in elementary music education* (Ph.D. dissertation), University of Washington, Seattle, WA.

Koza, J. E. (1992a). The boys in the band: Sexism and the construction of gender. *The Journal of Educational Foundations*, *6*(3), 85–105.

Koza, J. E. (1992b). Picture this: Sex equity in textbook illustrations. *Music Educators Journal*, *78*(7), 28–33.

Koza, J. E. (1993). The "missing males" and other gender issues in music education: Evidence from the *Music Supervisors' Journal*, 1914–1924. *Journal of Research in Music Education*, *41*(3), 212–232.

Koza, J. E. (1994a). Aesthetic music education revisited: Discourses of exclusion and oppression. *Philosophy of Music Education Review*, *2*(2), 75–91.

Koza, J. E. (1994b). Big boys don't cry (or sing): Gender, misogyny, and homophobia in college choral methods texts. *The Quarterly Journal of Music Teaching and Learning*, *4*(4), 48–64.

Koza, J. E. (1994c). Females in 1988 middle school music textbooks: An analysis of illustrations. *Journal of Research in Music Education*, *42*(2), 145–171.

Koza, J. E. (1994d). Getting a word in edgewise: A feminist critique of choral methods texts. *The Quarterly Journal of Music Teaching and Learning*, *5*(3), 68–77.

Koza, J. E. (2006). "Save the music"? Toward culturally relevant, joyful, and sustainable school music. *Philosophy of Music Education Review*, *14*(1), 23–38.

Koza, J. E. (2008). Listening for Whiteness: Hearing racial politics in undergraduate school music. *Philosophy of Music Education Review*, *16*(2), 145–155.

Kozol, J. (1991). *Savage inequalities: Children in America's schools*. New York: Broadway Paperbacks.

Kozol, W. (2017). White privilege and the pussy hat. *Reading the Pictures*, March 2. Retrieved from www.readingthepictures.org/2017/03/feminism-race-pussy-hat/ on November 23, 2018.

Kratus, J. (2013). Preparing music educators to facilitate songwriting. In M. Kaschub & J. Smith (Eds.), *Composing our future: Preparing music educators to teach composition* (pp. 267–282). New York: Oxford University Press.

Kratus, J. (2016). Songwriting: A new direction for secondary music education. *Music Educators Journal*, *102*(3), 60–65. doi:10.1177/0027432115620660

Kruse, A. (2016). Toward hip-hop pedagogies for music education. *International Journal of Music Education*, *34*(2), 247–260. doi:10.1177/0255761414550535

Kuntz, A. M. (2015). *The responsible methodologist: Inquiry, truth-telling, and social justice*. Walnut Creek, CA: Left Coast Press.

Ladson-Billings, G. (1995). Toward a theory of culturally relevant pedagogy. *American Education Research Journal*, *32*(3), 465–491.

Ladson-Billings, G. (1997). I know why this doesn't feel empowering: A critical race analysis of critical pedagogy. In P. Freire, J. W. Fraser, D. Macedo, T. McKinnon, & W. T. Stokes (Eds.), *Mentoring the mentor: A critical dialogue with Paulo Freire* (pp. 127–141). New York: Peter Lang.

Ladson-Billings, G. (1998). Just what is critical race theory and what's it doing in a nice field like education? *Qualitative Studies in Education*, *11*(1), 7–24.

Ladson-Billings, G. (2009). *The dream keepers: Successful teachers of African American children* (2nd ed.). San Francisco, CA: Jossey-Bass.

Ladson-Billings, G. (2015). You gotta fight the power: The place of music in social justice education. In C. Benedict, P. K. Schmidt, G. Spruce, & P. G. Woodford (Eds.), *The Oxford handbook of social justice in music education* (pp. 406–419). New York: Oxford University Press.

Laird, L. (2015). Empathy in the classroom: Can music bring us more in tune with one another? *Music Educators Journal, 101*(4), 56–61. doi:10.1177/0027432115572230

Lamb, R. (1987). *Including women composers in music curricula: Development of creative strategies for the general music classes, gr. 5–8.* (Ph.D. dissertation), Teachers' College, Columbia University, New York.

Lamb, R. (1994a). Aria senza accompagnamento: A woman behind the theory. *The Quarterly Journal of Music Teaching and Learning, 4/5*(5, 1), 5–20.

Lamb, R. (1994b). Feminism as critique in philosophy of music education. *Philosophy of Music Education Review, 2*(2), 59–74.

Lamb, R. (1996). Discords: Feminist pedagogy in music education. *Theory into Practice, 35*(2), 124–131.

Lamm, C., & Silani, G. (2014). Insights into collective emotions from the social neuroscience of empathy. In C. von Scheve & M. Salmela (Eds.), *Collective emotions: Perspectives from psychology, philosophy, and sociology* (pp. 63–77). Oxford, U.K.: Oxford University Press.

Lankshear, C., & McLaren, P. (1993). *Critical literacy: Politics, praxis, and the postmodern.* Albany: State University of New York Press.

Lareau, A. (2011). *Unequal childhoods: Class, race, and family life.* Berkeley: University of California Press.

Lareau, A., & Goyette, K. A. (Eds.) (2014). *Choosing homes, choosing schools.* New York: Russell Sage Foundation.

Lashbrook, S., & Mantie, R. (2009). Valuing subjugated experience: The One World Youth Arts Project. In E. Gould, J. Countryman, C. Morton, & L. Stewart Rose (Eds.), *Exploring social justice: How music education might matter* (pp. 292–303). Toronto, ON: Canadian Music Educators' Association.

Lather, P. (1998). Critical pedagogy and its complicities: A praxis of stuck places. *Educational Theory, 48*(4), 487–497.

Lewis, A., & Smith, D. C. (1993). Defining higher order thinking. *Theory into Practice, 32*(3), 131–137.

Lewis, J. (2016). *Musical voices from the margins: Popular music as a site of critical negotiation in an urban elementary classroom.* (Ed.D. dissertation), Teachers College, Columbia University, New York.

Lind, V. L., & McKoy, C. L. (2016). *Culturally responsive teaching in music education: From understanding to application.* New York: Routledge.

Lorde, A. (2007/1984). *Sister outsider: Essays and speeches.* Berkeley, CA: The Crossing Press.

Lundqvist, L.-O., Carlsson, F., Hilmersson, P., & Juslin, P. N. (2009). Emotional responses to music: Experience, expression, and physiology. *Psychology Of Music, 37*(1), 61–90. doi:10.1177/0305735607086048

MacDonald, D. B., & Hudson, G. (2012). The genocide question and Indian residential schools in Canada. *Canadian Journal of Political Science, 45*(2), 427–449.

MacDonald, R. A. R., Hargreaves, D. J., & Miell, D. (Eds.) (2002). *Musical identities.* Oxford: Oxford University Press.

Macedo, D. (1994). *Literacies of power: What Americans are allowed to know.* Boulder, CO: Westview Press, Inc.

MacKay, R. (2009). Teacher, teacher, can you reach me? What we can learn about teaching music from Canadian female pop musicians. In E. Gould, J. Countryman,

C. Morton, & L. Stewart Rose (Eds.), *Exploring social justice: How music education might matter* (pp. 184–198). Toronto, ON: Canadian Music Educators' Association.

MacKinnon, M. (2016). Is Austria's Norbert Hofer the Trump of Europe's far right? Not quite—he's learned how to play nice. *The Globe and Mail*, September 9. Retrieved from www.theglobeandmail.com/news/world/is-austrias-norbert-hofer-the-trump-of-europes-far-right-no-hes-learned-how-to-benice/article31792343/

Manne, K. (2015). Why I use trigger warnings. *The New York Times*, September 19, 2015. Retrieved from www.nytimes.com/2015/09/20/opinion/sunday/why-i-use-trigger-warnings.html

Marsh, S. (2017). "This is exactly what he wants": How Geert Wilders won by losing. *The Atlantic*, March 16. Retrieved from www.theatlantic.com/international/archive/2017/03/geert-wilders-won-by-losing-netherlands-vote/519834/

Martignetti, F., Talbot, B. C., Clauhs, M., Hawkins, T., & Niknafs, N. (2013). "You got to know us": A hopeful model for music education in schools. *Visions of Research in Music Education*, *23*, 1–27.

Masekela, H. (1977). Soweto blues. On *You told your mama not to worry*. (www.discogs.com/Masekela-You-Told-Your-Mama-Not-To-Worry/release/1674365). Casablanca—NBLP 7079.

Mato, D. (2004). Communication for social change in Latin America: Contexts, theories, and experiences. *Development in Practice*, *14*(5), 673–680.

McCarthy, M., & Goble, J. S. (2005). The praxial philosophy in historical perspective. In D. J. Elliott (Ed.), *Praxial Music Education: Reflections and Dialogues* (pp. 19–51). New York: Oxford University Press.

McLaren, P. (2000). *Che Guevara, Paulo Freire, and the pedagogy of revolution*. New York: Rowman & Littlefield Publishers, Inc.

Meiners, E. (2001). Exhibiting authentic ethnicities? The complexities of identity, experience, and audience in (educational) qualitative research. *Race, Ethnicity and Education*, *4*(3), 205–223.

Meyer, L. B. (1956). *Emotion and meaning in music*. Chicago, IL: University of Chicago Press.

Mills, C. (1997). *The racial contract*. Ithaca: New York University Press.

Moore, R. D. (2006). *Music and revolution: Cultural change in socialist Cuba*. Los Angeles: University of California Press.

Morrison, T. (1990). *Playing in the dark: Whiteness and the literary imagination*. Cambridge, MA: Harvard University Press.

Morton, C. (1994). Feminist theory and the displaced music curriculum: Beyond the "add and stir" projects. *Philosophy of Music Education Review*, *2*(2), 106–121.

Mulcahy, D. G. (2011). Liberal education, reading the word and naming the world. In A. O'Shea & M. O'Brien (Eds.), *Pedagogy, oppression and transformation in a 'post-critical' climate: The return to Freirian thinking* (pp. 69–85). New York: Continuum.

Mullen, J., Magnay, D., & Hanna, J. (2013). Imprisoned Pussy Riot band members released. *CNN*, December 23. Retrieved from http://edition.cnn.com/2013/12/23/world/europe/russia-pussy-riot-member-freed/

Narita, F. M., & Green, L. (2015). Informal learning as a catalyst for social justice in music education. In C. Benedict, P. K. Schmidt, G. Spruce, & P. G. Woodford (Eds.), *The Oxford handbook of social justice in music education* (pp. 302–317). New York: Oxford University Press.

Nattiez, J.-J. (1990). *Music and discourse: Toward a semiology of music* (C. Abbate, Trans.). Princeton, NJ: Princeton University Press.

Newton, A. Z. (1995). *Narrative ethics*. Cambridge, MA: Harvard University Press.

Noddings, N. (2013). *Caring: A relational approach to ethics and moral education* (2nd ed.). Los Angeles: University of California Press.

North, A. C., Hargreaves, D. J., & O'Neill, S. A. (2000). The importance of music for adolescents. *British Journal of Educational Psychology, 70*, 255–272.

Nowak, M., & Branford, B. (2017). France elections: What makes Marine LePen far right? *BBC News*, February 10. Retrieved from www.bbc.com/news/world-europe-38321401

O'Brien, M. (2011). Towards a pedagogy of care and well-being: Restoring the vocation of becoming human through dialogue and relationality. In A. O'Shea & M. O'Brien (Eds.), *Pedagogy, oppression and transformation in a 'post-critical' climate: The return to Freirian thinking* (pp. 14–35). New York: Continuum.

O'Neill, S. A. (2002). The self-identity of young musicians. In R. A. R. MacDonald, D. J. Hargreaves, & D. Miell (Eds.), *Musical identities* (pp. 79–96). New York: Oxford University Press.

O'Toole, P. A. (1994a). I sing in a choir but I have no voice! *The Quarterly Journal of Music Teaching and Learning, 4–5*(4, 1), 65–77.

O'Toole, P. A. (1994b). *Redirecting the choral classroom: A feminist poststructural analysis of power relations within three choral settings*. (Ph.D. dissertation), University of Wisconsin, Madison, WI.

O'Toole, P. A. (1997). Escaping the tradition: Tensions between the production of values and pleasures in the choral setting. In R. Rideout (Ed.), *On the sociology of music education* (pp. 130–137). Norman: University of Oklahoma.

O'Toole, P. A. (1998). A missing chapter from choral methods books: How choirs neglect girls. *Choral Journal, 39*(5), 9–32.

Paris, D., & Alim, H. S. (2014). What are we seeking to sustain through culturally sustaining pedagogy? A loving critique forward. *Harvard Educational Review, 84*(1), 85–100.

Paris, D., & Alim, H. S. (Eds.) (2017). *Culturally sustaining pedagogies: Teaching and learning for justice in a changing world*. New York: Teachers College Press.

Petchauer, E. (2009). Framing and reviewing hip-hop educational research. *Review of Educational Research, 79*(2), 946–978.

Piaget, J. (1972). Intellectual evolution from adolescence to adulthood. *Human Development, 15*, 1–12.

Pratt, M. L. (1991). Arts of the contact zone. *Profession, 91*, 33–40.

Racy, A. J., Marcus, S., & Solís, T. (2004). "Can't help but speak, can't help but play": Dual discourse in Arab music pedagogy. In T. Solís (Ed.), *Performing ethnomusicology: Teaching and representation in world music ensembles* (pp. 155–167). Berkeley: University of California Press.

Ranck, J. (2000). Beyond reconciliation: Memory and alterity in post-genocide Rwanda. In R. I. Simon, S. Rosenberg, & C. Eppert (Eds.), *Between hope and despair: Pedagogy and the remembrance of historical trauma* (pp. 187–211). New York: Rowman & Littlefield Publishers, Inc.

Ravitch, D. (2010). *The death and life of the great American school system: How testing and choice are undermining education*. New York: Basic Books.

Razack, S. (1998). *Looking white people in the eye: Gender, race, and culture in courtrooms and classrooms*. Toronto, ON: University of Toronto Press.

Razack, S. (2002). Gendered racial violence and spatialized justice: The murder of Pamela George. In S. Razack (Ed.), *Race, space, and the law: Unmapping a white settler society* (pp. 121–156). Toronto, ON: Between the Lines.

Razack, S. (2007). Stealing the pain of Others: Reflections on Canadian humanitarian responses. *The Review of Education Pedagogy, and Cultural Studies, 29*(4), 375–394.

Regelski, T. A. (1996). Prolegomenon to a praxial philosophy of music and music education. *Finnish Journal of Music Education, 1*(1), 22–59.

Regelski, T. A. (1998). The Aristotelian bases of praxis for music and music education as praxis. *Philosophy of Music Education Review, 6*(1), 22–59.

Regelski, T. A. (2005a). Critical theory as a foundation for critical thinking in music education. *Visions of Research in Music Education, 6*, 1–24.

Regelski, T. A. (2005b). Music and music education: Theory and praxis for "making a difference." *Educational Philosophy and Theory, 37*(1), 7–27.

Reimer, B. (1970). *A philosophy of music education*. Englewood Cliffs, NJ: Prentice-Hall.

Reimer, B. (1989). *A philosophy of music education* (2nd ed.). Englewood Cliffs, NJ: Prentice-Hall.

Reimer, B. (2003). *A philosophy of music education: Advancing the vision* (3rd ed.). Upper Saddle River, NJ: Prentice Hall.

Rhodes, A. M., & Schechter, R. (2014). Fostering resilience among youth in inner city community arts centers: The case of the artists collective. *Education and Urban Society, 46*(7), 826–848. doi:10.1177/0013124512469816

Riley, P. E. (2012). Exploration of student development through songwriting. *Visions of Research in Music Education, 22*. Retrieved from www-usr.rider.edu/~vrme/v22n1/visions/Riley_Student_Development_Through_Songwriting.pdf

Roberts, R. A., Bell, L. A., & Murphy, B. (2008). Flipping the script: Analyzing youth talk about race and racism. *Anthropology & Education Quarterly, 39*(3), 334–354.

Robinson, M. (2017). Music teachers' perceptions of high stakes teacher evaluation. *Arts Education Policy Review, 120*(1), 1–12. doi:10.1080/10632913.2017.1373380

Rosenthal, R. (2001). Serving the movement: The role(s) of music. *Popular Music and Society, 25*(3–4), 11–24. doi:10.1080/03007760108591797

Roy, W. G. (2010). *Reds, whites, and blues: Social movements, folk music, and race in the United States*. Princeton, NJ: Princeton University Press.

Ryan, A. (2011). Conscientization: The art of learning. In A. O'Shea & M. O'Brien (Eds.), *Pedagogy, oppression and transformation in a 'post-critical' climate: The return to Freirian thinking* (pp. 86–101). New York: Continuum.

Sahlberg, P. (2011). *Finnish lessons: What can the world learn from educational change in Finland?* New York: Teachers College Press.

Salverson, J. (2000). Anxiety and contact in attending to a play about land mines. In R. I. Simon, S. Rosenberg, & C. Eppert (Eds.), *Between hope and despair: Pedagogy and the remembrance of historical trauma* (pp. 59–74). New York: Rowman & Littlefield Publishers, Inc.

Sarath, E. (2002). Improvisation and curriculum reform. In R. Colwell & C. Richardson (Eds.), *The new handbook of research on music teaching and learning* (pp. 188–198). New York: Oxford University Press.

Sarath, E. (2013). *Improvisation, creativity, and consciousness: Jazz as integral template for music, education, and society*. Albany: State University of New York Press.

Schippers, H. (2010). *Facing the music: Shaping music education from a global perspective*. New York: Oxford University Press.

Schmidt, P. K. (2001). *The application of a problem-posing and dialoguing pedagogy for the teaching of history and philosophy of music education to graduate music education majors: An action research.* (Master's thesis), Rider University, Princeton, NJ.

Schmidt, P. K. (2005). Music education as transformative practice: Creating new frameworks for learning music through a Freirian perspective. *Visions of Research in Music Education, 6,* 1–14.

Schmidt, P. K. (2008). Democracy and dissensus: Constructing conflict in music education. *Action, Criticism & Theory for Music Education, 7*(1), 10–28.

Schmidt, P. K. (2016). Authority and pedagogy as framing. *Philosophy of Music Education Review, 24*(1), 8–23.

Scriven, M., & Paul, R. (1992). *Critical thinking defined.* Paper presented at the Critical Thinking Conference, Atlanta, GA.

Sheldon, D. A., & Hartley, L. A. (2012). What color is your baton, girl? Gender and ethnicity in band conducting. *Bulletin of the Council for Research in Music Education, 192,* 39–52. doi:10.5406/bulcouresmusedu.192.0039

Shepherd, J. (1991). *Music as social text.* Cambridge, U.K.: Polity Press.

Siddhartha. (2005). From conscientization to interbeing: A personal journey. In C. A. Bowers & F. Apffel-Marglin (Eds.), *Rethinking Freire: Globalization and the environmental crisis* (pp. 82–98). Mahway, NJ: Lawrence Erlbaum Associates, Publishers.

Simon, R. I., Rosenberg, S., & Eppert, C. (Eds.) (2000). *Between hope and despair: Pedagogy and the remembrance of historical trauma.* New York: Rowman & Littlefield Publishers, Inc.

Singleton, G. E., & Linton, C. W. (2006). *Courageous conversations about race: A field guide for achieving equity in schools.* Thousand Oaks, CA: Corwin Press.

Sinsabaugh, K. (2005). *Understanding students who cross over gender stereotypes in musical instrument selection.* (Ph.D. dissertation), Columbia University, New York.

Sloboda, J. (2015). Can music teaching be a powerful tool for social justice? In C. Benedict, P. K. Schmidt, G. Spruce, & P. G. Woodford (Eds.), *The Oxford handbook of social justice in music education* (pp. 539–547). New York: Oxford University Press.

Small, C. (1998). *Musicking: The meanings of performing and listening.* Hanover, NH: Wesleyan University Press, University Press of New England.

Smith, V. G., & Szymanski, A. (2013). Critical thinking: More than test scores. *National Council of Professors of Educational Administration International Journal of Educational Leadership Preparation, 8*(2), 16–26.

Smucker, J. M. (2017). Why we should stop using the word "activist." *In These Times,* May 30. Retrieved from http://inthesetimes.com/article/20125/the-trouble-with-activist on December 8, 2017.

Söderman, J., & Folkestad, G. (2004). How hip-hop musicians learn: Strategies in informal creative music making. *Music Education Research, 6*(3), 313–326.

Solís, T. (2004). Teaching what cannot be taught: An optimistic overview. In T. Solís (Ed.), *Performing ethnomusicology: Teaching and representation in world music ensembles* (pp. 1–19). Berkeley: University of California Press.

Solórzano, D. G., & Yosso, T. J. (2002). Critical race methodology: Counter-storytelling as an analytical framework for education research. *Qualitative Inquiry, 8*(1), 23–44.

Sotomayor, L., & Kim, I. (2009). Initiating social change in a conservatory of music: Possibilities and limitations of community outreach work. In E. Gould, J. Countryman, C. Morton, & L. Stewart Rose (Eds.), *Exploring social justice: How music education might matter* (pp. 225–239). Toronto, ON: Canadian Music Educators' Association.

Southcott, J. (2012). Nationalism and school music in Australia. In D. G. Hebert & A. Kertz-Welzel (Eds.), *Patriotism and nationalism in music education* (pp. 43–58). Burlington, VT: Ashgate.

Spruce, G. (2015). Music education, social justice, and the "student voice": Addressing student alienation through a dialogical conception of music education. In C. Benedict, P. K. Schmidt, G. Spruce, & P. G. Woodford (Eds.), *The Oxford handbook of social justice in music education* (pp. 287–301). New York: Oxford University Press.

Stauffer, S. (2017). *Whose imaginings? Whose future?* Paper presented at the Society for Music Teacher Education 2017 Conference: Imagining Possible Futures, Minneapolis, MN.

Stephenson, H. (2018). Tucson teacher being investigated over use of explicit rap song for sixth-grade homework. *Arizona Daily Star*, September 12. Retrieved from https://tucson.com/news/local/tucson-teacher-being-investigated-over-use-of-explicit-rap-song/article_2d901305-2d9e-5023-b0dc-89bd1fe70462.html on November 26, 2018.

Stokes, M. (Ed.) (1997). *Ethnicity, identity, and music*. Oxford & New York: Berg.

Style, E. (1996). Curriculum as window and mirror. *Social Science Record*, Fall 1996, 35–42.

Talbot, B. C. (2015). "Charleston, Goddam": An editorial introduction to ACT 14.2. *Action, Criticism & Theory for Music Education*, 14(2), 1–24.

Tan, E. (2017). How musician MILCK's 'Quiet' became a viral anthem for the Women's March. *NBC News*, January 24. Retrieved from www.nbcnews.com/news/asian-america/musician-milck-turned-quiet-viral-anthem-women-s-march-n711776 on December 22, 2017.

Tan, L. (2014). Towards a transcultural theory of democracy for instrumental music education. *Philosophy of Music Education Review*, 22(1), 61–77.

Tatum, B. D. (1997). *"Why are all the black kids sitting together in the cafeteria?": And other conversations about race*. New York: Basic Books.

Tayler, J. (2012). What Pussy Riot's 'Punk Prayer' really said. *The Atlantic*, November 8. Retrieved from www.theatlantic.com/international/archive/2012/11/what-pussy-riots-punk-prayer-really-said/264562/

Taylor, A. (2016). The uncomfortable question: Was the Brexit vote based on racism? *The Washington Post*, June 25. Retrieved from www.washingtonpost.com/news/worldviews/wp/2016/06/25/the-uncomfortable-question-was-the-brexit-vote-based-on-racism/?utm_term=.3654a90f58cc

Thompson, M. (2017). The hoods are off. *The Atlantic*, August 12. Retrieved from www.theatlantic.com/national/archive/2017/08/the-hoods-are-off/536694/

Tobias, E. (2012). Hybrid spaces and hyphenated musicians: Secondary students' musical engagement in a songwriting and technology course. *Music Education Research*, 14(3), 329–346. doi:10.1080/14613808.2012.685459

Trimillos, R. D. (2004). Subject, object, and the ethnomusicology ensemble: The ethnomusicological "we" and "them." In T. Solís (Ed.), *Performing ethnomusicology: Teaching and representation in world music ensembles* (pp. 23–52). Berkeley: University of California Press.

Trinka, J. L. (1987). *The performance style of American folksongs on school music series and non-school music series recordings: A comparative analysis of selected factors*. (Ph.D. thesis), University of Texas, Austin.

Turino, T. (2008). *Music as social life: The politics of participation*. Chicago, IL: The University of Chicago Press.

Turner, K. C. N. (2012). Multimodal hip hop productions as media literacies. *The Educational Forum, 76*(4), 497–509. doi:10.1080/00131725.2012.708617

Tusty, J., & Tusty, M. C. (Writers) (2007). *The singing revolution* [Film]. In B. Cram, A. Talvik, & P. Tibbo-Hudgins (Producers). United States: Abramorama.

U.S. Department of Health & Human Services, Administration for Children and Families, Administration on Children, Youth and Families, & Children's Bureau. (2017). *Child maltreatment 2015*. Retrieved from www.acf.hhs.gov/programs/cb/research-data-technology/statistics-research/child-maltreatment on June 26, 2018.

Vass, G. (2013). Hear no race, see no race, speak no race: Teacher silence, Indigenous youth, and race talk in the classroom. *Social Alternatives, 32*(2), 19–24.

Vaugeois, L. (2009). Music as a practice of social justice. In E. Gould, J. Countryman, C. Morton, & L. Stewart Rose (Eds.), *Exploring social justice: How music education might matter* (pp. 2–22). Toronto, ON: Canadian Music Educators' Association.

Vaugeois, L. (2013). *Colonization and the institutionalization of hierarchies of the human through music education: Studies in the education of feeling*. (Ph.D. dissertation), University of Toronto, Toronto, ON.

Vygotsky, L. S. (1978). *Mind in society: The development of higher psychological processes*. Cambridge, MA: Harvard University.

Waddell, K. (2017). The exhausting work of tallying America's largest protest. *The Atlantic*, January 23. Retrieved from www.theatlantic.com/technology/archive/2017/01/womens-march-protest-count/514166/ on December 22, 2017.

Walcott, R. W. (2000). Pedagogy and trauma: The middle passage, slavery, and the problem of creolization. In R. I. Simon, S. Rosenberg, & C. Eppert (Eds.), *Between hope and despair: Pedagogy and the remembrance of historical trauma*. New York: Rowman & Littlefield Publishers, Inc.

Walcott, R. W. (2009). Multicultural and creole contemporaries: Postcolonial artists and postcolonial cities. In R. Coloma (Ed.), *Postcolonial challenges in education* (pp. 161–177). New York: Peter Lang.

Walker, T. (2016). Goodbye "core subjects," hello "well-rounded education." *neaToday*, June 21. Retrieved from http://neatoday.org/2016/06/21/essa-well-rounded-education/ on December 23, 2017.

Washington, M. (2017). Kneeling isn't about patriotism—it's a distress signal. *CNN*, October 14. Retrieved from www.cnn.com/2017/10/14/opinions/what-nfl-protests-are-not-about-patriotism-washington-opinion/index.html on December 30, 2017.

Wass, H., Raup, J. L., Cerullo, K., Martel, L. G., Mingione, L. A., & Sperring, A. M. (1989/1988). Adolescents' interest in and views of destructive themes in rock music. *Omega, 19*(3), 177–186.

Wastvedt, S. (2017). Why this high school band is buying music from composers of color this year. *NPR News: Weekend Edition Saturday*, February 18. Retrieved from www.npr.org/sections/ed/2017/02/18/509133975/why-this-high-school-band-is-only-buying-music-from-composers-of-color on July 13, 2018.

Weiler, K. (1994). Freire and a feminist pedagogy of difference. In P. McLaren & C. Lankshear (Eds.), *Politics of liberation: Paths from Freire* (pp. 12–40). London: Routledge.

Williams, A. D. (2007). *The critical cultural cypher: Hip-hop's role in engaging students in a discourse of enlightenment*. (Ph.D. dissertation), University of Maryland, College Park, MD.

Williams, D. A. (2011). The elephant in the room. *Music Educators Journal, 98*(1), 51–57. doi:10.1177/0027432111415538

Williams, W. R. (2012). "Untold stories to tell": Making space for the voices of youth songwriters. *Journal of Adolescent & Adult Literacy, 56*(5), 369–379.

Willingham, L. (2001). *A community of voices: A qualitative study of the effects of being a member of the Bell'Arte Singers.* (Ph.D. dissertation), University of Toronto, Toronto, ON.

Willis, C. (2017). Parents outraged after teacher gives profanity-laced homework assignment. *WSB-TV2 Atlanta*, September 20. Retrieved from www.wsbtv.com/news/local/parents-outraged-after-teacher-gives-profanity-laced-homework-assignment/611724103 on November 26, 2018.

Winter, R. (2013). Language, empathy, archetype: Action-metaphors of the transcendental in musical experience. *Philosophy of Music Education Review, 21*(2), 103–119.

Woo, R. (2018). An open letter to people who love their pink pussy hats. *Together We Will*. Retrieved from http://twwusa.org/4809/member-voices-pink-pussy-hats/ on November 23, 2018.

Woodford, P. G. (2005). *Democracy and music education.* Bloomington: Indiana University Press.

Yancy, G. (2008). *Black bodies, White gazes: The continuing significance of race.* New York: Rowman & Littlefield Publishers, Inc.

Yosso, T. J. (2005). Whose culture has capital? A critical race theory discussion of community cultural wealth. *Race, Ethnicity and Education, 8*(1), 69–91. doi:10.1080/1361332052000341006

Young, J. O. (2008). *Cultural appropriation and the arts.* Malden, MA: Blackwell Publishing.

Zhang, Y. (2017). Walking a mile in their shoes: Developing pre-service music teachers' empathy for ELL students. *International Journal of Music Education, 35*(3), 425–434.

Zimmerman, J., & Robertson, E. (2017). *The case for contention: Teaching controversial issues in American schools.* Chicago, IL: The University of Chicago Press.

Credits

Song lyrics from "Quiet", "Mississippi Goddam", and "Soweto Blues" appear with the permission of the copyright holders. Lise Vaugeois' "musical life histories" are reprinted with the permission of the author and the Canadian Music Educators' Association. Credits are listed in the order they appear in the text. The author wishes to thank all artists, scholars, and copyright holders for permission to reprint their work.

"Quiet"
Written by Connie Lim and Adrianne Gonzalez.
Copyright © 2017 Connie Lim Music (ASCAP) and One Less Traveled Music Publishing o.b.o. BYAGINC (ASCAP)
Reprinted by permission.

"Mississippi Goddamn"
Words and Music by Nina Simone
Copyright © 1964 (Renewed) WB Music Corp.
All Rights Reserved
Used by Permission of Alfred Music

"Soweto Blues"
Words and Music by Stanley Todd and Hugh Masekela
Copyright © 1977 We've-Got-Rhythm-Music
Copyright Renewed
All Rights Controlled and Administered by Irving Music, Inc.
All Rights Reserved
Used by Permission
Reprinted by Permission of Hal Leonard LLC

Lise Vaugeois's Approaches to Studying Musical Life Histories table (pp.75-76 of this volume) is cited with permission of the author, Lise Vaugeois, and of the copyright holder, The Canadian Music Educators' Association (CMEA). It was published in E. Gould, J. Countryman, C. Morton, & L. Stewart Rose (Eds.), *Exploring social justice: How music education might matter* (pp. 2-22).

Index

Note: Activist-musicians are indexed under their first names or stage names to reflect the way they are referred to throughout the text, e.g.: Bryan (Bryan DePuy); tvu (Theresa "tvu" Vu). References to endnotes consist of the page number followed by the letter 'n' followed by the number of the note.

#MeToo Movement 137

24 (TV show) 51, 52

ableism 5, 11, 121, 122, 153
Abrahams, Frank 23, 24, 25, 28–29
abuse: child abuse statistics 106n9, 138; mandatory reporting of 97, 104–105, 106, 141, 145; *see also* trauma
action: concept as defined by Freire 15, 16–17, 20, 22; and creative music curriculum 90–91, 101, 102, 106; and culture of questioning 108; and dissent 119; and Kuntz' definition of activism 155; and music education 26, 28, 35, 36, 158, 161; and music education as political 118, 123, 125; and musicking 41–42; and musicking anti-oppression 123; *see also* dialogue; naming the world
active learner-centered approaches 15
active meaning-making 36, 38, 42, 60, 107
active music listening 91–92
activism: defining 6–7, 36–37, 149n9, 154–155; and Freire's notion of reflection 16–17, 159; in schools 146; and tri-faceted pedagogy 156–159
activist music education *see* activist music education, dangers of; activist music education, implementing; activist music education, redefining; activist-musicians in music education; creative music curriculum; tri-faceted pedagogy

activist music education, dangers of: chapter outline 127–128; connecting to others as fraught territory 128–141; dangers of enacting music education as political 145–148; risks of expressing lived experiences 141–145; summary 148–149; and tri-faceted pedagogy 154; *see also* connection, dangers of
activist music education, implementing: challenges and societal constraints 162; Global Education Reform Movement issues 162–164; navigating divided communities in classroom 164–165; not just "one more thing" 166–167; resistance from local communities 165–166; taking up the challenge 167–168
activist music education, redefining: activism as defined by Kuntz 154–155; critical pedagogy, activism and music education 155–156; material action and tri- faceted pedagogy 156–160
activist-musicians in music education: activism, music and anti-oppression pedagogy 4–6; activism defined 6–7; activist music education and critical pedagogy 7, 11, 12, 15, 60; activist music education for K-12 education 6, 9; activist-musicians and social movements 9–10; activist-musicians for this project, selection and biographies of 6, 7–9, 12, 169–176;

book outline 12–13; Ferguson, Missouri events and police violence 5; potential of music education 10–11; vignette 1 ("Quiet" at 2017 Women's March) 1–2, 4; vignette 2 ("Mississippi Goddam" by Nina Simone, Carnegie Hall, 1964) 2–3, 4; vignette 3 ("Nkosi Sikelel' iAfrica" at Soweto Uprising, 1976) 3–4; *see also* music, potential of; musicking; *separately listed activist-musicians*
Adorno, Theodor W. 55
Africanism 129, 133
Afro D *see* Pete (Pete Shungu, stage name Afro D)
Afro D All Starz, The (band) 54
Afrocentric history program 88–89
Afunakwa 149n2
ageism 11
Ahmed, S. 78
Aid to Children Without Parents (ACWP) 57
Akom, A. A. 29
Alibhai-Brown, Y. 149n6
Allsup, R. E. 25, 28, 82, 153
"alt-right" ideologies 4, 158–159
American Indian Movement 70
anti-oppression: anti-oppression pedagogy 5–6; anti-oppressive exemplars 118, 121–123, 125; musicking anti-oppression 123–125; *see also* oppression
anti-Semitism 5
Anyon, J. 84n8
apartheid (South Africa) 3–4, 9, 58, 71
Apple, M. 33, 84n8
Applebaum, B. 50
appropriation *see* cultural appropriation
Aristotle 23
art, role of in society 11
artists: and contexts 70–72; portrayal of women artists 113; as visionaries 101–102
Asgharzadeh, A. 102
audience desires, and storytelling 143–144, 154
authenticity 69, 134
authority figures: and dissent 119; and noticing ideologies 109–110, 116, 119, 125

"B" word, The 53–54
Baez, Joan 9
Baker, Jordan 5
"Balikbayan" song 47–48, 91
Bambu 54, 58
banking education (Freire) 19, 25, 36
Banks, J. A. 129
Bergman Ramos, Myra 19
Birkenshaw-Fleming, L. (ed.), *An Orff Mosaic from Canada* 74
Birmingham, Alabama, 1963 church bombing 2–3
Blocks Recording Club (record label) 65
Boler, M. 117
book outline 12–13, 37–38
Bowman, W. D. 23, 26, 27–28
Bradley, D. 44, 57, 79, 130, 132, 133, 135, 145
Britzman, D. 138, 140
Brooks, D. A. 3
Brooks, M. 83
Brown, J. 3
Brown, Michael, murder of (Ferguson, Missouri) 5, 70, 86, 152
Bruner, J. S. 15
Bryan (Bryan DePuy): biography 170; community building and music 43; connections between music and society 67–68; contextualizing classroom musics 79, 129; cultural appropriation 132; emotions and music 43, 48, 56, 146; instruments 72; role of music in communities 69; translating lyrics 73
Buck-Morss, S. 11
Buechner, Karl *see* Karl (Karl Buechner)
Bylica, K. 100–101

Campbell, N. I., *Shi-shi-etko* (Campbell and LaFave) 82, 83
Caruth, C. 137, 142, 143
Casey (Casey Mecija): "Balikbayan" song 47–48, 91; biography 173; colonial narratives and A Tribe Called Red 52–53; contextualizing music 68–69; cultural appropriation 80, 130, 131, 144; Girls Rock Camp program 80–81, 96–97, 113; Girls Rock Camp program, "The History of Women in Music" 119–121, 123–124, 125; instruments 72, 73; songwriting 96–97, 149n7
Chapman, Tracy 9
child abuse *see* abuse
Child Maltreatment (2015 report) 106n9
choirs (ensembles): dialogic relations in 64; hierarchies vs. mutuality 24

Chucky (Chucky Kim): biography 172; collective envisioning 101–102; community formation and music 43; connecting to larger narratives 46; educators to share their own stories 67; telling stories and musicking 47
cisgenderism 5, 11
Civil Rights Movement 3, 9, 56, 71
classical music, and hierarchization of musics issue 128–129
classism 5, 9, 11, 111, 112, 113, 122
classroom music, and music education industry/publishers 72, 110, 131, 135, 151
classroom spaces: as contact zones 78, 79, 81; as mutually supportive 62, 64–65, 66, 67, 93, 100, 121, 151
Clauhs, M. 24
Cochran, McKenzie 5
collective envisioning 101–102, 157, 161
Collins, Addie Mae 2
colonialism: b. hooks on 111; and Bambu's songs 58; and critical pedagogy 29, 32, 34, 37, 145; and Indigenous histories in Canada 53, 82, 139; postcolonial moment 102; and stereotyping 134; and Western European perspectives 130
Colwell, R. 25
coming to voice: concept as defined by Freire 17, 21, 22; and creative music curriculum 90–91, 94, 100, 101, 102, 106; and dissent 107, 123; and music education 28, 29, 37, 62, 66, 83; and music education as political 118, 123, 125; and musicking 46, 47, 48–50, 52, 60; and pedagogy of expression 157; and performance paradigm 99; and songwriting 95
coming-to-consciousness *see* conscientization (coming-to-consciousness)
communication, and musicking 46–50
community: and activist-musicians 9, 10, 35; and contextualizing musics 69–70, 72; and implementing activist music education 164–166; and musicking 10, 42–44, 47, 49; and role of music 69; *see also* community, practice of; pedagogy of community; place-based education
community, practice of: and ensemble as togetherness 62, 63–64; and mutually supportive spaces 62, 64–65, 100; and teachers-as-facilitators 66–67; and trusting youth with responsibilities 62, 65–66
composing, and gender 111
conducting, and gender 111
connecting *see* connection, dangers of; connection, music education as; connection, musicking as; pedagogy of community
connection, dangers of: cultural appropriation 130–132, 140–141; exoticization 135–137, 140–141; hierarchization of musics 128–130, 140–141; stereotyping 132–135, 137, 140–141; trauma 137–140, 141
connection, music education as: engaging with multiple musical traditions and cultural appropriation 77–82; navigating potential for re-experiencing trauma 82–83; practice of community 62–67; situated human practice 67–77; summary 83; *see also* community, practice of; pedagogy of community; situated human practice
connection, musicking as 42–46
conscientization (coming-to-consciousness): Freire's concept 16, 17, 18–19, 20, 21, 22, 147; and identifying lived conditions 116; and music education 25, 26, 27, 35–36, 38; and musicking 42, 51; and potential for colonialism 32; and teacher-student hierarchies 30, 31–32, 147–148, 154
constructivist learning 15
contact zones, classroom spaces as 78, 79, 81
content integration 129
contextualization: and cultural appropriation 79–80, 81; and pedagogy of community 151, 152; *see also* recontextualization; situated human practice
core subjects 84n5
counterstorytelling 60n6, 106n6
courageous conversations: and music education 117–118, 125, 147, 154; *see also* difficult truths
Crawford, John, III 5
creative music curriculum: collective identity and envisioning 101–102; creative curriculum and naming the world 90–91; exploring identity

91–94; learning to value others' assertions 100–101; musicking to share stories 94–100; summary 102, 106
critical music 122–123
critical pedagogy (Paulo Freire): action 15, 16–17, 20, 22; avoiding dogmatic implementation 29–30; banking education 19, 25, 36; colonialism and critical pedagogy 32, 34; coming to voice 17, 21, 22; conscientization 16, 17, 18–19, 20, 21, 22, 30, 31–32; dialogue 16, 17, 20, 22, 33; dreaming 17, 20–21, 22; empowerment 17, 21, 22, 30, 31–32; liberation 17, 21, 22, 31; lived experiences 17–18, 22; mutuality between students and teachers 17, 18, 20, 22, 31, 32; naming the world 7, 16, 17, 20, 22; patriarchy and critical pedagogy 33–34; praxis 7, 15, 16–17, 35; problem-posing education 17, 18, 19–20, 21, 22, 30, 31–32; racism and critical pedagogy 33–34; readings of the world 30–31; reflection 15, 16–17, 20, 22; teacher-student hierarchies and critical pedagogy 30–32, 34; transformation 15, 16–17, 20, 21, 22; *see also* critical pedagogy and music education; culturally responsive pedagogy; musicking; *separately listed concepts*
critical pedagogy and music education: action 26, 28, 35, 36; activist-musicians and critical pedagogy 7, 12, 15, 16, 22; actualizing tenets of critical pedagogy 34–35; coming to voice 28, 29, 37; conscientization 25, 26, 27, 35–36; dialogue 26, 27–28, 36–37; dreaming 26, 28, 36–37; empowerment 28–29, 37; ethics and praxis 23, 35; liberation 28, 29, 37; lived experiences 24, 25, 26, 35; mutuality between students and teachers 24–25, 35; naming the world 26–27, 28, 36–37; problem-posing education 25–26, 29, 35–36; reflection 26, 35; transformation 26, 28, 35, 36; *see also* critical pedagogy (Paulo Freire); musicking; place-based education; *separately listed concepts*
critical praxis 160–161
critical race theory 33, 60n7, 106n6
critical thinking: and activist-musicians 9, 108, 148; and courageous conversations 117; and critical music 122; and dreaming/imagining 155; and empowerment 28–29; Freire on 108; and Global Education Reform Movement 163; and Patrick's hip-hop program 108, 114, 153; and pedagogy of noticing 150, 153–154; and teacher-student hierarchies 147; and tri-faceted pedagogy 156
critique, practice of: and contexts 76; and critical music 122; and identifying lived conditions 116, 118; and music education as political 107, 125; and noticing ideologies 109, 113, 114–115, 116, 119; and standardized tests 163–164; *see also* culture of questioning; noticing, practice of; noticing ideologies
Cruz, C. 95
Cuba, activist-musicians and social movements 9
cultural appropriation: danger of 79–80, 81, 130–132, 140–141, 144–145, 148; and tri-faceted pedagogy 151, 152, 154
cultural genocide 80, 118
culturally relevant pedagogy 24, 85, 86, 122
culturally responsive pedagogy 23, 24, 25, 85, 86, 122, 152–153
culturally sustaining pedagogy 24, 85, 153
culture bearers 132–134, 135, 137
culture of questioning: and action 108; and dissent 119, 123; and identifying lived conditions 116, 118; and music education as political 107–108, 125, 145; and noticing ideologies 108–109, 116; and noticing representations 110, 114, 116; and pedagogy of noticing 153; and problem-posing education 25; and standardized tests 164; *see also* critique, practice of
curricula: and content integration 129; core subjects 84n5; and multicentricity 130; student-centered curricula 88–89; *see also* creative music curriculum
"Curriculum as window and mirror" (E. Style) 78, 81, 86–87, 89–90, 91, 132, 151–152

Dale, J. 17–18, 20, 22, 63, 117
Dan (Dan Matthews/DANakaDAN): biography 169–170; giving youth

time to be creative 92; "Is There Anybody Out There" song 47, 91; music and communicating feelings 48
Dane, Barbara 9
dangers of musicking 55–57; *see also* activist music education, dangers of; connection, dangers of
Darder, Antonia 22, 33, 36, 160–161
Davis, Angela 13n3
deejaying education 81
deficit discourses 11, 24, 52–53, 95, 144
dehumanization 77–78, 134–135; humanization 77–78, 79
Dei, G. J. S. 32, 33, 102
Deleuze, Gilles 14n16, 145
Delgado, R. 60n7
Delpit, L. D. 163–164
democracy: and Freirian dialogue 27–28; teaching to "do" democracy 165
democratic music education 64, 119
DePuy, Bryan *see* Bryan (Bryan DePuy)
Dewey, J. 15
dialogue: Freire's concept 16, 17, 20, 22, 33; and music education 26, 27–28, 36–37, 63, 66–67, 158, 161; and musicking 49; and musicking anti-oppression 124
difficult truths: and musicking 50; *see also* courageous conversations
Dirty Boots (band) 70
discomfort, pedagogy of 117
dissent (in classroom) 107, 118, 119, 123, 125, 148
"Dissent is Patriotic" signs 1
DJ L'Oqenz *see* El (DJ L'Oqenz)
DJ Phatrick *see* Patrick (Patrick Huang, a.k.a. DJ Phatrick)
The Doc Project (radio show) 47
Dr. Dre 111–112
dreaming: concept as defined by Freire 17, 20–21, 22; and creative music curriculum 102; and imagining musical practices 120, 121; and Kuntz' definition of activism 155; and music education 26, 28, 36–37; *see also* imagining musical practices
Dumlao, James *see* James (James Dumlao)

Earth Crisis (band) 71
Ebato, Taiyo *see* Taiyo Na (Taiyo Ebato)
El (DJ L'Oqenz): biography 172–173; growing up with arts and activism 53;

learning to deejay 81; potential of music for dividing people 56; vibrations and words 56, 114
Elliott, D. J. 23, 39n2, 40
Ellsworth, E. 29, 31, 32, 34, 127, 148
emotional expression: and musicking 48; and political music 103
empathy 115–116, 141–143, 148, 154
empowerment: Freire's concept 17, 21, 22; and music education 28–29, 37, 66; and potential for colonialism 32; and teacher-student hierarchies 30, 31–32, 147–148, 154
ensemble (togetherness) 62, 63–64, 167
ensembles (choirs): dialogic relations in 64; hierarchies vs mutuality 24
Eppert, C. 138
Epstein, Griffin *see* Griffin (Griffin Epstein)
Escobar, E. 11
Estonia, activist-musicians and social movements 9
ethics: and cultural appropriation 131, 132; ethic of care 65, 66; and praxis 23, 35; and traumatic histories 138
ethnocentrism 32
Eurocentricity 130
Evers, Medgar 2, 3
Every Student Succeeds Act (ESSA) 84n5
exoticization 129, 135–137, 140–141, 148, 154
experiences *see* lived experiences
expression: and musicking 46–50; *see also* emotional expression; pedagogy of expression

facilitators, teachers as 66–67
fascist agendas 56, 57; microfascism 14n16, 145–146, 148
Feld, S. 130, 131, 149n2
feminism: feminist critiques of critical pedagogy 33; feminist scholarship in music education 24; intersectional feminism 13n3
Ferguson, Missouri, shooting of Michael Brown (2014) 5, 70, 86, 152
Foucault, M. 127, 148–149
Frankfurt School 16
Freire, Paulo: critical pedagogy advocate 12; on critical thinking 108; *Education, the Practice of Freedom* 22; *Harvard Educational Review* articles 22; influence of in North America

22–23; on oppressed and their own liberation 143–144; on oppressors' dehumanization politics 77; *Pedagogy of the Oppressed* 19, 22, 30, 160–161; *The Politics of Education* 160–161; on reinventing pedagogy for specific contexts 12, 22, 29, 37, 86, 160, 166; on relationship between theory and practice 160–161; on respecting educands 109–110; on social life and academic subjects 68; on standardized curricula 85–86; *see also* critical pedagogy (Paulo Freire); critical pedagogy and music education; *separately listed concepts*
Frith, S. 49
"Fukushima" song 50

gangsta rap 112, 143
Garner, Eric 5
Gates, Henry Louis, Jr. 51
Gaye, Marvin 59
Gaztambide-Fernández, R. 27
gender: and critical pedagogy 33–34; and musical practices 111, 119–121; and musics/instruments 65, 111; and school musical education 110–111, 120–121, 123; *see also* cisgenderism; feminism; heterosexism; misogyny; sexism
genocide 118, 137, 139; cultural genocide 80, 118
Germany, Nazi Germany 56, 146
Girls Rock Camp program 53, 80–81, 96–97, 113; "The History of Women in Music" 119–121, 123–124, 125
Giroux, Henry A. 22, 25, 107, 108, 119, 145, 155, 158
Giroux, S. S. 25, 107, 108, 119, 145
Global Education Reform Movement 162–164
global song 132–133, 135
Gonzalez, Adrianne 1, 4
Gordon, M. 15
Gould, E. 28
Goulet, D. 25–26
Gowan, J. 23, 25
Gramsci, Antonio 16
Grande, S. 32
Great Leap (arts organization) 42
Green, Lucy 9, 25, 96, 110–111
Greene, M. 28, 101, 118
Griffin (Griffin Epstein): biography 170–171; contextualization and individuals' lives 70–71, 151; cultural appropriation 80, 132; gender and school music programs 120–121, 123; mutually supportive spaces 64–65, 100, 121, 151
Guattari, Félix 14n16, 145
Guthrie, Woody 9

Hall, S. 155
Hanisch, C. 9
Harvard Educational Review 22
Hawkins, T. 24
Haynes, D. J. 101–102
Hess, J. 145–146
heterosexism 1, 5, 11, 112, 114, 121, 122
Hickey, M. 94–95
hierarchies between teachers and students 30–32, 34, 147–148, 154; *see also* mutuality between students and teachers
hierarchization of musics 128–130, 140–141, 148
higher order thinking 163
Hill, M. L. 27, 103
hip-hop: and classism 122; and conscientization 25, 27; critical hip-hop pedagogy 27; and empowerment 29; "Hip-Hop Lit" class 103; and "inappropriate" language 74; music teachers' unfamiliarity with 81–82; and naming the world 117; and problem-posing education 117; and racism 52, 122; and social justice 54; *see also* Patrick (Patrick Huang, a.k.a. DJ Phatrick)
histories: and contextualizing musics 67–69; and music's connective role 44–46; *see also* counterstorytelling; narratives; storytelling
Holiday, Billie 9
Hollindale, P. 114
Home:Word (album) 49
homophobia 9
hooks, b. 34, 111–112, 121–122, 133, 135, 143
Horton, Myles 18, 22, 87, 115
Huang, Patrick *see* Patrick (Patrick Huang, a.k.a. DJ Phatrick)
humanization 77–78, 79; dehumanization 77–78, 134–135
Hwang, Jason *see* Jason (Jason Kao Hwang)

"hyphenated musicianship" concept 10
Hyslop-Margison, E. J. 17–18, 20, 22, 63, 117

identity: and coming to voice/naming the world in musicking 48–50, 91, 94; creative music curriculum and collective identity 101–102; creative music curriculum and exploring identity 91–94, 106; identity politics and musicking 47–48, 103; intersectional identities 65; and looking for larger narratives 93–94; and place-based education 87; and social justice 53
ideologies: and tri-faceted pedagogy 165–166; *see also* dissent (in classroom); noticing ideologies
imagining musical practices 118, 119–121, 123, 125; *see also* dreaming
immigrants: anti-immigrant sentiments 5; immigrant struggles and protest songs 9
implementing *see* activist music education, implementing
improvisation 49, 92–93
individual artists, and contexts 70–72
informal learning processes/strategies 9
instruments: and exoticization 135–137; exposing youth to different instruments 93; and gendered norms 65, 111; instrumental instruction and songwriting 96, 167; and situated nature of music 72–73; Yamaha instruments posters 112–113
internal social justice 54, 116
internalized oppression 20
intersectional critical pedagogy 34
intersectional feminism 13n3
intersectional identities 65
"Is There Anybody Out There" song 47, 91
Islamophobia 5

James (James Dumlao): biography 170; instrumental instruction and songwriting 96, 167; music and social movements 70, 91, 122–123, 124–125; world music ensembles 78–79
Jason (Jason Kao Hwang): biography 171; chants and multilingualism 87, 102; combining Chinese and Western instruments 135–137; giving kids space to improvise 92–93; jazz, improvisation and individual voices 49; music and human relationships 63; music as political act 49; unfamiliar musics and open-mindedness 44, 77, 156
Jim Crow laws 77
Juntunen, M.-L. 120

K-12 education, activist music education for 6, 9
Kaepernick, Colin 125n2
Kaminsky, Laura *see* Laura (Laura Kaminsky)
Karl (Karl Buechner): biography 169; contextualizing individual artists 71; risks of supporting social movements 105
Kaschub, M. 27, 106n2
Keenan, T. 142, 143
Keil, C. 145
Kelly, D. M. 83
Kertz-Welzel, A. 55, 57
Kim, Chucky *see* Chucky (Chucky Kim)
Kim, I. 14n3
Kirylo, J. D. 124, 147
Klinger, R. 134, 137
Kogawa, Joy, *Obasan* 138
Koza, J. E. 110, 111
Kuntz, A. M. 6–7, 36–37, 149n9, 154–155, 156, 157

Ladson-Billings, G. 33
Lady Gaga 9
LaFave, K., *Shi-shi-etko* (Campbell and LaFave) 82, 83
Lamm, C. 57
languages: "inappropriate" language 74–75; multilingualism 87, 102; translation of lyrics 73–74; *see also* lyrics
Lankshear, C. 17
Lareau, A. 84n8
Lashbrook, S. 60n4
Lather, P. 29, 34, 37, 148, 154
Laura (Laura Kaminsky): biography 171–172; soundscape for the classroom 99; *Vukovar Trio* 98–99
Lee (Phenner): biography 174; *A Pint of Understanding* 51; power of the arts and *24* (TV show) 51, 52
Lennon, John 59
Lewis, A. 163
Lewis, J. 106n8
LGBTQ/LGBTQQIA 53, 70

liberation: Freire's concept 17, 21, 22, 31; and music education 28, 29, 37
Lim, Connie *see* MILCK (Connie Lim)
Lind, V. L. 86
Linton, C. W. 117
Lise (Lise Vaugeois): biography 175; critical "musical life histories" questions 26, 75–76, 82, 115, 125n1, 132, 148; Eddy Robinson as First Nations musician 133–134; Indigenous issues and trauma 82–83, 117–118, 139; integrated approach to performance 99–100; moving youth beyond their lived experiences 89; Style's "Curriculum as window and mirror" 78, 132; White orchestral violinist as culture bearer 134
listening: active music listening 91–92; attentive listening 92; purposive listening 91, 92; reflective listening 67, 164–165
lived conditions 107, 108, 116–118, 123, 125
lived experiences: concept as defined by Freire 17–18, 22, 87, 88–89, 141; and creative music curriculum 90–102, 106; and multiple music traditions 81, 83; and music as situated human practice 76–77; and music education 24, 25, 26, 35, 62, 67; and musicking 42, 46, 60; and pedagogy of expression 150, 152, 153; and performing 99; and place-based education 85–90, 106; risks associated with sharing experiences 103–106, 141–145; and teacher as facilitator 67; *see also* creative music curriculum; place-based education
Liz (Liz Stookey Sunde): biography 175; listening to music 91–92; music and analysis of current events 122–123; Music2Life: Soundtrack for Social Change 91–92, 122–123
L'Oqenz, El *see* El (DJ L'Oqenz)
Lorde, A. 163
lyrics: and ideologies 114–116, 125; translation of 73–74; writing of 96–97; *see also* hip-hop languages; songwriting

Macedo, Donaldo 17, 22, 25, 39n1, 86, 88–89, 141
McKoy, C. L. 86

McLaren, P. 17, 22, 76–77
McNair, Carol Denise 2
Magali (Magali Meagher): biography 173; catering curriculum to context 86, 152; Girls Rock Camp program 53, 96, 113; instrumental instruction and songwriting 96, 167; trusting youth with responsibilities 65–66
Magnetic North (band): "Fukushima" song 50; *Home:Word* (album) 49; "New Love" song 53
Makeba, Miriam, "Soweto Blues" 3–4
"Mama Paquita" song 74
Mammalian Diving Reflex 65
mandatory reporting (of abuse) 97, 104–105, 106, 141, 145
Manne, K. 139
Mantie, R. 60n4
Marcus, S. 133
Martignetti, F. 24
Martin, Trayvon 59
Marx, Karl 16
Masekela, Hugh 3–4
mash-up/remix 97–98, 132, 144; *see also* sampling (music process)
mass shootings 137
Matthews, Dan *see* Dan (Dan Matthews/DANakaDAN)
Meagher, Magali *see* Magali (Magali Meagher)
Mecija, Casey *see* Casey (Casey Mecija)
Meiners, E. 133
"The Message" (song) 54, 116
Mexico/U.S. border, forced separation of children from parents 137–138
microfascism 14n16, 145–146, 148
MILCK (Connie Lim) 1–2, 4
Mills, C. 111
misogyny: and 2016 presidential election campaign 1; and gangsta rap 112; and hip-hop 114–116, 121–122; and rap music 121–122; *see also* sexism
"Mississippi Goddam" (song) 2–3
Miyamoto, Nobuko *see* Nobuko (Nobuko Miyamoto)
Mock, Janet 13n3
Morrison, T. 129, 133
Moses, Johnny 137
Mulcahy, D. G. 18
multicentricity 130
multicultural education 74, 129
multiculturalism 149n6

multilingualism 87, 102
"music" (as a verb) 10
music, potential of: inherently social nature of music 40–41; musicking, activist-musicians and critical pedagogy 41–42; musicking as connection 42–46; musicking as dangerous 55–57; musicking as expression and communication 46–50; musicking as learning site 58–59; musicking as political 50–55; summary 59–60; *see also* musical practices; musicking
music education: and coming to voice 28, 29, 37, 62, 66, 83; and dialogue 26, 27–28, 36–37, 63, 66–67, 158, 161; and empowerment 28–29, 37, 66; and lived experiences 24, 25, 26, 35, 62, 67, 76–77, 83; and multicultural movement 74; potential of 10–11; and problem-posing education 25–26, 29, 35–36, 62, 83; *see also* connection, music education as; place-based education; political, music education as
music education industry/publishers, and classroom music 72, 110, 131, 135, 151
music industry: and misogyny/rape culture 121–122; and representations/ideologies 113–114
Music2Life: Soundtrack for Social Change 91–92, 122–123
Musical Futures program 96
musical practices: and gender 110–111, 119–121; imagining 118, 119–121, 123, 125
musicking: and action 41–42; and anti-oppression 123–125; and coming to voice 46, 47, 48–50, 52, 60; and community 10, 42–44, 47, 49; as connection 42–46; and conscientization 42, 51; as dangerous 55–57; and dialogue 49; as expression/communication 46–50; as human encounter 62; as learning site 58–59; and lived experiences 42, 46, 60; "music" (as a verb) 10; and naming the world 42, 46, 48–51, 52, 54–55, 60; as political 50–55; and transformation 41–42; *see also* creative music curriculum
mutuality between students and teachers: Freire's concept 17, 18, 20, 22, 31, 32; and music education 24–25, 35; *see also* hierarchies between teachers and students
mutually supportive spaces 62, 64–65, 66, 67, 93, 100, 121, 151

naming the world: concept as defined by Freire 7, 16, 17, 20, 22, 90–91, 145; and creative music curriculum 90–91, 94, 100, 101, 102, 106; and hip-hop 117; and identifying lived conditions 107, 118; and Kuntz' definition of activism 155; and music education 26–27, 28, 36–37, 156; and musicking 42, 46, 48–51, 52, 54–55, 60; and noticing ideologies 107; and pedagogy of expression 153, 157, 158; and pedagogy of noticing 157; and performance paradigm 99; and songwriting 95; and trauma/abuse issue 104, 105; and writing lyrics 96–97
Narita, F. M. 25
narratives: connecting to larger narratives and musicking 44–46, 71; looking for larger narratives in classroom 93–94; *see also* counterstorytelling; histories; storytelling
National Football League (NFL) protests 125n2
Nattiez, J.-J. 40
Nazi Germany 56, 146
"New Love" song 53
Newton, A. Z. 138
Niknafs, N. 24
"Nkosi Sikelel' iAfrica" song 3–4, 61n17
No Child Left Behind Act (NCLB) 84n5
Nobuko (Nobuko Miyamoto): biography 173; music as community-building tool 42; music to generate change 51–52; youth creating their own songs 94
Noddings, N. 65
noticing, practice of: and the "B" word 53–54; and conscientization 36, 38, 42, 116; and identifying lived conditions 118; and music industry 113–114; and musicking 60; and musicking anti-oppression 123, 125; *see also* critique, practice of; culture of questioning; noticing ideologies; pedagogy of noticing
noticing ideologies 108–109; authority figures 109–110, 116, 119, 125;

lyrics 114–116, 125; representations 110–114, 125; summary 116; *see also* culture of questioning; dissent (in classroom); pedagogy of noticing
Nussbaum, M. 77

Obama, Barack 51
O'Brien, M. 65, 77
Occupy Movement 70
O'Donnell, Darren 65
Ohbijou (band) 47
One World Youth Arts Project 60n4
one-drop rule 77
open-mindedness 44, 77, 79, 81, 156
oppression: internalized oppression 20; music as resistance against 4–5, 6, 10; and pedagogy of noticing 153–154, 157; *see also* anti-oppression; trauma
An Orff Mosaic from Canada (Birkenshaw-Fleming, ed.) 74
O'Toole, P. A. 24

Palestinian resistance 9
participatory musical culture 61n18
patriarchy: and critical pedagogy 33–34; and critique of critical pedagogy 29, 34; in music 114; and music education 121; and popular culture 111, 112; and rap music 121–122; and representations of artists 113
Patrick (Patrick Huang, a.k.a. DJ Phatrick): biography 171; hip-hop program 95–96; hip-hop program and challenging misogyny 114–116, 121–122, 123; hip-hop program and critical thinking 108, 114, 153; hip-hop program and musicking anti-oppression 124, 125, 147; hip-hop program and recognition of systemic conditions 157; internal social justice and music education as political 54, 116–117, 118; learning via music and Bambu 58; "The Message" (song by Grandmaster Flash and Furious Five) 54, 116
pedagogy of community: classroom community 151, 152; contextualization 151, 152; emphasis on connectivity 150; exposure to multiple musics 151–152; implementation issues 165–166; potential dangers 154; setting the conditions for activism 156, 158–159
pedagogy of discomfort 117

pedagogy of expression: emphasis on storytelling 152, 153; implementation issues 165–166; lived experiences 150, 152, 153; place-based education 152–153; potential dangers 154; setting the conditions for activism 156–157, 158–159; songwriting 153, 156–157
pedagogy of noticing: emphasis on critical thinking 150, 153–154; implementation issues 165–166; potential dangers 154; setting the conditions for activism 156, 157, 158–159
pedagogy of respect 17
performance paradigm 99
performing (in school) 99–100
Petchauer, E. 27
Pete (Pete Shungu, stage name Afro D): biography 174–175; Black youth and Afrocentric history program 88–89; music reinforcing status quo 55; music representing different things to different people 58; spoken-word piece about the "B" word 53–54; teachers' ideologies and practice of critique 109, 114, 119; trying different instruments 93
Peter, Paul & Mary (band) 92
Phenner, Lee *see* Lee (Phenner)
The Phonemes (band) 53
phronesis 23
phronesis 35
Piaget, J. 15
place-based education: concept 85–86; critical pedagogy and culturally responsive teaching 86; reflecting and extending worlds 89–90; reflecting and validating youth in school programs 86–88, 152–153; student-centered curricula in music education 88–89; summary 89–90, 106
police violence 5, 9, 11, 70, 125n2, 137
political, music education as: dangers of enacting music education politically 145–148; defining political 107–108; dissent in the classroom 107, 118, 119, 123; exemplars of anti-oppressive possibilities 118, 121–123; identifying lived conditions 107, 108, 116–118, 123; imagining musical practices 118, 119–121, 123; musicking anti-oppression 123–125; noticing ideologies 108–116; summary 125; *see*

also culture of questioning; noticing ideologies; pedagogy of noticing
political change: and musicking 50–55; and musicking as dangerous 55–57
political movements: and musicking 44–46; *see also* social movements
political music 9–10, 103, 105, 106
popular culture: and patriarchy 111, 112; and racism 111–112
Post-Traumatic Stress Disorder (PTSD) 139
potential of music *see* music, potential of
Pratt, M. L. 78, 79, 81
praxial music education 14n10, 23, 33, 39n2
praxis: and constructivist learning 15; critical praxis 160–161; and ethics 23, 35; Freire's approach 7, 15, 16–17, 35
problem-posing education: Freire's concept 17, 18, 19–20, 21, 22; and hip-hop 117; and materials from students' experiences 86; and music education 25–26, 29, 35–36; and music education as connection 62, 83; and potential for colonialism 32; vs. problem-solving 25–26, 163, 164; and teacher-student hierarchies 30, 31–32
problem-solving, vs. problem-posing 25–26, 163, 164
protest songs 9–10; *see also* political music
punk music 43
pussy hats 1
Pussy Riot (band) 123–124

questioning *see* culture of questioning
"Quiet" (song) 1–2, 4

race/racism: and anti-oppression pedagogy 5; b. hooks on 111; and the "B" word 53–54; and critical pedagogy 33–34; and critique of critical pedagogy 29, 34; and difficult truths 50; and hip-hop 52, 122; and intersectional feminism 13n3; and Jim Crow laws 77; and music education 11; and music education discourse 111; musicians against racism 9; and mutually supportive spaces 121; and National Football League (NFL) protests 125n2; and Nina Simone's "Mississippi Goddam" 2–3; and pedagogy of noticing 153; and popular culture 111–112; proliferation of racist ideologies 4;

and representations of women in music 119–120; and stereotyping 133; and Western European perspectives 130; and Yamaha instruments posters 112–113; *see also* critical race theory; White supremacy
Racy, A. J. 133
Rankin, John 142
rap music 58, 111–112, 121–122; gangsta rap 112, 143
rape culture 121–122
Ravitch, D. 168n1
Razack, S. 115, 142, 143
recontextualization 69–70, 132, 134
Reece, Florence, "Which Side Are You On" 5
reflection: concept as defined by Freire 15, 16–17, 20, 22, 159; and creative music curriculum 90–91, 101, 102, 106; and Kuntz' definition of activism 155; and music education 26, 35; and tri-faceted pedagogy 158; *see also* conscientization (coming-to-consciousness); problem-posing education
reflective listening 67, 164–165
Regelski, T. A. 23, 25–26, 39n2
Reimer, B. 60n1
remix/mash-up 97–98, 132, 144; *see also* sampling (music process)
representations, and noticing ideologies 110–114, 125
respect, pedagogy of 17
responsibilities, trusting youth with 65–66, 67
Rice, Tamir 5
Robertson, Carole 2
Robertson, E. 165
Robinson, Eddy 133–134
Rosenberg, S. 138
Ryan, A. 112

Sahlberg, P. 162
salvationism 143–144
Salverson, J. 138, 140
sampling (music process) 80, 130, 149n2; *see also* mash-up/remix
Schafer, R. Murray 149n1
Schippers, H. 69
schizophonia 130, 144
Schmidt, Patrick K. 23, 25, 26, 27, 29
schools: activism in 146; gendered musical roles in 110–111, 120–121, 123; performing in 99–100; violence in 11

Seeger, Pete 9
sexism: and 2016 presidential election campaign 1; and anti-oppression pedagogy 5; and music education 11; musicians against 9; and portrayal of women artists 113; and representations of women in music 119–120; sexual stereotypes in music 112; and Yamaha instruments posters 112–113; *see also* feminism; gender; heterosexism; misogyny
Shakur, Tupac 9
Shepherd, J. 40
Sheth, A. 33
Shi-shi-etko (Campbell and LaFave) 82, 83
Shor, Ira 22
Shungu, Pete *see* Pete (Pete Shungu, stage name Afro D)
Silani, G. 57
Silverman, M. 23, 39n2, 40
Simon, R. I. 138
Simone, Nina, "Mississippi Goddam" (Carnegie Hall, 1964) 2–3, 4
Singleton, G. E. 117
situated human practice: contextualizing musics 67–69; individual and community contexts 69–72; instruments 72–73; languages 73–75; questions to develop contextual knowledge 75–76; summary 76–77; *see also* cultural appropriation
SKIM: biography 174; connecting to larger narratives 45, 71, 93; using music for or against status quo 52, 55
slavery 134, 137, 142
Sloboda, J. 158
Small, C. 10, 40, 52, 55, 61n18, 62, 63
Smith, D. C. 163
Smith, V. G. 163
Smith, Yvette 5
social justice: and anti-oppressive exemplars 122–123; defining 149n9; internal social justice 54, 116; and music education 158; and musicking 52–54; and pedagogy of noticing 154
social justice education 7, 146
social movements: and activist-musicians 9–10, 157; and music education 70, 91, 94, 122–123, 124–125, 151; and musicking 44–46, 51; risks in supporting 105
Solís, T. 133
Solórzano, D. G. 106n6

songwriting: and anti-oppression 123–125; and audience desires 143–144, 154; and cultural appropriation 144–145; as curriculum 94–96, 153; and instrumental instruction 96, 167; and pedagogy of expression 153, 156–157; and sharing stories 104; writing lyrics 96–97; *see also* lyrics; mash-up/remix; soundscapes
Sotomayor, L. 14n13
soundscapes 99, 100–101
South Africa, apartheid 3–4, 9, 58, 71
"Southern Man" song 105
"Soweto Blues" (song) 3–4
Soweto Uprising (1976) 3–4
Spoils (band) 43, 64
Spruce, G. 25
standardized tests 163–164, 168n1
Starr, Edwin 9
Stauffer, S. 164
Stefancic, J. 60n7
stereotyping 132–135, 137, 140–141, 148, 154
Stookey, Paul 92
Stookey Sunde, Liz *see* Liz (Liz Stookey Sunde)
storytelling: and audience desires 143–144, 154; and musicking 47–48; and pedagogy of expression 152, 153; without lyrics 98–99; *see also* counterstorytelling
student-centered curricula 88–89; *see also* teachers
Style, E., "Curriculum as window and mirror" 78, 81, 86–87, 89–90, 91, 132, 151–152
Sunde, Liz *see* Liz (Liz Stookey Sunde)
Szymanski, A. 163

Taiyo Na (Taiyo Ebato): biography 173–174; community and musicking 43–44, 49, 64, 152; community and telling underrepresented stories 47, 60n7; integration of youth's critical music into curriculum 122, 123; multi-faceted role of music 40; pie-in-the-sky concert/class 58–59, 100; political music and emotions 103; seeing humanity and beauty in youth music-making 87–88; solo and lecturing space 44, 64, 151, 159; teachers-as-facilitators 66–67
Talbot, B. C. 3, 24

Index   211

teachers: as "fellow adventurers" 25, 153; ideologies of 109–110, 116, 119, 125; mutuality between students and teachers 17, 18, 20, 22, 24–25, 31, 32, 35; teachers-as-facilitators 66–67; teacher-student hierarchies 30–32, 34, 147–148, 154
techne 23
telling stories *see* storytelling
testimonios 95, 124
three-fifths clause (U.S. Constitution) 77
Tobias, E. 10
Todd, Stanley 3–4
togetherness (ensemble) 62, 63–64, 167
tolerance 141, 142–143, 148, 149n6
transformation: concept as defined by Freire 15, 16–17, 20, 21, 22, 108, 145; and creative music curriculum 90–91, 101, 102, 106; and culture of questioning 108; and Kuntz' definition of activism 155; and music education 26, 28, 35, 36, 156; and musicking 41–42; *see also* dialogue; naming the world
trauma: and music education 82–83, 117–118, 137–140, 141, 148, 151; and musicking 48, 52; and pedagogies of community and noticing 154; and pedagogy of expression 153, 154; and sharing experiences in classroom 104–105, 106; and songwriting 95; *see also* abuse
travel, and connecting 78
Tribe Called Quest, A (band) 9
Tribe Called Red, A (band) 52–53
tri-faceted pedagogy: critical praxis for music education 160–161; implementation issues 165–166; pedagogy of community 150–152; pedagogy of expression 150, 152–153; pedagogy of noticing 150, 153–154; redefining activist music education 154–160; remaining aware of potential dangers 154; *see also* activist music education, redefining; pedagogy of community; pedagogy of expression; pedagogy of noticing
Trimillos, R. D. 133
Trinka, J. L. 84n7
True Believers (band) 64
Trump, Donald J. 1, 9, 125n2
Turino, T. 56, 63

tvu (Theresa "tvu" Vu): biography 176; demystifying songwriting 95, 96; experience with music industry 113; finding one's own voice 49; mash-up/remix 97–98; music as conduit 57; music to communicate difficult truths 50, 161; "New Love" song 53

uAspire 54
United Farm Workers 70
U.S. Constitution, three-fifths clause 77
U.S. presidential election campaign (2016) 1
U.S./Mexico border, forced separation of children from parents 137–138

Vaugeois, L. *see* Lise (Lise Vaugeois)
Vietnam war 9, 71
violence: and musicking 56; police violence 5, 9, 11, 70, 125n2, 137; school violence 11
visionaries: artists as 101–102; *see also* collective envisioning
Vu, Theresa ("tvu") *see* tvu (Theresa "tvu" Vu)
Vygotsky, L. S. 15

Walcott, R. W. 102, 155
Wesley, Cynthia 2
Western classical music, and hierarchization of musics issue 128–129
"Which Side Are You On" (song) 5
White, Victor, III 5
White supremacy 111, 113, 114, 158
Wilson, Darren 84n6, 86
Women's Liberation Movement 70
Women's March (Washington, D.C., January 2017) 1
Wonder, Stevie 59
Woodson, Tyree 5
world music 79, 133, 135

Yamaha instruments posters 112–113
Yancy, G. 34
Yosso, T. J. 24, 106n6, 160
Young, J. O. 130
Young, Neil, "Southern Man" song 105

Zimmerman, J. 165